The Human Right to Dominate

THE HUMAN RIGHT TO DOMINATE

Nicola Perugini and Neve Gordon

OXFORD
UNIVERSITY PRESS

Oxford University Press is a department of the University of Oxford.
It furthers the University's objective of excellence in research, scholarship,
and education by publishing worldwide. Oxford is a registered trade mark
of Oxford University Press in the UK and in certain other countries

Published in the United States of America by
Oxford University Press
198 Madison Avenue, New York, NY 10016,
United States of America

Cataloging-in-Publication data is on file at the Library of Congress

978-0-19-936501-2 (hbk.)
978-0-19-936500-5 (pbk.)

To Farah, Catherine, Ariel, and Aviv

Among the natural rights of the Colonists are these: First, a right to life; Secondly, to liberty; Thirdly, to property; together with the right to support and defend them in the best manner they can.

> —Samuel Adams, "The Rights of the Colonists," *The Report of the Committee of Correspondence to the Boston Town Meeting*, November 20, 1772

My conflict with the Other revolves around one single question: who between us, today, deserves the status of victim? I often told the Other, joking: "let's exchange our roles. You are a victorious victim. . . . I am a dominated victim."

> —Mahmoud Darwish, interview with the Lebanese poet Abbas Beydoun, *Al Wasat* (London), 1995

CONTENTS

ACKNOWLEDGMENTS

This book is the result of a friendship and a fertile scholarly exchange. Over the last few years, hardly a day has passed in which we have not bounced ideas or thoughts off each other. Each one of us has intervened in practically every paragraph, sentence, and word in this book. Every line has been constantly questioned, revisited, rearticulated, and at times erased—to such an extent that our individual contributions are currently almost unrecognizable. We consequently share equal responsibility for both the contributions and the mistakes the book might contain. The intellectual curiosity and affinity we have developed during the writing of *The Human Right to Dominate* is already consolidating into a new book project about human shielding, a topic that we begin to develop in chapter 3. We have therefore, by mutual consent, decided to let Nicola Perugini be the first author of *The Human Right to Dominate*, while Neve Gordon will be the first author of the second book *On Human Shielding*, which we expect to publish in the near future.

Our encounter was made possible by generous fellowships awarded to both of us by the Institute for Advanced Study at Princeton. The School of Social Science and the IAS campus's beautiful environment provided us with an incredible space for exchanging ideas. We are particularly grateful to Joan Scott and Didier Fassin for inviting us to the IAS and for encouraging us to complete this project. Danielle Allen, Lucas Bessire, Vincent Dubois, David Eng, Sara Farris, Moon-Kie Jung, Peter Thomas, Jens Meierhenrich, and Laurence Ralph have all read parts of the manuscript during our stay at IAS and offered very helpful suggestions.

Another person who made this book possible is Clifford Bob, a coeditor of Oxford's Culture and Politics series. Cliff pushed us to embark on this project and read drafts of the manuscript at different stages while providing us with meticulous and insightful comments, which then forced us to rethink some of our claims and to reformulate others. Lisa Hajjar, Catherine Rottenberg, and Rebecca Stein have also read the whole manuscript and pushed us to make our arguments clearer and more precise, as did James Cook, the sociology editor at OUP.

Different people read earlier drafts of chapters or commented on them during various presentations. We are grateful to Nasser Abourahme, Ala Alazzeh, Lorenzo Alunni, Merav Amir, Valentina Azarov, Roberto Beneduce, Nitza Berkovitch, Eduardo Cadava, Alice Cherki, Gerard Daniel Cohen, Yinon Cohen, Elliott Colla, Armando Cutolo, Emilio Dabed, Joyce Dalsheim, Dani Filc, Michal Givoni, Saleh Hijazi, Sandi Hilal, Thomas Keenan, Nadim Khoury, Hagar Kotef, Omar Jabary Salamanca, Stefano Jacoviello, Luciano Li Causi, Miriam Lowi, Anne Norton, Zia Mian, Sunaina Maria, Julie Peteet, Alessandro Petti, Kareem Rabie, Amnon Raz-Krakotzkin, Noga Rotem, Tommaso Sbriccoli, Majid Shihade, Pier Giorgio Solinas, Simona Taliani, Oraib Toukan, Lorenzo Veracini, Eyal Weizman, Niza Yanay, Oren Yiftachel, Tirdad Zolghadr, and Francesco Zucconi.

After the year at IAS, the Al Quds Bard College in Palestine gave further support to Nicola during the writing process, allowing him to adapt his courses and workload to his writing needs. The University of Siena provided Nicola with a postdoctoral fellowship that allowed him to write the article "The Human Right to the Colony" with Kareem Rabie, which inspired chapter 4 of this book. Nicola is also extremely grateful to Brown University, where he completed the book as a Mellon Postdoctoral Fellow at the Cogut Center for the Humanities with a fellowship in Italian and Middle East Studies. Special thanks go to Beshara Doumani, Michael Steinberg, Suzanne Stewart and Massimo Riva for giving him the opportunity to continue his work and research at Brown.

Neve wishes to thank Gal Ariely, Dani Filc, Michal Givoni, Becky Kook, David Newman, Jennifer Oser, Sharon Pardo, Renee Poznanski, Ahmad Sa'adi, Lynn Schler, and Haim Yacobi, members of the Department of Politics and Government at Ben-Gurion University, for their ongoing support over the years.

The Human Right to Dominate

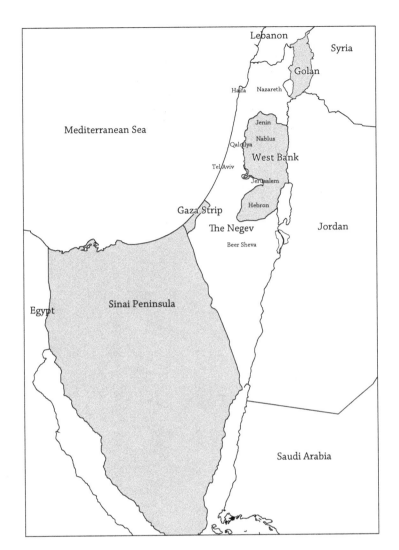

Figure 1.
Map of Israel/Palestine.
Source: Neve Gordon, Israel's Occupation.

Human Rights as Domination

The Grand Duchess: "And to whom better to speak of crime than a murderer?"

Kaliayev: "What crime? All I remember is an act of justice."
                                                    —Albert Camus

On a cool spring day in May 2012, the members of the North Atlantic Treaty Organization (NATO) met in McCormick Place, Chicago. The 28 heads of state comprising the military alliance had come to the Windy City to discuss the impact of the Arab Spring on security, a missile shield system for Europe, and the withdrawal of NATO forces from Afghanistan. Nearly a decade before, in August 2003, NATO had assumed control of the International Security Assistance Force, a coalition of 46 countries that had sent soldiers to occupy the most troubled regions in Afghanistan (i.e., south and east). Not long before the Chicago summit, President Barack Obama had publically declared that the United States would begin pulling out its troops from Afghanistan and that a complete withdrawal would be achieved by 2014.[1] NATO was therefore set to decide on the details of a potential exit strategy.

A few days before the summit, placards appeared in bus stops around downtown Chicago urging NATO not to withdraw its forces from Afghanistan. "NATO: Keep the progress going!" read the posters, thus creating a clear connection between the military occupation of Afghanistan and "progress." The caption was spread over a photograph of two Afghani women walking in an unrecognizable street, wearing burkas that covered their entire body, including head and face. Walking between them is a girl who seems surprised by the voyeuristic photographer; hers is the only visible face, which looks neither frightened nor happy, but is nonetheless alert. The photograph's subtext seems clear: the burka is this child's future. Connecting the caption with the image, one understands that, according to the logic of the placard, NATO needs to continue its mission in Afghanistan in order to emancipate Afghani women, particularly Afghani girls. Indeed, military resolve and even violence is needed to ensure these women's freedom. Just in case the viewer misses the connection, on the top left-hand side of the poster one reads in large bold letters, "Human Rights for Women and Girls in Afghanistan" (figure I.1).

The poster was part of a public campaign against President Obama's declared intention of withdrawing US and NATO troops from Afghanistan. Under the banner "NATO: Keep the progress going!" there was notification about a "Shadow Summit for Afghan Women" that was to take place alongside the NATO summit. "Admission," the public is notified, "is free." Sponsoring the event was not a Republican think tank or a defense corporation, such as Lockheed Martin, but Amnesty International,

Figure I.1.
Amnesty International campaign on the eve of the NATO summit.
Source: Amnesty International.

the first and one of the most renowned human rights organizations across the globe.[2] Amnesty also prepared a letter that emphasized the importance of NATO's continued intervention in Afghanistan and managed to secure the signature of former secretary of state Madeleine Albright, among others.[3] During the shadow summit itself, participants made remarks that dovetailed nicely with the US State Department's "Responsibility to Protect" doctrine, otherwise known as "humanitarian intervention."[4]

The idea that the most prominent international human rights NGO (nongovernmental organization) was campaigning against the withdrawal of US and NATO military forces from a country halfway around the globe is something worth dwelling on. The assumption underlying Amnesty's campaign that the deployment of violence is necessary to protect human rights suggests that violence and human rights are not necessarily antithetical. Violence protects human rights from the violence that violates human rights.[5] Violence is not only the source of abuse, but, as Amnesty's placard clearly implies, can also be the source of women's liberation.[6] Yet if violence is traditionally associated with domination and human rights with emancipation, then the connection between the two seems odd. Are human rights unavoidably connected to domination, or is this campaign just an exceptional case?

Domination in this book refers to a broad array of relationships of subjugation characterized by the use of force and coercion. Our focus on domination is twofold: we are interested in violent practices deployed against individuals and groups in order to dominate them; but we want to examine also how by enacting different relationships of domination these practices are rationalized, legitimized, and made sense of by appealing to human rights. What, in other words, is the relation between human rights and domination?

While we assume that all forms of domination are violent, it is important to note that violence is not always or necessarily a manifestation of domination. Anticolonial history teaches us, for instance, that violence can be deployed to resist, liberate, and disentangle people from colonial relationships of domination.[7] The same could be said about the struggle in South Africa, where for several decades various anti-apartheid groups resorted to violence. Ironically, Amnesty International was unwilling to adopt Nelson Mandela as a political prisoner because he refused to renounce the use violence, since in his view it was a legitimate weapon in the struggle against the apartheid regime.[8] Even the United Nations, the main international institution responsible for protecting human rights, has reaffirmed "the legitimacy of the peoples' struggle for liberation form colonial and foreign domination and alien subjugation by all available means, including armed struggle."[9]

Amnesty's keep-the-progress-going campaign is interesting because it implores a group of states to deploy violence and prolong a foreign military occupation in another country in order to defend women from radical Islam; the complex political situation in Afghanistan is thus reduced to religion-driven human rights violations against which protracted violent intervention is needed.[10] Yet, unlike Arundhati Roy, who exposes the duplicity of the war in Afghanistan when she notes that if women's rights were indeed the objective, then it is unclear why the Western military forces failed to stop on their way for a short excursion in Saudi Arabia, we are interested in the reasons why human rights are deployed to justify military occupation.[11] If all forms of domination are violent, then all forms of mobilization of human rights in support of domination are functional to the reproduction of dominant violence, and ultimately to the protection and legitimization of domination itself.

Behind the campaign urging NATO forces to remain in Afghanistan was Suzanne Nossel, Amnesty International USA's executive director at the time. Several years earlier, Nossel had published a *Foreign Affairs* article entitled "Smart Power," where she called upon progressives, including, we infer, human rights activists, to "learn from the example of the U.S. military's" use of power in a "smart" way. The military, she said, "has long recognized that its comparative advantage comes not from size or firepower but from farsighted strategy, sophisticated intelligence, professionalism, and precise weaponry. Although the military's weapons systems have been calibrated to conserve firepower and minimize collateral damage, the same cannot be said of U.S. foreign policy."[12] While Nossel's use of the US military as an example of smart power is based on a shaky argument,[13] what is more interesting to us here is how the military becomes the paradigm for progressive action, including human rights work. A renewed liberal internationalist strategy, Nossel explains, "recognizes that military power and humanitarian endeavors can be mutually reinforcing."[14] This, we believe, is an intriguing claim that deserves some attention, since the welding of military clout with forms of humanism, including human rights, has become a prominent feature of contemporary global politics.[15]

Nevertheless, in her *Foreign Affairs* article, Nossel does not interrogate the relationship between human rights and domination. Instead, she is upset at progressives, whom she describes as "flummoxed," and suggests that they (meaning her tribe) should fight against the appropriation of liberal internationalist tenets by conservatives who invoke "the rhetoric of human rights and democracy to further the aggressive projection of unilateral military power."[16] She thus identifies a process whereby conservative forces are appropriating human rights to legitimize and justify former president George W. Bush's wars in Afghanistan and Iraq. Yet her criticism is not directed against this appropriation per se—since, after all, she initiated the "NATO: Keep the progress going!" campaign—but against its use to justify the deployment of unilateral violence. What really bothers her is the identity of the actors (unusual suspects) that suddenly appropriate human rights discourse, and the fact that they use it to advance policies that she, at the time, rejected. We, by contrast, are interested in the appropriation itself, the significance of the multifarious appropriations of human rights that we have been witnessing over the past decade and a half, and what the implications of this phenomenon may be, since this will enable us to better understand the connection between human rights and domination.

HUMAN RIGHTS APPROPRIATIONS

Amnesty International's campaign against the withdrawal of NATO troops from Afghanistan is merely a paradigmatic example of a much wider trend whereby human rights are being deployed in the service of domination. If during the 1980s and 1990s, conservatives in the United States tended to reject the expanding human rights culture and were often even hostile to it,[17] at the turn of the new millennium they began to alter their strategy, embracing human rights language. This shift is part of a global phenomenon.[18] In fact, there are many parallels to be drawn between the way the Bush administration (aided by some international human rights and humanitarian organizations) invoked women's rights to help justify the war in Afghanistan and similar appropriations in other areas of the world. For some time now, the French nationalist Marine Le Pen has been advocating women's rights as part of her campaign against French and migrant Muslims. Her ideological counterparts in Denmark have become the most outspoken champions of the basic right of freedom of expression as they support the publication of vilifying caricatures of the Muslim prophet Muhammad in local newspapers.[19] Geert Wilders, the founder and leader of the conservative Freedom Party in Holland, who compared the Koran to Hitler's *Mein Kampf*, has invoked the discourse of gay and women's rights to attack and undermine religious freedoms in his country and elsewhere.[20] Human rights discourse has become a desired resource for those seeking political influence and power, providing its diverse advocates "legitimacy for their struggles and . . . an aura of respectability that no other rhetoric can supply."[21]

These appropriations, whereby human rights have become the new lingua franca of global moral speak, underscore that human rights have been increasingly serving as a common horizon for political traditions of different stripes.[22] Human rights, as Costas Douzinas has cogently observed, "have become the new morality of international relations, a way of conducting politics according to a moral norms and rules . . . human rights are now the canonical text for the moral disposition of world affairs."[23] Their widespread deployment as a dominant moral currency has also propelled institutional change, whereby conservatives began to introduce the language and strategies of human rights within existing organizations, while simultaneously creating an array of new human rights NGOs, which, until recently, seemed to be the sole turf of liberals.

In the United States, well-established conservative think tanks, such as the Heritage Foundation and the American Enterprise Institute, have become home to scholars whose expertise includes human rights, while a plethora of conservative NGOs are now invoking human rights to advance their political objectives. The World Congress of Families, a US-based global NGO founded in 1997, joined, for example, 100 groups, many of which define themselves as human rights NGOs, to support President Vladimir Putin's 2014 antigay law.[24] On its home page the World Congress describes itself as "an international network of pro-family organizations, scholars, leaders and people of goodwill from more than 80 countries that seek to restore the "natural" family as the fundamental social unit and the 'seedbed' of civil society (*as found in the UN Universal Declaration of Human Rights, 1948*)."[25] If in Holland conservatives mobilize gay rights to advocate the infringement of religious freedoms, in this case conservatives invoke human rights to advocate the violation of gay rights.

A spate of other conservative NGOs have adopted a human rights agenda and are mirroring not only the language and institutional scaffolding of liberal human rights groups, but also the methodologies and strategies they have developed. They understand that human rights are a powerful organizing tool. Advocacy campaigns that name and shame perpetrators of abuse are no longer the prerogative of liberal human rights groups, which developed these strategies in the 1970s and 1980s, while international human rights and humanitarian law, once the signature of liberal human rights groups, such as the International Commission of Jurists and the American Civil Liberties Union, now appears in petitions filed by the conservative Rutherford Institute (to maintain prayers in schools), the National Rifle Association, and the American Center for Law and Justice (ACLJ).[26] Affiliated with the Christian Right in the United States, the ACLJ uses "U.S. constitutional law, European Union law and human rights law" to advance its pro-life and religious freedom agenda. The NGO engages in litigation, provides legal services, offers advice to individuals and governmental agencies, and counsels clients on "global freedom and liberty issues." It also supports "training law students from around the world in order to protect religious liberty and safeguard human rights and dignity."[27] Even though it is affiliated with the ideology of the Republican Tea Party, it has opened European offices in Strasbourg so that it can more easily file suits in the European Court of Human Rights. By 2013 it had already intervened in 15 cases before this court.[28]

The appropriation of human rights language, institutions, and strategies by conservative actors points to an increasing convergence between liberals and conservatives on a global scale. In this introductory chapter we provide a thumbnail sketch of these convergences, while in the following chapters we offer a more extensive analysis in relation to the case of Israel/Palestine. Significantly, the condition of possibility of these convergences is the mutual agreement on some fundamental assumptions. First, both liberal and conservative human rights NGOs share certain juridical assumptions about the law's authority, the courts' decisive role as the arbiters of disagreement, and what constitutes adequate language to discuss evidence—in this case the legal vocabulary of human rights. Second, during the past decade liberal and conservative human rights NGOs have adopted increasingly similar strategies of human rights advocacy. This form of convergence includes an agreement on the appropriate methodology and techniques for gathering data, what constitutes valid data, and, consequently, what constitutes evidence. Different actors might disagree on the interpretation of the data, but they tend to concur upon which data have the capacity to serve as proof. Third, both liberals and conservatives use the evidence of human rights abuses to generate meanings and allocate guilt and innocence.[29] Such convergences suggest that human rights lawyers, activists, and experts representing a variety of organizations with different objectives ultimately share assumptions about the predominant role of the law and about certain methodological standards that need to be satisfied for the data to actually produce evidence.[30] Hence it is no surprise that they often use similar strategies to advance their objectives. We define the deployment of the same strategies by different organizations as *mirroring*.

Liberals and conservatives from different geographical areas aiming to advance different political goals mirror each other in numerous ways. These include the way they formulate the petitions submitted to courts, the invocation of international law in these petitions, the kind of advocacy campaigns they launch, and even the iconography used in their campaigns. One example is the utilization of the burka as the prime symbol of women's oppression.[31] Amnesty International framed its pro-NATO placard in a way that is reminiscent of numerous Islamophobic campaigns initiated by conservative organizations such as the poster distributed by the conservative Frankfurt-based International Society for Human Rights, which used the image of a burka as a prison (figure I.2), and the poster used by the Swiss People's Party in a successful referendum campaign to ban the construction of minarets on mosques (figure I.3).[32] Hence, convergence is predicated on a basic agreement of underlying assumptions and systems of symbols, and serves as the condition of possibility of these kinds of mirrorings.

However, because of the diverse political proclivities of these groups, we not only witness convergences and mirroring, but also numerous *inversions*. Organizations with different political agendas struggling around the same moral dilemmas launch uncannily similar types of campaigns articulated through the language of human rights, but the ideals and beliefs these campaigns convey may be radically different. According to liberal human rights groups worldwide, legislation against gays constitutes a

Figure I.2.
A campaign by the conservative NGO the International Society for Human Rights.
Source: www.igfm.de (IGFM), Internationale Gesellschaft für Menschenrechte.

Figure I.3.
A campaign by the Swiss People's Party against the construction of minarets.
Source: Swiss People Party.

violation, whereas conservative NGOs invoke article 16 of the Universal Declaration of Human Rights (which deals with the "universal" family) to show how antigay legislation secures human rights. In the United States, the Coalition to Stop Gun Violence invokes human rights against the widespread circulation of weapons and ensuing massacres, while the National Rifle Association depicts gun owners as a persecuted minority, victims of human rights violations.[33] In Israel, several liberal NGOs are fighting against settlement expansion and oppression in the Occupied Palestinian Territories, denouncing human rights violations against the Palestinian inhabitants, while their conservative counterparts characterize the Palestinian population as invaders and perpetrators of abuse, and Jewish settlers as indigenous victims. As these examples illustrate, victims, according to one human rights group, are perpetrators in the eyes of another. Human rights discourses have the power to shape moral legal categories (victims and perpetrators), and to invert and subvert the definition of the relationships of power within which they are mobilized.

These inversions help expose that human rights, which most people assume to be progressive and liberating, can just as easily be connected with domination. This is not to say that the relation between human rights and domination is new, but rather that it has become much more apparent as soon as the new appropriations we are describing became pervasive across the globe. There are several reasons why we are currently witnessing this proliferation of human rights appropriations. One of these has to do with the larger politics of managing consent and dissent at home and abroad, whereby the deployment of human rights by conservative think tanks, NGOs, and philanthropy organizations is part of a response to the perceived success of liberals in advancing policy objectives. Another reason for the increasing appropriation has to do with the efficacy of human rights in framing history.[34] The appropriations informing the inversions we mentioned and those from Israel/Palestine, which we will closely explore in this book, reflect a struggle over the narration of history, or more precisely the struggle over the interpretation of the history of violence *as* domination. Rights, as Duncan Kennedy points out, are extremely poignant because their invocation "allows you to be right about your value judgments, rather than just stating 'preferences'."[35] They frame events legally and morally, and ultimately, as we show, help legitimize certain interpretations of domination while delegitimizing others.

Given this *epistemic* function of human rights, and given the intrinsic link between violence and the modern concept of the human,[36] it is not surprising that state security institutions that hold the monopoly over legitimate violence also began invoking international humanitarian and human rights law in their work.[37] We described above how a liberal human rights NGO campaigned for militaries to deploy violence in order to secure human rights, but it is also important to note that militaries the world over have integrated human rights as part of their training. At Fort Benning, the home of the US Army's Armor and Infantry schools, soldiers who are "prepared and equipped to fight and win" wars are also required to take a human rights class.[38] The objective of the course is to "impress upon the students that democratic values, international human rights law, and international humanitarian law are essential to leadership skills in the armed forces."[39] The human rights class consists of three distinct segments: ethical foundations, legal imperatives, and operational considerations. The institute's chaplain teaches ethics, while the judge advocate teaches international human rights and humanitarian law.

Amnesty International estimates that each year in addition to training its own soldiers, the US government trains approximately 100,000 foreign police and soldiers from more than 150 countries in approximately 275 military schools and installations while offering over 4,100 human rights courses.[40] And although Amnesty International is critical of some of the messages conveyed in these courses, the organizers of the course at Fort Benning welcome "the participation and observations of human rights NGOs."[41] The military, as we show in chapter 3, deploys human rights to frame its actions. As Laleh Khalili maintains, the invocation of law and legality often structures the conduct of war, which helps explain why states must invoke human rights as a means of ensuring regulatory and ethical compliance.[42]

The integration of human rights classes in military training also points to another shift within the field of human rights. If international humanitarian law was once considered to be the legal corpus dealing with armed conflict, and international human rights law was considered to be the corpus employed during times of peace, the two bodies of law are no longer thought to be totally separate. In their reports and petitions, human rights NGOs deploy these two legal frames simultaneously in the struggle to secure human rights in times of armed conflict and military occupation, and since conflict has become the norm in many parts of the world, it is now common practice to *discard* the so-called separation theory.[43] In other words, human rights norms are no longer considered part of a field that is completely separated from the humanitarian norms of the *jus in bello,* for as the International Committee of the Red Cross maintains, "there is a convergence between the protection offered by human rights law and that of international humanitarian law."[44]

Within this context of convergences, mirroring, and inversions, the instrumentalist conception of human rights—according to which conservatives or militaries deploy human rights merely as a *pretext* for attaining other political objectives—is revealed to be both theoretically and empirically flawed. While we agree that the phenomenon we describe does not sit well with central parts of the social and political history of human rights, we do *not* think that the conservative and security actors we depict are simply distorting human rights. Put differently, the connection between human rights and domination that we examine in this book is not created through legal errors or the misapplication of human rights.

Human rights are, no doubt, used as tools to advance political goals, but, in the process of being appropriated, they do much more; they become an organic part of a social and political *text*, and not only a pretext for some other hidden objective. In this respect there is no fundamental difference between the liberal and conservative appropriation of human rights, since both camps adopt the same reasoning: they appropriate human rights to develop a legal and moral framework in which historical events and political objectives are given a specific meaning. In this way, human rights help produce a certain narration of history, which simultaneously confers a specific political meaning on human rights. They constitute a highly flexible political discourse with the capacity to be constantly appropriated, translated, performed, and retooled in different political arenas. It is within such processes, we argue, that the relationship between human rights and domination reveals itself.

Thus, the claim that the military or conservative think tanks and NGOs are merely distorting or perverting the meaning of human rights, as if liberal NGOs in some way own human rights or are the only actors that use them "correctly," needs to be problematized. In fact this claim prevents us from investigating the politics of human rights and the multifaceted forms in which they are performed by both liberal and conservatives. By the politics of human rights we mean the struggle over the translation and interpretation of human rights not as pretext but as text, whereby diverse actors integrate the grammar of human rights within their own worldview while their worldview, in turn, is informed by this integration of human rights. In other words, the rhetoric of human rights is both a political tool and, just as importantly, an *epistemic framework* that shapes the way different actors conceive their own position within social space and the political significance of events that they witness or are concerned about. One of the objectives of this book is precisely to show how human rights are able to confer a very specific meaning to the contexts of power within which they are invoked.

The Human Right to Dominate is accordingly an exploration of both epistemic and political processes of appropriation. As the title suggests, we are particularly interested in how both liberal and illiberal forces appropriate and deploy human rights in a way that corroborates, reinforces, and rationalizes domination instead of destabilizing it. Rather than laying claim to a morally adequate conception of human rights, we aim to unveil how human rights and domination intersect.[45] Indeed, the book is not a moral condemnation of a presumed misapplication and perversion of human rights. Rather, it is an interrogation of how human rights—whose assumed and stated goal is the protection of human dignity—can lend themselves to the enhancement of domination.

AGAINST THE HYDRAULIC MODEL OF HUMAN RIGHTS

The global convergences between liberals and conservatives, rights activists and militaries, cause lawyers and government officials are manifestations of the changes the culture of human rights has been undergoing. In order to map out these developments in the human rights sphere in the following chapters we focus on Israel/Palestine, analyzing an array of materials, including legal petitions, advocacy reports, military reports, media campaigns, and protocols of parliamentary discussions. In addition, we have interviewed directors of human rights NGOs, cause lawyers, and other practitioners. Through a careful examination of empirical evidence, we criticize the widely accepted "hydraulic model"—namely, that more human rights equals less domination—which normally associates the promotion of human rights with the empowerment of the weak.[46] Michael Ignatieff argues that human rights are universal "because they define the universal interests of the powerless."[47] Indeed, the prevalent assumption of this model is that the proliferation of human rights mitigates and subverts the asymmetrical relationship between oppressors and oppressed. Human rights discourse, in other words, is generally conceived as an intrinsically counterhegemonic tool and an instrument for righting historical injustices; exposing violations and abuse embarrasses and even threatens the strong while paving the way for the rehabilitation of the weak.

In the following chapters we show that this linear and indeed progressive narrative—held by most human rights practitioners and taught in most human rights courses—is informed by two central elisions and fallacies. First, insofar as human rights discourse is deployed by the weak in order to make demands on the dominant actor to exert its power more ethically, then human rights end up empowering the dominant actor since this discourse expands the spheres of legitimate sovereign intervention. This is precisely how Jack Donnelly describes the struggle against racial segregation in South Africa. After explaining to his readers that human rights are the language of the victims and dispossessed, he notes that "the struggle against apartheid in South Africa was a struggle to change South African laws and practices so that average South Africans could turn to the legislature, courts, or bureaucracy should they be denied, for example, equal protection of the laws or political participation."[48] Insofar as human rights empower the legislature, courts, and bureaucracy to secure the rights of the weak, then the claim that international human rights law is a form of exogenous intervention aimed at limiting state power or sovereignty is inaccurate. Even though the majority of scholarly publications on human rights accept the idea that human rights limit and restrain the state, the threat that human rights produce, as we show in the following chapters, is not really a threat to the state.

Second, when the weak or those who claim to represent them invoke human rights to demand action from the dominant, they may, as Amnesty International USA did in 2012, demand the deployment of violence in order to protect human rights.[49] As mentioned earlier, when this occurs, often rights-abusive policies are instituted to protect a right, revealing the inadequacy of the linear progressive assumptions of the hydraulic model. When the protection of one right entails the violation of another right, a paradox is produced, whereby the human rights discourse adopted in order to fight injustice through a humanitarian war may engender new forms of injustice. The hydraulic narrative precludes the understanding of such political dynamics, because it flattens the analysis into a moral polarization cut off from concrete social and political relations of power. It thus obscures the dialectic of power between the perpetrators of abuse and their victims and obfuscates situations whereby the oppressors can claim, reshape, and translate human rights and thus create their own human rights culture in order to rationalize the perpetuation of domination.

Interestingly, major human rights books such as *The Power of Human Rights* and *Activists beyond Borders* do not really engage with the limitations of the hydraulic model.[50] Yet once one becomes aware of the intricate ties between human rights and domination, it becomes apparent that this book's title, *The Human Right to Dominate*, is not really an oxymoron. In spite of its ostensible contradiction, the counterintuitive title we chose reflects a constantly evolving convergence between human rights and domination.

To be sure, the claim that human rights can reproduce existing relations of power is not new. Several thinkers have argued that human rights are actually bound by power and often operate in its service, without really threatening it. This critique can be traced back to Karl Marx's discussion of political rights in *On the Jewish Question*,[51] and has more recently been invoked by governmentality theorists, who have examined how human rights can be deployed by states to manage the conduct of populations and individuals.[52] Human rights, according to this perspective, help refine forms of government. They are not merely a normative framework embraced by NGOs and other nonstate actors, but are also employed by the state to entrench its own rationality and shape the comportment of populations and individuals it administers. In this sense, human rights help create new subjectivities since through the evolving inventory of rights they define what it means to be a fully human subject. We accordingly show in the following chapters on Israel/Palestine that state and nonstate actors define who the subject of human rights is, thus producing a certain *economy of human rights*. By economy of human rights we mean the mechanisms through which human rights are developed, appropriated, and circulated by state and nonstate actors, and then allocated unevenly to different individuals and social groups. Consequently, some groups may be bearers of a more extensive inventory of rights and therefore be considered more human than other groups. The form a state takes on and the way it deploys power in its relations with nonstate actors can, as we show in chapter 4, be revealed and ascertained from an analysis of the economy of human rights.

THE ILLUSION OF THE ORIGINAL

A different kind of critique that also emphasizes the deployment of human rights by the powerful argues that human rights are a Western construct and have been utilized as an apparatus to advance Western imperial or colonial projects.[53] Still other commentators have insisted that the recourse to sanctions, embargos, and different forms of "humanitarian intervention" in order to enhance the diffusion of human rights is actually part of a strategy for maintaining control and influence in which the old colonial trope of the "civilizing mission" is being rearticulated.[54] The universalist discourse of human rights is, according to such critics, epistemologically, historically, and normatively inscribed within Western culture, which aspires to expand and cement its own domination.

While this latter critical literature offers several significant insights, we disagree with some of its basic assumptions. Makau Mutua, for example, exposes and criticizes the savages-victims-saviors schema through which human rights advocacy often operates. Human rights NGOs, he correctly claims, tend to depict Third World abusers as savages, Third World populations that are subjected to violations as victims, and the human rights defenders from the West as saviors. He then calls upon all proponents of human rights to reject this schema and in its stead "seek a truly universal platform."[55] Mutua's idea that people can invoke a truly universal platform as if human rights are signifiers with a stable universal meaning that needs to be revealed is, we believe, misguided.

We also do not subscribe to the arguments advanced by scholars such as Jean Bricmont who maintain that human rights emerge as essential characteristics of Western culture and are always deployed to spread imperial projects.[56] This is an extension of the Marxist critique, and it assumes that human rights are *innately* the weapon of the strong, ignoring, for instance, the complexity of a postcolonial world in which the weak are increasingly appropriating human rights and contributing to the production of new political meanings. As we show, human rights discourse has the power to reframe history, as when Palestinians adopt it in order to define themselves as victims of colonial abuse. Similar to the historical relationship between humanism and domination, the *human* of human rights discourses has the contradictory power to legitimize domination as well as oppose it. There is no historical or logical necessity in the relationship between human rights and domination or human rights and liberation.[57] Hence, this critique, like Mutua's, risks overshadowing the historical malleability of human rights, reducing human rights to a tool of an essentialized Western imperial bloc.

Ultimately, the underlying assumption of both these critiques is that human rights have some kind of stable core that is either inherently good and therefore needs to be uncovered and deployed, or inherently bad and consequently cannot be used under any circumstances. By contrast, we maintain that "human rights" is a contested and overdetermined concept.[58] When they are claimed, they have an ever-present potential to acquire new political meanings, which may mirror or invert existing ones.[59] This is one of the "perplexities of human rights," which Hannah Arendt discusses in the *Origins of Totalitarianism*. Human rights have universal pretensions, but upon examination turn out to be time-bound in their articulations, codifications, and applications.[60] Circumscribed by the time and place and, not least, the given language in which its very terms are formulated, human rights discourse speaks of the universal in a mode that is always less and other than universal.[61] This is why we assume that human rights are adopted by a wide array of political actors who translate them, often in dissimilar ways, into local idioms.[62] During this process of translation, human rights, as Sally Merry has pointed out, "are remade in the vernacular," which inevitably produces fragmentation of meanings and thus destabilizes the ostensible international consensus on what universal human rights are.[63]

The point is that in every translation, as Walter Benjamin held, "the original undergoes a change."[64] Yet each deployment of human rights is a translation that routinely claims to be an original in a way that corresponds with the construction of a specific understanding of history. Laying claim to an original is an act that aims to provide validity and authority to the human rights utterance, since the original is supposedly unrelated to particular political relations and struggles; it is universal, neutral, and nonpolitical. Precisely, its guise as an original is what bestows power upon a human rights claim. Abandoning the illusion of the original may be very difficult and be perceived as a betrayal, but we think that the effort not to lay claim to an original can contribute to a clearer understanding of what people do with human rights. And, as we maintain in the concluding chapter, it can open the door for a different kind of human rights, even after their entrenchment within forms of domination.

More specifically, human rights declarations and conventions pose as a *depoliticized* original even though they too are translations and appropriations of earlier enunciations. But it is crucial to notice that the translations from these "original" conventions take place in relation to a variety of political forces that invoke and mobilize them, regardless of these forces' ideological orientations or the power differential between them.[65] There are three dimensions to this claim. First, the adoption of human rights as a language of struggle and of making sense of events is in itself a political choice: human rights are mobilized in place of, and sometimes at the expense of, other political discourses of justice. Hence, the decision to adopt human rights discourse as a political language is already a political decision. Second, when they are adopted in a concrete context, human rights are also shaped by the context itself. In other words, the specific translation of human rights tends to be determined through a struggle among different forces within a given society. Therefore, the struggle over the "legitimate" appropriation and meaning of human rights concomitantly reflects and produces sociopolitical relations. Third, precisely because human rights present themselves as universal, their appropriation and vernacularization in a local context are beneficial for both hegemonic and counterhegemonic projects, which often operate by reframing group interests as universal in order to acquire global legitimacy. The combination of these three dimensions produces what we call the politics of human rights, and its existence underscores that human rights are fundamentally political, rather than a tool that can or cannot be politicized.

Political relations help shape and are concomitantly shaped by the meaning of human rights and the two words that make it up: the *human* and *rights*. Every translation of human rights is informed by this dual process in which the tension between existing political forces that mobilize human rights and a presumed universal produces potentially endless significations and political scenarios. The meaning of the human and the social allocation of various degrees of humanity have changed from one historical and geographical context to another.[66] Within colonial regimes, for instance, the indigenous were often considered to be subhuman, while in Nazi Germany the Jews became subhuman, as did the Muslims in Bosnia. The same can be said about the term *right*. The right to property was interpreted in one historical context as the right to be employed and in another context as the right to own. And education, once merely a privilege enjoyed by the few, is currently considered a basic human right in most countries around the globe. A relatively recent example of the struggle over the meaning of human rights involves the attempt to introduce the new category "unlawful combatant" to international humanitarian law (IHL). For over a century IHL was based on the distinction between two categories of humans—combatants and noncombatant—and developed rules of moral conduct toward each category. Those who are in favor of introducing the category of "unlawful combatant" claim that there is a new phenomenon that is not captured by IHL and therefore it is vital to introduce a novel category and determine new rules of conduct toward it. Their opponents claim that the category is being introduced in order to legitimize immoral forms of conduct against the enemy, such as torture and detention without due process.[67] All these examples underscore the dynamic character of human rights, their multiple significations and appropriations, as well as the diverse forms of vernacularizations that they take on. They reveal that the idea of some primordial existence of original human rights is an illusion.

Once one acknowledges the ultimate instability of human rights and that their signification reflects, reproduces, and potentially transforms existing power relations, it becomes difficult not to be suspicious of claims often made by human rights practitioners about the "distortion," "misappropriation," or "perversion" of human rights. The fact that human rights are unstable signifiers does not mean, however, that they fall outside the normative sphere. On the contrary, it is precisely this instability that allows the constant redefinition, resignification, and transformation of the normative realm. After all, human *rights* produce notions of right and wrong and in this way provide a normative frame to history. Their political mobilization is carried out in order to "seize the rules of history" and define their acceptable content.[68]

Consider, in this context, the allegation often made by liberal human rights NGOs about authoritarian regimes that suddenly appropriate the language of human rights to justify certain policy choices. Condemning the deployment of human rights in this way in a discussion one of us had with a former chairperson of Amnesty International USA, he did not draw a connection between his criticism of a dictator who supposedly distorted the language of human rights and the fact that during the Cold War his own organization dealt solely with political and civil rights and was unwilling to monitor or condemn the violation of economic and social rights.[69] The dictator's so-called distortion is accordingly considered political, but Amnesty's omission is objective and neutral. Indeed, for years Amnesty's justification for this policy was that civil and political rights are first-generation rights, while economic and social rights are second generation, which is a way of producing the illusion of an original (and a hierarchy of rights) in order to provide a specific normative frame to history.[70] This, to be sure, is a politicization of human rights, and is not fundamentally different from the dictator who uses human rights discourse to justify his policies. Our claim is that human rights cannot be deployed in any other way, since every appropriation is a translation, and every translation is a form of politicization. Therefore the challenge is not to understand when human rights are politicized and when they are not. The challenge is to comprehend the ways in which they are politicized, and what the epistemic and political implications of these processes are.

HUMAN RIGHTS AND THE STATE

Our work aims to identify the meanings human rights acquire within a situation of vast power differentials and to show how human rights have been mobilized to justify, produce, and reproduce domination. The types of translation and appropriations of human rights that we describe in the chapters dealing with Israel/Palestine are taking place also across the globe. But the fact that these transformations are part of a growing global culture does not suffice to announce the death of the local and its dissolution into a decentralized form of global politics. Our emphasis on the local leads us to reject another kind of critique, the one voiced against human rights by Antonio Negri and Michael Hardt. The two authors maintain that human rights are the weapons of an amorphous form of decentralized power they call empire, which has emerged as a result of the state's ongoing disintegration.[71]

This, we believe, is a misguided critique. Empirically we are *not* witnessing the state's dissolution, the disappearance or withdrawal of state sovereignty, or the succumbing of the state from its status as the central unit within the existing global order. The state is still "the source and a target" of human rights activism.[72] Consider for a moment refugees attempting to enter Italy or Australia in order to enjoy the human rights provisions offered by these states. When refugee boats approach the promised shores, often the states in which they seek asylum send the vessels back to deep waters. As a result, over the years, thousands of refugees have ended up drowning in the sea.[73] In spite of the transformation of their seas into migrants' cemeteries, these states preserve their international legitimacy as defenders of human rights. To be sure, the European Court of Human Rights and some international NGOs condemned these states and asked them to rectify their policies, but they never questioned the relationship between human rights and the state.[74]

A similar example involves the International Criminal Court's (ICC) decision to avoid opening an investigation into alleged war crimes carried out in Gaza during Israel's 2014 military campaign "Protective Edge." Responding to criticism, the ICC's chief prosecutor, Fatou Bensouda, explained that she can only "investigate and prosecute crimes committed on the territory or by the nationals of states that have joined the ICC statute or which have otherwise accepted the jurisdiction of the ICC through an ad hoc declaration to that effect." This means, she continued, "that the alleged crimes committed in Palestine are beyond the legal reach of the ICC" since the Palestinian Authority had not signed the Rome Statute (which established the ICC).[75] The point is that without the consent of the state, one of the major international human rights bodies can neither investigate war crimes nor prosecute alleged offenders. In this way war crimes and human rights violations can be condoned in the name of the principle of sovereignty. Thus, the claim that the state is disintegrating in the face of empire seems empirically inaccurate.

In order to lay bare the complexity of the relationship between the state and human rights, we discuss in chapter 1 the state's central role within the post–World War II human rights regime. We demonstrate how the same form of political organization that was historically responsible for the most egregious human rights violations was, in turn, elevated to the protector of human rights. Not only is the state concomitantly the major perpetrator of abuse and the one responsible for securing human rights, but the postwar human rights regime also offers the state itself protection by bestowing upon it the authority to arbitrate and protect human rights. Simultaneously, the state provides this regime with legitimacy since the human rights conventions making up the regime only come into force after a certain number of states have signed and ratified them.[76]

This does not mean that the state should be considered as a totalizing structure of power, or as a coherent and autonomous actor that is external to society yet somehow fully controls it.[77] In the following pages, we unpack the relationship between the state, civil society, and human rights, showing that they are intricately imbricated, while illustrating this relationship through the creation of Israel and its colonial policies against Palestinians. Describing the contradictions informing the notion of human rights as external to the modern nation-state, we thus underscore that the relation between human rights and domination is not accidental but rather tied to the way human rights were constructed following World War II. We stress that the postwar human rights regime helped legitimize the state as the central entity within the global order. Human rights legitimize the state and are, in turn, ultimately implemented by the state through its positive laws. The legitimacy of human rights does not exceed the legitimacy of the state. If the state ever dissolves, then human rights as we know them today would also disappear.

AT THE BORDERS OF THE HUMAN

Like in many other places around the globe, in Israel/Palestine the state continues to be the primary framework through which human rights are allocated. However, within the context of the changing culture of human rights new actors constantly appear and interact with the state in different ways employing a variety of practices. Thus, in order to understand the relation between human rights and domination, we examine human rights organizations of different stripes that have mushroomed in the last two decades and analyze how their work, wittingly or unwittingly, aligns with state violence. As we show, the struggle for human rights helps determine who the subject of human rights is through the demarcation of the borders of the human, while domination operates in order to create and guard these borders.[78]

This process of determining who the subject of human rights is becomes apparent when analyzing the *inversions* taking place in Israel/Palestine.

Settler human rights NGOs portray, for instance, the indigenous Palestinians as the invaders and thus perpetrators of human rights violations, while Jewish settlers are conceived of as natives and depicted as victims of abuse. Through such processes of translation and narration human rights shape the borders of the human by determining who the subject of human rights is. For these settler NGOs the Israeli Jew is the subject of human rights, while the Palestinian is not. In fact, once human rights are identified with the Jew, they serve to bolster the Zionist project of sustaining Israel's Jewish character. Some of the organizations we analyze explicitly frame their activities as protecting "Zionist human rights."[79] These settler NGOs, which very often mirror the advocacy campaigns of liberal NGOs struggling for the human rights of Palestinians while inverting their claims of justice, underscore that human rights do not need to be grounded in a cosmopolitan worldview or in the assumption of a universal subject in order to be deployed as an effective political tool.

It could accordingly be argued that there is an essential difference between liberal human rights NGOs that strive to be inclusionary by appropriating a universal perspective and conservative NGOs that tend to be informed by an exclusionary worldview. Liberal NGOs often perceive "the human" as a more extensive category, and they resort to human rights in order to criticize government policies that discriminate against people because they are not citizens, or belong to a different ethnic group, class, or religion, or because of their gender or sexual orientation. Their work is fundamentally inspired by international law and their discourse is marked by a canonical reference to universal human rights. Settler and more broadly conservative NGOs tend to reduce the borders of the human to a specific community. Thus, among the different groups adopting human rights language and deploying human rights practices there are significant variances in relation to how the category of the human is employed.

While we are fully aware of these distinctions, in the following pages we show that they are often not clear cut, particularly because of the increasing convergences between liberals and conservatives and because the universal always acquires a specific meaning once it is articulated within the local idiom as a legal-political claim. Insofar as the universal is always contaminated or particularized by power relations within the contexts in which human rights are mobilized, then the difference between liberal and conservative or settler NGOs is not between universal and nonuniversal human rights (since the former are also nonuniversal), but is one of pretension toward what we call a "symbolic" universal.[80] Our objective is to understand how this pretension is formulated and how it affects political practices. The liberal NGOs aspire toward what they consider to be a more universal claim. Yet, as we illustrate in chapter 3, when it comes to the definition of what is legal and illegal violence, this symbolic universalism is state-centered and it enhances a particular definition of the human that is bound by citizenship. International law, which the liberal human rights NGOs incessantly invoke in their work, is aligned with the state, and often with powerful states, in a profound way.

In order to illustrate this claim we show that when Israeli liberal human rights organizations use international law to analyze an armed conflict, they can end up condemning organizations like Hamas for carrying out war crimes because of their deployment of "indiscriminate weapons," while exonerating Israel because it uses "precise weapons" from the air. The fact that Israel killed many more civilians than Hamas is beside the point, according to the liberal NGOs. Unwittingly then, liberal human rights organizations also produce a hierarchy between civilians. The people who were not intentionally targeted by states using "precise weapons" are collateral damage according to liberal human rights NGOs, while those killed by "indiscriminate weapons" are victims of war crimes.

To be sure, the different political orientations of conservative and liberal human rights NGOs lead them to appropriate human rights in different ways. The settler NGOs adopt an explicit ethnic register when they translate human rights, while liberals underscore the technological difference that is ostensibly neutral vis-à-vis the human. In reality, however, both of these camps demarcate the borders of the human in ways that often advance the political objectives of the dominant, albeit through different processes. The crux of the matter is that within the context in which they operate, the technological distinction between weapons corresponds to the ethnic distinction between Jews and Palestinians. For both settler and liberal human rights NGOs Palestinian life ends up being worth less: for the settlers because of ethnicity, for the liberals because the fact that international law favors high-tech states. As we show, one effect of these two translations of international law (one purely settler, the other liberal) is that the colonized is effectively dehumanized, while the ethnocratic-colonial ethos and its correspondent political regime are entrenched.

Israel/Palestine is not unique in this sense. During colonialism the right to employ violence and dispossess the indigenous population was framed as a sovereign right to dispose.[81] Many modern democracies were colonial powers, and the ethos of rights informing the democratic regimes was used to frame colonialism as an emancipatory and civilizing project that enhances the rights of the indigenous populations.[82] Simultaneously, though, colonization was sustained through acts of violation, ranging from massacres and rape to expropriation and dispossession.[83]

"The [liberal] illusion that basic human rights in the colonies were being respected" ended up, according to Alice Conklin, legitimating "a regime [of conquest] based on force in the age of democracy."[84] The convergence of rights and colonialism was made possible through the circumscription of the *subject* of the rights of man, so that not every human being was considered a subject worthy of enjoying full rights.[85] Colonial legal codifications translated rights that allowed for a series of distinctions between indigenous and nonindigenous rights.[86]

The difference between the colonizers of old and Israel-Palestine, though, is that Israel's right to dominate is articulated within a global landscape in which the human rights culture presents itself with more universal pretensions as a result of the development of the international human rights regime. The colonizers of the past did not conceive themselves as part of a global human rights movement devoted to the creation of universal human rights standards; they did not create or work with human rights NGOs; they did not celebrate international Human Rights Day (as settler NGOs recently did in Israel); they did not struggle over the definition of who the legitimate human rights defender is; they did not monitor or denounce other human rights organizations for their "politicization" or "distortion" of human rights or their incapacity to understand the correct definition of the borders of the human. Interrogating these transformations can, we maintain, help us gain insight into the relation between human rights and domination.

* * *

In order to illustrate how human rights can help institutionalize, legitimize, normalize, and reproduce existing relations of domination in a given historical context, we examine the deployment of human rights in Israel/Palestine, focusing primarily on the last decade. The next chapter offers a historical overview of human rights in Israel, while showing how human rights are bound by the state in profound ways. Entitled "The Paradox of Human Rights," this chapter begins by drawing a connection between the establishment of the international human rights regime and the creation of the State of Israel in 1948, showing that the Allies considered the creation of Israel as a form of human rights reparation for the horrific crimes carried out against the Jews in Europe. It then uses the Eichmann trial to illustrate how the so-called universal human rights discourse was nationalized in Israel and how human rights informed by a universal aspiration reappeared in Israel/Palestine only after the eruption of the first Intifada in 1987. The chapter goes on to describe the second

Intifada and the military campaigns against Gaza, while showing that at least in the local political arena human rights also served to normalize the colonial relations between Israelis and Palestinians.

The following three chapters focus on the deployment of human rights in Israel/Palestine over the past decade. In "The Threat of Human Rights," we show how human rights activism began to be conceived as a threat in Israel, while describing the institutional response to this threat. We demonstrate how Israeli conservative actors began to frame liberal human rights NGOs as a national security threat not in order to reject human rights tout court but in order to counter the liberal NGOs' attempt to palliate and restrict state violence, and in order to ultimately legitimize Israeli military warfare. In the next chapter, "The Human Right to Kill," we describe the convergence between Israeli military, government officials, and security think tanks on the one hand, and liberal human rights NGOs on the other. Focusing on Israel's military campaigns against Gaza, we show how international humanitarian law is used by Israel to legitimize and justify the killing of Palestinian civilians. We go on to demonstrate that liberal human rights NGOs adopt international law in a way that rationalizes the deployment of lethal violence against Palestinians. In the fourth chapter, "The Human Right to Colonize," we describe the emergence of settler human rights NGOs and show how they use human rights discourse to advance colonial dispossession both in the Occupied Palestinian Territories and in Israel. Not unlike chapter 3, we show how this form of "human rights activism" takes place in a political, legal, and strategic space of convergence with liberal NGOs that support the human rights of Palestinians.

In the concluding chapter, we ponder whether human rights can still be used in a counterhegemonic way after they have been appropriated to advance domination. Far from rejecting human rights and their political potential to correct social wrongs, we argue that human rights can still be a potent tool for advancing justice. Hence for us "to be for human rights means," following Edward Said, "to be willing to venture interpretations of those rights *in the same place and with the same language* employed by the dominant power."[87] It means, in other words, to understand human rights as a form of power, and to understand power as a mechanism that increasingly adopts human rights as its lingua franca. Consequently, the political and ethical obligation is not only to interrogate the intersection of power and human rights so as to better understand its epistemological and political implications, but also to constantly interpret and reinterpret human rights in a way that subverts forms of domination.

CHAPTER 1

The Paradox of Human Rights

There was hardly a Western liberal during the late 1940s through to the 1970s who did not explicitly say that the establishment of Israel in 1948 was one of the great achievements of the postwar era, and who did not think it at all necessary to add that this was so for its victors in particular. From the point of view of the survivors of the dreadful massacre of the European Jews it was a central achievement: there is no point at all in denying that. The Jews who came to Palestine were the victims of Western civilization, totally unlike the French military who conquered Algeria, the British felons forced to settle Australia, or those who have ravaged Ireland for several hundred years, or the Boers and the British who still rule in South Africa. But to admit that the difference in identity between Zionists and white settlers in Africa, Europe, Asia, Australia, and the Americas is an important one, is not to underplay the grave consequences that tie all the groups together.

—Edward Said

As the victors of World War II became fully aware of the ghastly consequences of the Nazi death machine, the idea of creating a regime to protect human rights rapidly surfaced in the international arena. A human rights vocabulary was developed in order to make sense of the horrors of the past and to help shape a new geopolitical order controlled by the war's victors. These efforts were propelled by the desire to find a way to prevent the repetition of such horrific acts in the future. "Crimes against humanity" became a common expression among the representatives of the postwar international community, while "never again" was adopted as a human rights truism against the recurrence of those crimes. From this moral and political framework, the Universal Declaration of Human Rights emerged and was adopted by the United Nations in 1948.

Many prominent human rights exponents, including René Cassin, Raphael Lemkin, and Louis Henkin, interpreted the postwar ascendency of human rights as a mechanism that limits state power.[1] Universal human rights, according to this narrative, emerged after World War II to counter the excesses of the state by limiting the violence to which it can subject its own citizenry.[2] As Jack Donnelly, a leading human rights scholar in the United States, put it: "International law, including international human rights law, is the record of restrictions on sovereignty accepted by states."[3] Leading organizations such as Amnesty International and Human Rights Watch also adopted this account and have been advocating human rights to help secure the freedom and liberation of individuals struggling against oppressive governments for decades. Aryeh Neier, the first executive director of Human Rights Watch, explains that human rights are "a series of limits on the exercise of power. The state and those holding the power of states are forbidden to interfere with freedom of inquiry or expression. They may not deprive anyone of liberty arbitrarily. They are prohibited from denying each person the right to count equally and to obtain the equal protection of the laws. They are denied the power to inflict cruelty. And they must respect a zone of privacy."[4] The assumption is that human rights are in some way external to the state and are most often deployed in an effort to protect citizens from the state and indeed restrict its abuses.

This linear narrative of global salvation and redemption through human rights—a narrative that is reproduced in most scholarly books and taught in most human rights courses—disintegrates, however, once one examines more closely the explicit paradoxes of the postwar human rights regime.[5] In the following pages, we problematize this process through the analysis of its political underpinnings and implications in Israel/Palestine. In particular, we discuss how the new regime bestowed upon the nation-state a central role in the postwar human rights order. We highlight how the nation-state was granted responsibility to protect human rights, while simultaneously the human rights regime provided the state with international legitimacy. We then turn to explain how the creation of Israel as the state of the Jewish people reveals one of the central paradoxes of human rights. Finally, we show how during different historical moments—the Eichmann trial, Oslo years, and second Intifada—the international human rights discourse was appropriated to enhance domination.

Let us turn to the Universal Declaration of Human Rights. According to this foundational charter of the contemporary human rights regime, "Member States have pledged themselves to achieve, in co-operation with the United Nations, the promotion of universal respect for and observance of human rights and fundamental freedoms."[6] Hence, out of the atrocities perpetrated mainly by European nation-states, aspirations for justice were articulated through a universal vocabulary of human rights. Human rights thus became the moral standard for scrutinizing political violence and evaluating the relationships among states themselves and between states and the people living within their borders, while the nation-state was instated as the pillar of the new moral order in a very specific way.

First, it was restored as the constitutive unit of a global family (the so-called "family of nations") responsible alongside the UN for securing "harmony, peace and freedom."[7] Second, the authority to implement the emerging human rights regime was bestowed upon the state. In other words, human rights served to restore the legitimacy of this political entity, both as the central unit of global politics and as the juridical actor responsible for the people under its governance. By reproducing the complex bond between the universal and the state, the post–World War II human rights regime helped resurrect the nation-state from the ruins it had engendered. Simultaneously, the nation-state conferred upon the Universal Declaration and international instruments emanating from it legitimacy. After all, human rights conventions only come into force once a certain number of member states have signed and ratified them. It is because of these interrelated tensions that we can speak of an epistemic and political paradox intrinsic to the post–World War II human rights regime.

This paradox is characterized by a tripartite configuration, operating as a complex and supposedly self-evident combination of *protection from*, *protection by*, and *protection of* the state. The 1948 Convention on the Prevention and Punishment of the Crime of Genocide exemplifies this clearly. First, it identifies the state and its officials as the potential perpetrators of genocide and human rights violations, thus instituting the *protection from* the state. Second, it requires state-parties to recognize the crime of genocide as a constitutive element of international law and to punish persons guilty of genocide, thereby ascribing to the state the responsibility to protect. Hence, the citizen is simultaneously protected *from* and *by* the state. Finally, as an instrument that empowers the state to protect the citizen, the convention offers the state itself protection; it serves as the *protection of* the state within the postwar world order by offering it continuous recognition and legitimacy as the central unit of the order itself and primary enforcer of the convention. In all the major human rights conventions and treaties the three forms of protection—from, by, and of—are combined and the centrality of the nation-state is thus reiterated.[8] This combination, we maintain, lies at the core of a paradox and points to an intricate link between human rights and domination.

Despite its universal pretentions, human rights, as several scholars have already pointed out, are bound by the state and acquire different meanings in different historical and geographical contexts.[9] Yet an extremely important element has remained constant within the diverse post–World War II adoptions and articulations of human rights: not only has the nation-state persisted as the key political form responsible for the organization and management of human communities, but also belonging to a nation-state has become the fundamental condition for acquiring human rights and becoming a member of an internationally recognized community.[10]

The struggle for human rights was considered by dominated people— women, colonized, disenfranchised minorities, and so on—as a way to achieve freedom from oppression and exploitation, and acquire the "right to be human."[11] This struggle came to embody a process through which dominated groups could either achieve self-determination or become full citizens in an existing state and thus enter the family of nations. By becoming a sovereign people or citizens of a sovereign state, the stateless believed they would be protected and acquire international legitimacy, independence, and dignity—the conditions for being fully recognized as human by those who had already attained citizenship. Entering the family of nations, a process enshrined in the Declaration as a universal human right, thus became one of the ultimate goals of the stateless. Consequently, alongside the struggles for human dignity and defense from state abuses, human rights were conceived as synonym of the struggle for national statecraft. Universal human rights thus provided the framework for the creation of new states in the name of self-determination. Simultaneously, a central role in securing human rights was bestowed upon the state, even though colonial and World War II history demonstrates that the sovereign state is among the most egregious human-rights-violating entities.

Developments in the international arena after World War II and throughout the decolonization process are similar to the changes taking place in colonial Egypt analyzed by Samera Esmeir. Esmeir poignantly shows how in Egypt the definition of the human was constituted through modern law under colonial rule. She calls this process "juridical humanity" and describes it as a mechanism through which modern colonial law "endows itself with the power of humanization, and declares that its absence signals dehumanization," binding the definition of the human to (colonial) state power.[12] Along similar lines, but on a global scale, the treaties and conventions that followed the publication of the Universal Declaration can be interpreted as the articulation of an *international juridical humanity.* They laid out the conditions for having one's (individual) or a people's (collective) humanity recognized and protected within the postwar international order.

Anticolonial and, more broadly, post–World War II self-determination struggles can thus be understood as struggles for obtaining access to a full (previously denied) condition of humanity recognized by the community of nations, with all of its paradoxical implications. Self-determination transforms the victims of human rights violations into full human beings, since only after the collective enters the framework of the state does it become an active agent of history. When in 1952 the UN General Assembly adopted the resolution "The Right of Peoples and Nations to Self-Determination," it couched self-determination as "the prerequisite to the full enjoyment of all fundamental human rights."[13] Hannah Arendt made a similar point when she claimed that at the very moment when the refugee appears on the political scene, when the individual is divorced from citizenship and all forms of political community so that only the so-called human remains, at that moment all human rights are lost.[14] It is, she infers, the state that bestows rights on people.

But what were the political implications of granting the state the responsibility to protect people from human rights violations? What kind of new political agencies were developed as a result of this process? And how does this process help us better understand the relationship between human rights and domination? In order to explore these and other questions we will now turn to Israel/Palestine, not because this case study is necessarily unique, but because it exposes the implications of the paradox of human rights in a clear and urgent way.

REPARATION FOR HUMAN RIGHTS VIOLATIONS

The European Holocaust, undoubtedly one of the major triggers propelling the development of the language and political practices that constitute the contemporary human rights regime, produced in Palestine—far from the territorial and geographical setting in which the extermination of the Jews took place—one of the most illuminating examples of the paradoxical welding of human rights with national statecraft. In fact, the history of Israel's creation illustrates very clearly the paradox of the international human rights regime and the constitutive interrelationship between human rights, national statecraft, and domination. It does so because during the mid-1940s the Allies conceived Israel's foundation as a type of humanitarian reparation for the crimes committed against Jews in Europe during the Holocaust, while this reparation assumed the form of a settler nation-state (in Palestine) whose colonial practices generated new human rights violations.[15]

Israel's establishment coincided with the international response to the genocide that took place in Europe, the foundation of the UN, and the publication of the Universal Declaration.[16] Debated within a framework of self-determination for both Arabs and Jews, the 1947 partition plan of Palestine was meant to provide two stateless peoples with two states by dividing a single territory—the British colony of Palestine.[17] According to the plan, the indigenous Palestinian majority, comprising 68 percent of the population, was to receive about 43 percent of the land, whereas the Jewish minority, comprising 32 percent of the population, was allocated 57 percent of mandatory Palestine.[18] Self-determination through the creation of a state was discussed by the UN member states as a post-Holocaust humanitarian solution for those Jews living outside of Mandatory Palestine as well, and was therefore conceived within the broader framework of human rights.

Hence, Jewish migration to Palestine alongside national settler statecraft was first contemplated and then implemented as a way out from the protracted condition of refugee-hood in which Jewish survivors were left after the Holocaust. As Daniel Cohen points out, in contrast with other ethnic groups assisted by the International Refugee Organization (i.e., a UN agency), postwar Jewish refugees occupied a position of political centrality in international relations. Unlike other refugee communities in Europe, the UN did not limit itself to providing assistance to the stateless Jews, but rather morphed the "political victims" into a state-forming "political nation."[19] The UN drew a connection among three issues: the genocide and other egregious human rights violations carried out against the Jews during World War II; its efforts to find a solution for the postwar Jewish refugee problem in Europe; and the establishment of a state for the Jewish people in Palestine.

Consequently, it is not surprising that Zionist scholars like Alexander Yakobson and Amnon Rubinstein have described the creation of Israel as embedded in the global history of human rights. "Everything that naturally derives from [the] definition [of the Jewish state], including the Law of Return,[20] meets human rights norms as accepted by the free world today, not just acceptable in 1947," the two scholars argue.[21] And, indeed, when one carefully examines the connection between Israel and human rights, a prominent feature emerges: namely, that the establishment of a nation-state, in this case Israel, was considered by the international community as a natural reparation for human rights violations carried out by Nazi Germany and other European states.

After World War II, the Allies referred to the extermination of millions of European Jews as an unprecedented moment in human history. The notion of genocide was introduced into international legal and moral debates on human rights as the primal form of violation against which the international community should adopt a politics of permanent mobilization—a new politics against those "acts committed with intent to destroy, in whole or in part, a national, ethnical, racial or religious group."[22] But while the extermination of people was framed as a relatively new phenomenon, and as "the primal murder that founds contemporary Human Rights Discourse,"[23] authors from Hannah Arendt and Aimé Césaire to Frantz Fanon and Mahmood Mamdani subsequently underscored that the European Holocaust had a long history, since systematic mass killing along racial lines was first developed in the European colonies before being redeployed in the continent.[24] In brief, the extermination of the European Jews cannot be fully understood without examining its colonial and imperial antecedents. This historical recontextualization of the Holocaust in the broader genealogy of genocides (especially in their settler form) is essential for understanding the paradox of human rights in our context, as we show momentarily.

The international recognition that a state should be granted to the "Jewish nation" as post-Holocaust reparation for collective human rights violations became commonsensical because of a number of factors. Not least among these was the intensive work of the Zionist movement, which for years had lobbied state leaders and international organizations in order to legitimize its aspiration to create a homeland for the Jews in Palestine.[25] In 1945, the Jewish Agency—the organization in charge of buying and settling land in Palestine on behalf of the Zionist movement— tried to lobby the member states at the UN conference in San Francisco as they signed the UN Charter, in which for the first time human rights were referred to as one of the constitutive elements of the international order.[26] In this context, the objective of the Jewish Agency was to generate further international legitimacy for the creation of a Jewish state by introducing into the conference's agenda the relation between the plight of European Jewish survivors and the creation of a Jewish homeland in Palestine.

The memoires of Eliahu Elath, representative of the Jewish Agency's Political Department and later the first Israeli ambassador to the UN, shed light on this process. He describes how the Zionist efforts to weld the Jewish aspiration to self-determination in the British colony of Palestine and the emergence of an international community coalesced around the principles of human rights. In *Zionism at the UN*, Elath writes that "One of the most urgent problems awaiting solution is that of the survivors of the

Holocaust. Will the [San Francisco] conference rise to this challenge? Will it understand the problem and draw the necessary practical conclusions affecting the future of Palestine, the only country where their national life and dignity can be fully restored?"[27]

The notion of *Israel as reparation*—a state where Jewish human dignity could be "fully restored"—was espoused by the Great Powers, especially by President Truman, who closely followed the plight of the Jewish refugees in Europe. In 1945, the president sent Earl G. Harrison—a dean from the University of Pennsylvania—to carry out a survey on displaced persons in Europe. "Harrison reported that the one million Jewish survivors still living in temporary refugee camps throughout Europe were behind barbed-wire fences in what had been concentration camps, and they survived on a diet consisting of bread and coffee. . . . Harrison concluded his study by recommending that the 'only real solution' would be the immediate evacuation to Palestine of those Jews who desired to leave Europe." Immediately after reading the report, Truman started to exert pressure on the British government to allow Jewish immigration to Palestine.[28]

Two years later, Britain agreed to raise the issue of Palestine at the UN. The relationship between Israel's creation and the plight of Jewish refugees in Europe was at the center of a thorny debate in the UN's Special Committee on Palestine (UNSCOP). During the proceedings, several member states sent their representatives to the European camps where Jewish survivors were hosted after the end of the war and assessed their "attitude regarding resettlement, repatriation or immigration into Palestine."[29] The idea of settling Jews in Palestine as a solution for the humanitarian crisis in Europe became a central point in the debate on the partition of Palestine.

In his decisive 1947 testimony at UNSCOP, Chaim Weizman, the UN representative of the Jewish Agency who later became Israel's first president, called upon the member states to "encourage intensive colonization" in the territory that the international community would soon decide to recognize as the state of Israel.[30] Weizman's invocation became reality, since Israel's state-building process amounted to the destruction of hundreds of Palestinian villages, the systematic expulsion of the indigenous population, and the settlement of hundreds of thousands of Jews in their stead.[31] The reparation of a human rights violation through settler colonialism was bound to generate a new cycle of violence.[32] The firm connection between the humanitarian solution for the European Jews who survived the Holocaust and were subsequently dispersed in refugee camps and the creation of a settler Jewish state in Palestine after decades of Zionist mobilization serves as a powerful example of the paradox of the post–World

War II human rights regime. While human rights were announced and enunciated as tools of protection from violent and dispossessive nation-states, dispossessed Jews were entitled to create a nation-state whose foundational form was settler colonialism. As we noted earlier, the genealogy of the European genocide can be traced back to the forms of violence first instituted by settler colonialism.

In this paradoxical context, the framing of Israel's establishment as a humanitarian solution provided its settler colonial nature with an aura of international legitimacy. It also reveals that the two apparently irreconcilable discourses of human rights and domination can and do coincide, as well as how the first can be deployed to legitimize and normalize the second. This historical process is significant since it serves as a paradigmatic example of how the birth of post–World War II human rights regime was located in a space in which human rights, nation-state, and domination are entangled in a Gordian knot.

THE EICHMANN TRIAL AND THE SUBJECT OF HUMAN RIGHTS

The Specialist, the name given to Adolf Eichmann in an inspiring courtroom documentary, was one of the masterminds of the extermination of Europe's Jews.[33] In charge of a subdepartment of Jewish affairs at the Gestapo (the Nazi secret police), Eichmann was one of the architects of the Nazi system of deportation and annihilation. When in 1960 Israeli secret service agents kidnapped Eichmann in Argentina and brought him to be tried in Israel, the survivors of the "Final Solution" were, for the first time, directly confronted with the dilemma of what to do with a perpetrator of some of the most horrendous crimes documented in human history.

Often identified as a constitutive moment in the creation of an international legal regime of universal jurisdiction, the Eichmann trial did not dissolve the post–World War II paradoxes of human rights.[34] On the contrary, it further revealed the contradictions of the evolving human rights regime in several ways. First, Eichmann was kidnapped by the Mossad (the Israeli secret services) in Argentina, where he had fled after World War II. Thus, Israel violated international law to bring to trial a criminal of international law. Second, and more fundamentally in the context of our discussion, as Hannah Arendt and other critics have already highlighted, the Nazi genocide that triggered the development of the universal vocabulary of human rights was investigated in Jerusalem in a local court, where this ostensible universal discourse was translated into an ethnonational one. Arendt consequently concludes that "the very monstrousness of the events is 'minimized' before a tribunal that represents one nation only."[35]

During the trial, the new Jew, the Israeli Jew who was unprotected before the state's creation, was transformed into the subject of human rights, while the new state was deemed responsible for this transformation and for securing these rights. Human rights were accordingly made to coincide with the rights of Jews by completely ignoring the horrific violations Eichmann carried out against non-Jews. Indeed, reading the transcripts of the prosecution, one is left under the impression that human rights violations were committed during the European extermination against Jews and only Jews.[36] In this way, the trial helped reproduce an existing Israeli moral framework that privileges the Jew over the non-Jew, but now the framework was rationalized through the invocation of international law—and the identification of the Jew with the subject of human rights. Moreover, the appeal to international law bolstered an existing moral framework that helped further rationalize certain laws and policies that already existed in Israel, such as the Law of Return, which provides any Jew (and only Jews) the exclusive right to "return" to Israel and immediately become a citizen, or the policies that allow the state to expropriate land from Palestinians and allocate it to Jews.[37] Hence, the trial, with all its universal pretensions, was subsumed by a local idiom and given a specific meaning; it served both to articulate an existing logic connecting the Jewish character of the state and the human subject, and as a vehicle through which this logic was further rationalized and disseminated.

However, pushing our reflection beyond the historical moment, one can gain a glimpse of how the Eichmann trial continued to inform the relationship between human rights and domination. Building on Talal Asad's insights on the practical effects of human rights when they are translated into the local language of the nation-state, we have to ask ourselves what role human rights played after Eichmann was hanged in 1962.[38] Indeed, the unprecedented configuration of the Eichmann trial, and the legal-political mechanism through which it was performed, generated a situation whereby human rights for Jews were nationalized and the state assumed sole responsibility for their protection. This nationalization buried the universal human rights discourse within the Israeli political arena, and for almost three decades following the trial one witnesses the promulgation of an ethnocentric nationalism without direct mobilization of human rights discourse. But even though human rights had almost disappeared from the discursive landscape, they continued to produce an array of political effects. In the following section we examine how human rights were further transmuted into nationalism and thus contributed to the enhancement of ethnonational domination even without being directly invoked.

THE RETERRITORIALIZATION OF THE THREAT

Due to a convergence of various historical processes, the Eichmann trial exacerbated the instrumentalization of the Holocaust by helping to facilitate the articulation of two interconnected projections: temporal and spatial. It helped project the genocidal threat of the past into Israel's present, and was used as a mechanism to expedite the geographical displacement of the threat of egregious human rights violations from a European territorial setting to a Middle Eastern one. The combination of these two projections accelerated the progressive equation between the European human rights violators of World War II and Arab populations of the Middle East. This is the twofold nature of what we define as the reterritorialization of the threat, and it is relevant here because it exposes more clearly how the paradox of human rights manifests itself even when this discourse is not invoked.

As Idith Zertal convincingly argued, in order to comprehend the political impact of the Eichmann trial we must analyze it in its relation to the 1967 War between Israel and the Arab armies. Before the trial Israel had adopted a strategy of "selective amnesia," "suspension of the grief," and "organized silence" in which the Holocaust and the experience of exile were all but disavowed by the state in order to construct a new Jewish identity—namely, the "new Jew" who escaped a vulnerable condition of exile and achieved self-determination in Israel. However, the Eichmann trial marked a return of the vulnerability discourse and transformed the Holocaust's memory of suffering into a national discourse of existential threat.[39] In other words, through the trial the Holocaust's threat was projected into Israel's current present and into a new territorial setting different from the one in which it had originated.

Eichmann, who was guilty of crimes against humanity committed in Europe, was judged in the Middle East, in the territorial setting of the state that was considered by the Western powers as reparation for those very crimes. Concomitantly, the Arab states in the region as well as the Palestinians who were displaced as a result of Israel's establishment were progressively equated with Eichmann. In fact, following the trial Ben-Gurion and other political leaders carried out a fundamental discursive operation that Zertal defines as the "nazification of the enemy."[40] The connection between the Holocaust and the Arabs was produced through the latter's transformation into an existential threat, reinforcing the idea of Israel as an entity in a permanent state of emergency.

During and after the 1967 War, the Israeli conquest of new Palestinian and Arab territories was constructed as an answer to this state of permanent emergency.[41] When in 1969—two years after his post–1967 War speech at the UN in which he defined the war as an Arab "collective assault [against] the last sanctuary of a people which had seen six million of its sons exterminated by a more powerful dictator two decades before,"[42]— Abba Eban, Israel's foreign minister at that time, defined the return to the pre-1967 borders as "something of a memory of Auschwitz."[43] He thus evoked the temporal persistence of the Holocaust into the present. In this way, through the metaphor of "Auschwitz lines"—a metaphor that was later remobilized by other Israeli political actors—he reterritorialized the threat in the context of Israel's conquests. A withdrawal from the territories occupied in 1967 would have corresponded, according to Abba Eban's logic, to the return of history: the potential repetition, in a new temporal and spatial setting, of the horrific events that triggered the creation of the contemporary international human rights regime.

The paradox of human rights in Israel after the Eichmann trial is precisely this process through which the crimes against humanity committed in Europe served to rationalize and justify the rights-abusive expansionist process of Israeli national statecraft in the Middle East. The "eternal presence" of the horrific violations perpetrated during the Holocaust served, in other words, to validate the claim that Israel was constantly threatened by the potential repetition of these violations.[44] Thus, the spatial and temporal displacement of the Holocaust into the Palestinian Middle East served to justify practices of forced relocation and dispossession of the area's indigenous population; it helped legitimize settler colonial practices (in the territories occupied in 1967), because it enabled Israel to evoke the past in order to provide the domination of the present with moral justification. Conquest and colonization were normalized and legitimized as a sort of preemptive measure against the rematerialization of Auschwitz.

Fundamentally, this discourse of permanent emergency resulted in a twofold reification. First, it transformed the Arabs into an ultimate threat. Second, it re-emphasized and crystallized the position of Israeli Jews as the perpetual victims of human rights violations. In another local manifestation of the global paradox we have been examining in this chapter, human rights were subsumed by the nationalist ethnocentric rhetoric and therefore made to disappear.

A DIFFERENT HUMAN RIGHTS DISCOURSE?

During the 1970s and the beginning of the 1980s human rights continued to play a role in the background of Israel's policies in the Middle East. Israel's rights-abusive policies were condemned in different UN resolutions, which used the language of international law while emphasizing the Palestinian right to self-determination. However, these resolutions were like empty words voiced merely to fulfill a ceremonious obligation. The human rights vocabulary was hardly invoked—within Israel, the territories it had occupied in 1967, or the international arena—at the popular level even though the Palestinians in the West Bank and Gaza had been living under Israeli military rule for an extended period and had been subjected to various human rights violations and forms of state violence on a daily basis.[45]

Only following the outbreak of the first Palestinian uprising (known as the Intifada) in December 1987 did the discourse begin to change. When the first Intifada erupted, protesters in the Occupied Palestinian Territories (OPT) filled the streets, demonstrating against the occupying power; they blocked the major arteries with burning tires and large rocks and threw stones and Molotov cocktails at military patrols. Preservation of law and order in the OPT had come to be perceived among the general Palestinian public as serving the interests of an illegitimate government, indicating that violation of the law and challenging Israel's authority were considered to be acts of patriotism, loyalty, and heroism. Fundamentally, the uprising was an attempt to unveil the oppressive character of what had been primarily couched by the occupying forces as a bureaucratic rule. The goal was to force Israel to replace the colonial rule of law and its administrative apparatus with more soldiers and, in this way, to undercut all attempts to present the occupation as normal. Israeli rule, in other words, would apply only where soldiers were present to enforce it. The objective was to undo Israel's twenty-year efforts to normalize the occupation in the West Bank and the Gaza Strip.

It is within this context that the human rights discourse reappeared on the political scene under a new guise. After decades in which Israel strengthened its collective nationalist identity and the Palestinian liberation movement shaped its struggle as a nationalist anticolonial one based on armed resistance, and almost twenty years (starting from the 1970s) in which the world had witnessed the increasing mobilization of individual human rights as tools for international campaigns of advocacy, Palestinians adopted the language of human rights and used it both to justify their resistance and as a critique of Israel's military rule. Human rights were progressively adopted as the language spearheading the struggle for self-determination.[46]

The uprising, which was informed by an array of anticolonial actions ranging from demonstrations and strikes to a boycott of Israeli goods, was met with harsh measures, including extrajudicial executions, massive administrative arrests, curfews, closure of schools and universities, and severe restrictions on movement[47] But an important transformation occurred: Palestinians as well as Israeli and international media that covered the ongoing events started to frame the confrontations between the Palestinian resistance and the Israeli military using the vocabulary of human rights. This international coverage of the uprising, particularly in major English-speaking outlets, seems to have had some impact on those reporters who covered the events for the local press as well as on the public relations apparatuses of the Israeli government and military, all of which responded to allegations of abuse using similar language and emphasizing that they too were concerned with the humanitarian plight of the Palestinians.

Furthermore, within an extremely short period, human rights were institutionalized, and numerous new NGOs emerged. Before the uprising erupted, only one human rights NGO existed in Israel, while about 15 human rights NGOs were established in the years immediately following its outbreak. In the OPT, the impact of the uprising on the institutionalization of human rights was just as striking. Only two human rights NGOs existed before the Intifada, and about six others were established within a very short period following its eruption.[48] This proliferation took place with the help of international funding.[49] In some cases, Palestinian human rights NGOs helped fill the void created in 1967 following Israel's banning of all Palestinian political parties. These NGOs instantly created networks among themselves and with a range of international human rights groups, from Amnesty International and Middle East Watch (a predecessor of Human Rights Watch) to the International Commission of Jurists and Physicians for Human Rights USA. They imported, translated, reinterpreted, modified, and contextualized the global human rights discourse in order to connect it to the local political landscape.

The new NGOs began using the human rights vocabulary in their press releases, reports, and correspondence with Israeli authorities (government, military, civil administration). Some of them focused on Palestinian victims of torture, introducing the language of clinical trauma as a tool for advocating human rights in the Palestinian political arena. Other organizations centered their activities on monitoring forms of violations that became the basic grammar of human rights activism for Palestine:

deportations, house demolitions, administrative detention, dispossession, denial of the freedom of movement.[50] In addition, several of the new rights organizations adopted the direct litigation strategy and filed literally hundreds of petitions to the Israeli courts, invoking both international humanitarian and human rights law in their petitions.[51] The media covered some of these cases so that the rights discourse also entered the public domain via the Israeli judicial system, after it had infiltrated from the international sphere to domestic NGOs that employed it in their appeals.

Thus, the first Palestinian popular uprising and the diffusion of the global human rights discourse helped reframe the Palestinian question. For the first time after Israel's establishment, the abuses committed by the occupying state against the Palestinian population were systematically framed as human rights violations. Palestinians in the West Bank and Gaza Strip slowly gained access to the international "circle of victims" of human rights violations, producing a new situation whereby human rights claims were no longer the prerogative of the Jewish population of Israel/Palestine. This reframing process triggered an incremental shift in international public opinion toward the plight of the Palestinians, first among activists and later among wider segments of civil society.

A PARADOXICAL SITUATION

This "globalization of Palestine" through the language of human rights ended up having a significant impact on the region's political landscape.[52] The framing of the conflict using human rights and the increasing international preoccupation with the violations perpetrated against Palestinians helped force Israel to the negotiating table. After Israeli prime minister Yitzchak Rabin and PLO leader Yasser Arafat signed the Oslo Accords on the White House lawn in September 1993, international donors continued funding human rights NGOs both in Israel and in the OPT in order to help promote the implementation of the peace process. The rights groups were expected to monitor and denounce Israel's practices of dispossession of Palestinian land as well as to expose other rights abusive policies. Within Palestinian society, human rights NGOs also acquired a prominent role in promoting and assisting the so-called state-building process managed by the Palestinian Authority.[53] They often became an alternative to grassroots initiatives and traditional political parties in what critics have since called the NGOization of civil society.[54]

This new "human rights boom" did not, however, produce a rupture in the region's history of political violence. Notwithstanding the increasing activism, the NGOs did not manage to even create a dent within the local framework of colonial sovereignty. One example will have to suffice here. During the first Intifada, NGOs filed petitions to the Israeli High Court of Justice against the violation of Palestinian human rights. While these petitions seemed to be challenging government policies, and in some sense they partially did, for the most part the court ended up discharging Israel from any kind of responsibility for egregious violations.[55] Indeed, Israel's High Court of Justice enabled the government to continue carrying out home demolitions; it authorized holding Palestinians in prison for years on end without trial (administrative detention); it justified the expropriation of Palestinian land and the deportation of Palestinian leaders, and it took well over 10 years after human rights NGOs launched an international campaign before it decided to outlaw torture.[56] In the absence of an international body able to enforce international human rights conventions, cause lawyers and activists remained trapped in the paradox of human rights whereby the colonized had to resort to the colonizer's court to seek protection. These practitioners found themselves requesting the dominant state to secure the human rights of the stateless Palestinians.[57] Ultimately, human rights were incorporated by Israeli courts, in the sense that the court began to use the language of human rights to reinforce "discretionary justice."[58]

Wittingly or not, by filing petitions the human rights NGOs helped legitimize the very same Israeli courts that many Palestinians had boycotted during the occupation's first decades. The human rights discourse brought the Israeli regime and the colonized closer, creating a convergence, but in a way that was far from the coexistence and peace that this discourse intended to produce. Through their daily interaction with these courts as well as with the Israeli military and different government offices, human rights practitioners helped validate the institutional framework of the settler colonial state. The state that was responsible for extrajudicial executions, torture, home demolitions, and dispossession, was asked to be both the arbitrator of and protector from the violations that it was carrying out.

During this period, the first discussions concerning the correct proportion between national security and respect of human rights (see chapter 2) emerged among Israeli legal experts. Invoking the principle of proportionality—requiring belligerents to refrain from causing damage disproportionate to the military advantage to be gained—Justus Reid Weiner, a senior attorney at the Israeli Ministry of Justice during the first

Intifada and currently a researcher at the Jerusalem Center for Public Affairs, displaces the context of violence in which proportions are calculated. Writing in 1991, in the midst of the first Intifada, Weiner claims that

> A good part of the criticism Israel has faced is the result of the prolonged nature of the uprising. Israel is the only state in the Middle East that would have tolerated an insurrection like the Intifada and allowed it to persist for more than three years. Indeed, it is the great good fortune of participants in the Intifada that their adversary in this struggle is the state of Israel, a democracy committed not only to its own citizens' security, but to human rights for those non-citizens living under its rule.[59]

Human rights, the language that NGOs adopted in order to unveil the nature of the Israeli regime in the OPT, was beginning to be adopted by those "organic" legal experts whose ultimate political objective was the preservation of the ethnonational regime itself.[60] Indeed, this is one of the first instances we have come across in which a state official frames the state's policies toward Palestinians using the language of human rights.

On the one hand, then, the introduction of a human rights discourse in Israel/Palestine during the first Intifada—focusing on the human rights of the colonized rather than on the human rights of the colonizer—produced new practices echoing a broader transformation in global advocacy. Most importantly, it spurred the reframing of the conflict and began to alter the perspective regarding the identity of victim and perpetrator, particularly in the international arena. This rearticulation of the discourse facilitated the reframing of the historical understanding of the relationship between domination and human rights in the area, and triggered a different discourse from the one that had dominated the previous decades. Jews no longer had sole proprietorship of victimhood.

On the other hand, however, human rights did not materialize as a tangible or effective counterhegemonic political force, particularly not within the local context in which they were deployed.[61] The human rights NGOs helped numerous Palestinians patients cross checkpoints to reach hospitals; they postponed several house demolitions; they located thousands of political prisoners who had been taken from their homes in the middle of the night; they, at times, even pressured the military to lift a curfew; but they had no effect on the occupation's structure and did not even destabilize the routine of domination that had led to their emergence. Moreover, the introduction of the global human rights discourse that was among the main causes of the NGOization of Palestinian society in many ways undermined other Palestinian political cultures of resistance. Thus, even though (or perhaps because) human rights had become a hegemonic discourse, it did not manage to alter the asymmetry of power in the area. On the contrary, as the quote from Justus Reid Weiner exemplifies, the circulation of human rights discourse in Israel provided the settler state with a new tool to corroborate its legitimacy.

Prominent Israeli human rights lawyer Michael Sfard emphasized this point when he claimed that the mobilization of human rights within the Israeli legal system has generated a paradoxical situation that enables the state to criticize itself while in effect producing its own legitimization:

> The human rights lawyer's dilemma is ... complex. Arguably, internal opposition may lead, eventually, to a symbiosis between resistance movements and the authorities. The authorities need internal opposition to better assess the feasibility and ease of implementing its policies. It needs human rights litigation as a policy "fine-tuner." This insight is overwhelming: the opposition, when it uses only internal means of combat, becomes part of the practice to which it objects. Its resistance is nicely boxed and is given an official role as a phase in the policy structuring procedure.[62]

Hence, human rights, in spite of the new framework in which they were deployed following the eruption of the first Intifada, conserved their paradoxical characteristics. At the end of the day, state institutions structurally embedded in the colonial system appropriated the human rights critique in order to constitute themselves as both legitimate and lawful. The performance, whereby the human rights lawyers appear in court, and judges arbitrate between plaintiffs and government institutions that carry out violations, helped the state constitute an image of equanimity and morality. In this sense, the human rights critique became a legitimizing tool for state domination. In another manifestation of the paradox, the *protection from* the state merged with the *protection of* the state.

NORMALIZING DOMINATION

In September 2000, after the failure of the Oslo peace process and the continuous expansion of Israel's settling activities in the OPT the second Intifada erupted. The Israeli military defined the events in the OPT as an "armed conflict short of war," and thus expanded the range of situations in which soldiers were permitted to fire live ammunition even in cases when there was no immediate life-threatening danger.[63] Another feature of the change involved expanding the use of extrajudicial executions.

Up until December 2008 the assassination policy led to the death of 384 Palestinians.[64] While the assassination policy was, in fact, the continuation of a long-established practice, the year 2000 was the first time that Israel officially acknowledged its use of extrajudicial executions.[65] In this way, Israel transformed the West Bank and Gaza Strip into the international military lab for aerial assassinations.[66]

In the military operation dubbed Defensive Shield still other changes in Israel's repertoires of violence became apparent. The massive attack was launched in the West Bank on March 29, 2002, in response to a suicide attack where a Palestinian blew himself up during a Passover meal in a hotel dining room, killing twenty-eight people. This was the culmination of a bloody month for Israel, perhaps the bloodiest one in Israel's history in terms of civilian deaths, with eighty-one Israelis killed in daily attacks. Call-up notices for 20,000 reserve soldiers were issued, the largest draft since the 1982 Lebanon War. Tanks rolled into Palestinian cities and towns throughout the West Bank, as population centers were placed under prolonged curfews.[67] In March and April alone, close to 500 Palestinians were killed.

Over the following months many West Bank cities, towns and villages were transformed into restricted military zones, and their residents were held under sustained (often 24-hour) curfew for days on end. On occasion, nearly 900,000 West Bank residents in 74 communities were held under curfew, so that, for example, during the six-and-a-half-month period between June 17 and December 31, 2002, 37 localities and 547,000 people were, on average, confined to their homes.[68] Israel also developed a dense network of both fixed and movable military checkpoints, numbering some 140 in the West Bank and 25 to 30 in the Gaza Strip. In addition it set up literally hundreds of unmanned physical obstacles in the form of concrete blocks, piles of dirt, or trenches, which were used to prevent access to and from towns and villages. Palestinian movement was thus almost completely curtailed.

The extensive recourse to dehumanizing forms of state violence, on the one hand, and the Palestinian resort to armed struggle and suicide attacks as techniques of resistance, on the other, increased the efforts to make sense of political violence through the invocation of the human rights discourse. The international NGOs operating in the area and the local Israeli and Palestinian organizations that had become prominent during the first Intifada and the ensuing peace process published report after report about the violent confrontations. Often framed fatalistically by the media and human rights practitioners as a new chapter in an "endless conflict," the increasing documentation and denunciation of human rights violations paradoxically decreased the focus on the structural elements and political rationales producing them. With the exception of exposing the state's dispossessive land regime, the major mode of critique espoused by the liberal human rights NGOs focused on uncovering instances of violations rather than on the structural underpinnings of domination.[69]

The move away from structural critique manifests itself in several ways, of which we will mention three: (1) the constitution of the violation as a case and the appeal to the violating state to correct the violation; (2) the constitution of the violation as a routine to be administered according to human rights standards; and (3) the reduction of structural colonial violence to a series of symptoms. First, by adopting a legalistic strategy and demanding justice from the High Court of Justice, the human rights NGOs, as Gad Barzilai has pointed out, often translate the violation into a "case," categorizing, differentiating, and insulating it and thus obfuscating the structural underpinnings of the violation.[70] Moreover, by continuously appealing to the court that for years helped legitimize Israel's violations, the NGOs cover up the human rights paradox of the perpetrator as arbitrator, and in this sense also help conceal some of the structural dimensions of abuse. Second, one notices a routinization of violations, which occurs, inter alia, when there is a convergence between human rights NGOs and the perpetrator of abuse. Analyzing the work of the liberal NGO Checkpoint Watch—created in 2001 to monitor military checkpoints and primarily the restriction of the Palestinian right to free movement—Irus Braverman reveals a link between the organization's surveillance of checkpoints and the Israeli military's capacity to bureaucratize its procedures at the checkpoints and frame them as abiding by human rights standards. She concludes that human rights groups "have become part of the system [of occupation]: an instrument for improving the system from within and a way for Israel to legitimize its border operations to the outside world by attending to the demands of human rights groups."[71] Facilitating this convergence is the fact that the Israeli military has been meeting, interacting, and exchanging information routinely with these human rights NGOs, and has started to speak the same language, which helps normalize its restrictions of the right to movement.

Finally, the way human rights organizations portray the violations at times allows for the perpetuation of the political power that carries out the violations. Didier Fassin has shown how, during the second Intifada, human rights organizations operating in support of Palestinians began invoking the clinical discourse of trauma. This discourse and the techniques through which Doctors Without Borders and local human rights practitioners tried to produce evidence of Israel's human rights violations reinscribed the Palestinian question within an internationally emerging hegemonic framework of interpretation: one of psychological trauma, whose main effect was the reduction of a long history of colonial violence to a series of mental scars and symptoms to be healed by human rights and mental health practitioners. This process, which in the following years led to a proliferation of mental health support in the OPT, helped routinize domination, recovering its psychic symptoms, as in a medical routine, but often obscuring its underlying political causes and transforming a collective question of justice into individual experiences and cases of mental suffering and human rights violation.[72]

In this way, human rights have helped normalize relations of domination. We understand this process of normalization differently from the way it is usually evoked in Israel/Palestine. By normalization we do not merely mean the normalization of the relationships between colonizers and colonized, whereby the two people continue to meet, conduct "business as usual," and cooperate while ignoring the relations of domination between them. The sense of normalization invoked here refers to our claim that human rights activism, while developing new tools of monitoring and advocacy, has often elided the fundamental mechanisms of domination that produce the very actions this advocacy denounces and classifies as human rights violations.

Human rights NGOs and researchers operating within and in support of Palestinian society further systematized and professionalized their techniques of evidence production. New human rights training programs were developed in Israel and in the OPT through international funding; video cameras were distributed to Palestinian farmers asking them to record violations; munition experts were flown in to analyze the architecture of destruction; airplanes were commissioned to provide aerial photos of expropriated land; and the West Bank was mapped by human rights activists using GIS technology.[73] Such techniques helped further reveal Israel's breach of international human rights and humanitarian law and helped spur advocacy campaigns for the *protection from* state violations. To be sure, alongside the normalizing effect of human rights work, NGOs did at times analyze the state's practices of land grab, settlement building, seizure of Palestinian resources, collective punishment, and violence, and produced reports that examined not only the effects of domination but also elements of its structure. But this professionalization of human rights through the increasing sophistication of investigation techniques also generated a sense of normalcy of human rights violations and the apparatuses producing them. When violence and human rights violations are normal and become the object of a "denunciation routine," they are, as Lori Allen has noted, everywhere and nowhere in particular.[74]

To recapitulate, the normalization of domination, in the context of this book, is a key feature of the human rights paradoxes we have analyzed. We have shown that Israel's foundation as a Jewish state in the Middle East was connected to the new international human rights regime through the notion of reparation for violations, and that in this way the ensuing settler project was legitimized. In the following decades, the state itself continued this process of normalization by framing different state practices of domination and dispossession as the prevention of the repetition of "another genocide"—Abba Eban's Auschwitz lines. But with the introduction and circulation of a human rights discourse during the first Intifada, its consolidation during the Oslo years, and its further proliferation during the second Intifada, normalization became even more complex, taking on new shapes and practices.

To be sure, we are not claiming that human rights organizations and actors operating in Israel/Palestine deliberately aim to obfuscate domination, but this, as we show in chapter 3, has been one result of human rights activism in the area. However, in spite of this, normalization was not a linear process. In fact the reframing of the conflict as an issue of human rights protection of Palestinians did have an impact on how it has been perceived, mainly in the international arena. Over the years, the human rights discourse managed to transform the lens through which the international community understands Israel/Palestine, and this new framing altered the conception about which side is inflicting systematic human rights violations. In spite of the normalizing effect of mainstream human rights activism, the Israeli government, alongside a group of NGOs and scholars, began to perceive Palestinian and pro-Palestinian human rights campaigns as a threat. We accordingly turn now to examine some of the dangerous effects human rights continued to produce in the wake of the new millennium.

CHAPTER 2

The Threat of Human Rights

Today the trenches are in Geneva in the Council of Human Rights, or in New York in the General Assembly, or in the Security Council, or in the Hague, the ICJ.
            —Danny Ayalon

The military campaign began on a cold winter day. Israel launched a series of aerial strikes on the Gaza Strip on December 27, 2008, targeting over 100 sites. Gaza, which for many years had been under a military and economic siege, was now under fire. By the end of the first day, over 200 Palestinians had been killed, while hundreds more had been wounded.[1] Calling the campaign Operation Cast Lead—to create an association among Israeli Jews between the military offensive and the holiday Hanukkah that commemorates the Maccabee struggle for religious freedom against the Hellenistic Syrians in year 165 B.C., which is symbolized by a dreidel made of cast lead upon which the acronym "A Great Miracle Happened There" is inscribed—Israel continued bombing the Gaza Strip for several days, unleashing its F-16 fighter jets, Apache helicopters, and drones from the air, and naval warships from the sea. Israeli spokespeople justified the offensive, claiming that it had been initiated in retaliation to artillery being fired from the Gaza Strip on Israel's southern cities and towns. The Hamas government in Gaza countered this accusation by pointing out that a successful truce had been in place from June until November and that the fray had resumed only after Israeli fighter jets violated it by killing a number of militants and moving its tanks across the Strip's border. Notwithstanding the mutual charges, the assault continued, and on January 3, Israel embarked on a ground offensive that lasted until January 18, 2009. Even before the fighting had subsided, it was obvious that the magnitude of the harm to Gaza's population and its vital infrastructures was extensive.

After the soldiers had pulled out, the Israeli human rights organization B'Tselem assessed the damages on both sides, reporting that 1,389 Palestinians had been killed, of whom 759 had not taken part in the hostilities. Of these, 318 were minors under the age of eighteen. The rights group went on to note that more than 5,300 Palestinians had been wounded, 350 of them seriously. In addition, Israel had caused enormous damage to residential dwellings, industrial buildings, and agriculture, as well as infrastructure for electricity, sanitation, water, and health, which was already on the verge of collapse prior to the military operation. Citing a United Nations report, the human rights group estimated that Israel had destroyed more than 3,500 residential dwellings, rendering an estimated 20,000 people homeless. B'Tselem also pointed out that during the operation Palestinians had fired hundreds of rockets and mortar shells at Israel, "with the declared purpose of striking Israeli civilians." These attacks ended up killing three Israeli civilians and one member of the Israeli security forces, and wounding dozens more. Nine soldiers were killed within the Gaza Strip (four of them by friendly fire) and more than 100 soldiers were wounded, one of them critically.[2] In the history of the Israeli-Palestinian conflict, Cast Lead was a watershed, not only owing to the extent of unfettered violence, but also because of the legal debate that it propelled.

Following the Israeli attack, the UN Human Rights Council appointed Judge Richard Goldstone to head a fact-finding mission to examine the hostilities in Gaza.[3] Originally, the commission's mandate was to investigate only possible Israeli violations of international law, but before accepting the appointment Judge Goldstone demanded that the mandate include the investigation of "all violations of international human rights law and international humanitarian law that might have been committed at any time in the context of the military operations that were conducted in Gaza during the period from 27 December 2008 and 18 January 2009, whether before, during or after."[4] As a precondition for leading the fact-finding mission, he insisted that the international commission would investigate Hamas as well, since he conceived the symmetry of the investigation as the only way to carry out a balanced enquiry into possible violations of international law. Impartiality is, after all, considered to be a basic principle of human rights and humanitarianism, and international investigations have to present themselves as unbiased in spite of the fact that they assess political contexts marked by vast asymmetries of power and violence.

Irrespective of the broadened mandate, the Israeli government refused to cooperate with the UN fact-finding mission and even denied the commission entry into Israel in order to interview Israelis who had been subjected to rocket fire launched from the Gaza Strip. Nonetheless, in July 2009 the Israeli Ministry of Foreign Affairs published a 159-page legal defense of the military campaign that was cited by the international commission in its final report. So even though the mission did not meet Israeli officials and could not question them, it was aware of the Israeli perspective as it was drafting what came to be known as the Goldstone Report.[5] After carrying out numerous interviews and on-site visits in Gaza as well as reading dozens of human rights reports, the UN team concluded that both Israel and Hamas had breached international humanitarian law and had committed potential war crimes and crimes against humanity.[6] The brunt of the criticism was directed toward Israel, claiming, inter alia, that it had intentionally targeted civilians. In its recommendations, the UN team demanded that each side open criminal investigations and prosecute the persons responsible for the alleged war crimes.[7]

Legally, however, the findings do not amount to judicial proof beyond reasonable doubt, and therefore are considered conditional, serving as pointers for independent investigations that should be conducted by the Israeli and the Palestinian authorities.[8] Israel understood the charge of breaching international humanitarian and human rights law as a threat to its sovereignty, and decided to forcefully counter the so-called attack. Immediately following its publication, a smear campaign was launched against Richard Goldstone, portraying the report as a blood libel against the Jewish state.[9] "There are three primary threats facing us today," Prime Minister Benjamin Netanyahu averred, "the nuclear threat, the missile threat, and what I call the Goldstone threat."[10] President Shimon Peres called Goldstone "a small man, devoid of any sense of justice," and Harvard law professor Alan Dershowitz depicted Goldstone as "an evil, evil man," and harshly questioned his Jewish belonging by describing him as "a traitor to the Jewish people," the UN's "token court Jew" and a "despicable human being."[11] Youval Steinitz, Israeli finance minister at that time, accused Goldstone of being an anti-Semite, a "self-hating" Jew.[12]

International human rights and humanitarian law served as the lens through which Goldstone examined the fray, the same lens used by liberal human rights NGOs, but this time it was deployed by an international commission representing the UN and therefore signified even more blatantly the threat of human rights for the Israeli establishment. His team's report was threatening because it was an official UN body, and, following the cue of local NGOs, it used human rights to frame the conflict between

Israel and Palestinians in a way that depicts Israelis as aggressors and violators of human rights, rather than victims of abuse, bestowing upon this framing further legitimacy in the international arena. While the politicians responded by depicting the report as a threat to the Jewish people as a whole, and not only to Israel, the Israeli Intelligence and Terrorism Information Center, a think tank operating from within the Israel Defense Forces (IDF), prepared a 349-page monograph aimed at undermining the accuracy of the UN mission's findings.[13]

As this multifaceted offensive was waged, Israeli conservative groups started to blame Israeli and international human rights organizations for providing Goldstone's international commission with evidence, testimonies, and forensic materials to substantiate accusations against Israel. Human rights NGOs were closely scrutinized and transformed into a national security threat. In this chapter, we maintain that conservative actors no longer conceive human rights as a threat per se. For them the menace originates from what they call the "politicization of human rights," by which they mean the use of human rights to criticize the state and its political order. Consequently, the assault they wage against liberal human rights advocacy is aimed at defining the legitimate meaning of human rights.

We accordingly show how conservative NGOs working together with well-funded think tanks, government officials, and academics introduced the term *lawfare* in order to portray liberal human rights NGOs and their donors as carrying out an assault against the State of Israel. After describing the campaign carried out against these liberal actors, including "naming and shaming" and the introduction of laws aimed at curtailing their work, we show how the major liberal donor in Israel and the leading liberal human rights organization internalized some of the accusations made against them. Finally, we argue that through this process of self-censorship these liberal organizations prevented themselves from mobilizing human rights as a real threat to the state and its colonial order.

THE "POLITICIZATION" OF HUMAN RIGHTS

Leading this campaign against human rights organizations in Israel is NGO Monitor. Founded in 2002 by Gerald Steinberg, a political scientist from Bar Ilan University whose research focuses on "the politics of human rights and non-governmental organizations," NGO Monitor analyzes reports and press releases of local and international NGOs and investigates the international donors funding them.[14] Its self-declared goals are to expose "distortions of human rights issues in the Arab-Israeli conflict" and "to end the practice used by certain self-declared 'humanitarian NGOs' of exploiting the label 'universal human rights values' to promote politically and ideologically motivated agendas."[15] In 2013, NGO Monitor was accredited as a member in the UN Economic and Social Council and as such can participate in the UN Human Rights Council meetings.[16]

NGO Monitor's assault on liberal NGOs is directed against what it conceives to be the "politicization of human rights" and not against human rights *tout court*. When political actors like Gerald Steinberg and NGO Monitor refer to the notion of "politicization" of human rights, they mean a "distortion of the true sense of human rights" and their alteration into a threat. They are, at least partially, mirroring the critique of liberal human rights NGOs against conservatives and dictators. Much of NGO Monitor's research and political activism is directed against the "'halos' of perceived objectivity" surrounding liberal human rights NGOs, which have historically "succeeded in gaining immense power in placing human rights issues—as they interpret them—high on governmental agendas."[17] Placing itself in a peculiar position of proximity to—rather than in contrast to—human rights, NGO Monitor has been developing a stance centered on the necessity to depoliticize human rights and to liberate them from "self-appointed moral guardians" who "subjugated" them to "partisan interests."[18] This line of criticism is part of a broader global trend, whereby NGO Monitor merely follows the cue of other organizations that have been leading an international campaign in the name of NGO accountability. These groups have affinities and direct interactions with Steinberg's organization, forming what could be defined as the conservative front for the "salvation of human rights."

Linked together by a shared mission, common political targets and similar discourses, conservative NGOs from numerous countries have created a united front and a network that increasingly challenges liberal human rights NGOs like Amnesty International and Human Rights Watch. For instance, UN Watch, an NGO based in Geneva founded in 1993 by Morris B. Abram (former US permanent representative to the United Nations), aims to monitor the "just application of UN Charter principles" and combat the "disproportionate attention and unfair treatment applied by the UN towards Israel."[19] Headed by former diplomats and scholars, this organization is funded, inter alia, by Zionist advocacy groups like the American Jewish Committee.[20] Another example is Global Governance Watch (previously NGO Watch), a joint project of the American Enterprise Institute and the Federalist Society for Law and Public Policy Studies. "Its goal is to raise awareness about global governance, to monitor how international organizations influence domestic political outcomes, and to address issues of transparency and accountability within the United Nations, related to intergovernmental organizations, and other non-state actors."[21]

The discourse about NGO accountability and politicization promoted by these conservative groups echoes internal discussions carried out by many traditional liberal human rights NGOs, which in the last two decades have been preoccupied by issues of politicization, accountability and transparency of their organizations. The convergence between liberals and conservative helps explain the prominence of this discourse at the UN and exposes a space where political adversaries, in spite of their different agendas, speak a common language. It reveals how diverging groups adopt similar moral imperatives—transparency, accountability, prevention of politicization—and concur that the attempt to uphold a neutral and objective stance through some kind of "ethical transcendence" is a necessary moral good that can be accomplished through human rights work.[22] Thus, the philosophy of human rights of both liberal and conservative NGOs is grounded in what we called in the introduction "the illusion of the original"; namely, the belief in the existence of something called human rights that is external to empirical-historical social relationships.

The assumption shared by these diametrically opposed NGOs is that the politicization of human rights undermines their orthodox meaning and is ultimately a perversion. The practitioners who aim to repress the politicization of human rights may accede that their own work has concrete political implications, but, in order to claim credibility, they maintain that human rights themselves, as they appear in legal documents and treaties, are not political. The ostensible nonpolitical nature of human rights—their so-called objective, neutral, and universal character—is considered by liberal and conservative practitioners alike to be both the prime source of power of human rights and the source of their moral legitimacy. Human rights, in other words, are conceived to be legitimate only insofar as they are nonpartisan, and their power stems from their universality and the assertion that they do not represent particular interests.

We, by contrast, maintain that human rights, like all rights discourses, are intrinsically *political* in the sense that the very process of adopting, claiming, and deploying human rights—a process for which people receive training and education—is always politicized.[23] The translation of any struggle into the language of human rights is already a political choice and consequently an integral part of the political. Thus, in spite of the illusion of the original, human rights do not constitute an alternative to politics, or an extrapolitical and pure tool confined to the realm of ethics, as many NGOs concerned with reasserting their neutrality and nonpolitical reputation claim.[24] Rather, the deployment of human rights is always a *partisan* operation (in its literal meaning of *taking part*) in which determined historical-political situations of conflict, struggle, exploitation, and domination become the object of political debates and practices whose outcome aims to determine who are the moral and immoral actors in a given political context. This is the power of human rights to strengthen or destabilize power, and to ultimately frame history and give it different kinds of meanings.

Thus, instead of rejecting the expanding human rights discourse and culture as they had in the past, the current objective of conservative scholar-activists à la Steinberg is to create their own alternative human rights idiom that is used to undermine the human rights idiom that had been developed and historically embraced by liberal human rights NGOs worldwide.[25] Their struggle—which they share with liberal human rights practitioners around the globe—is over the legitimate articulation of an essentialist conception of rights, one that claims to be founded on the abstention from politics through a perspective that purports to be extraneous to the political processes.

Lawfare

One of the most common ways of challenging the existing human rights discourse is by pitting it against national security concerns and against real and constructed existential threats. This strategy has become pervasive among conservatives who attempt to limit the impact of human rights campaigns by reframing events—that liberal NGOs had described as breaching human rights norms—as a security threat to the government's authority or the country's territorial integrity.[26] During this process (that we describe in detail in this chapter's next sections), liberal human rights organizations themselves are constituted as a threat to the state and become an object of a national debate as well as a site of repressive legislative and policy interventions. The conservative struggle against the politicization of human rights thus coincides with the struggle for the protection of the nation-state. In this sense, the politics of human rights acquires an even more profound connection with sovereign politics since human rights is equated with the state's security.

NGO Monitor was the first Israeli organization to couch its criticism of liberal human rights organizations in security parlance. Its line of reasoning was articulated in an article entitled "NGOs Make War on Israel" penned by its founder, Steinberg,[27] who in a different venue also claimed that human rights are being exploited as a "weapon against Israel."[28] Steinberg thus tapped into the post-9/11 conservative trend in the United States, which began employing the term *lawfare* in order to describe the endeavor of individuals and groups who appeal to courts against certain practices of state violence emanating from the so-called global war on terrorism—such as torture, extrajudicial executions, and the bombing of civilian urban infrastructure.

The genealogy of the debate surrounding lawfare—a genealogy whose exhaustive reconstruction goes beyond the scope of this chapter—can be traced back well before 9/11 and deserves serious consideration. Here, however, we would like to note that lawfare combines the words *law* and *warfare* and is increasingly defined by state officials, scholars, and experts dealing with the various international fronts of the "war on terror" and "asymmetric conflicts" as *the use of law for realizing a military objective*.[29] It is, however, not only used to describe attempts of human rights groups to submit warfare and conflict to legal oversight, but is, we argue, also a speech act that aims to *reconstitute the human rights field as a national security threat* and in this way to counter a certain kind of deployment of human rights deemed threatening to the state.[30] Lawfare, as we show below, has been used as the point of entry through which numerous securitizing actors—NGOs, think tanks, academics, policymakers, legislators—have mobilized the media, shaped public opinion, lobbied legislators and policymakers, introduced new laws, and pressured donors in an attempt to construct human rights as a security threat in order to pave the way for a form of exceptional intervention against—mainly liberal—human rights organizations.[31]

Originally, though, conservative actors hinged the term *lawfare* to the exercise of universal jurisdiction by national and regional courts that tried officials from the United States and Israel. Universal jurisdiction is predicated on the notion that there are acts that are so universally appalling that states have an interest in exercising jurisdiction to combat them.[32] Indeed, a basic principle of universal jurisdiction is the extraterritoriality of international law; the idea that international law can be applied to alleged criminal acts that have occurred outside the state/territory where it is being deliberated, even if the alleged violation has been perpetrated by a nonnational and even if the state's nationals have not been harmed.[33] Acts that are subject to universal jurisdiction include extrajudicial executions, deliberate targeting of civilians in military operations, torture, enslavement, enforced disappearances, the use of indiscriminate weapons, collective punishment, intentional destruction of civilian infrastructure, and numerous other acts that constitute war crimes, crimes against humanity, or genocide.

In point of fact, the deployment of universal jurisdiction is not new. The International Court of Justice (ICJ) has been providing advisory opinions for half a century about interstate disputes concerning the conduct of armed conflict. But the ICJ only hears cases filed by states, and only in the past two decades has it become more common for individuals and groups to use universal jurisdiction to file suits against alleged criminals. The ad hoc tribunals for the former Yugoslavia (1993) and Rwanda (1994), as well as the establishment of hybrid tribunals in Cambodia, East Timor, and Sierra Leone a few years later marked the beginning of a new era. Currently nonstate actors have three kinds of venues for filing such suits: the ICC, a few regional courts (e.g., European Court of Human Rights and the Inter-American Court of Human Rights), and scores of national courts.[34]

A paradigmatic and early example of the use of universal jurisdiction in domestic courts occurred in 1998 when Spain requested that the United Kingdom extradite fascist General Augusto Pinochet on grounds of widespread torture carried out during US-led Operation Condor in which Pinochet was implicated.[35] Since then hundreds of suits have been filed in countries such as Belgium, France, Italy, the Netherlands, Spain, Switzerland, Turkey, New Zealand, Norway, and the United Kingdom, primarily against military personnel and government officials from Africa, Latin America, and the former Yugoslavia, but the term lawfare, in its negative connotation, gained credence as a threat when suits were filed against officials from the United States and Israel.[36] International humanitarian and human rights law becomes a weapon of lawfare not when this body of law is deployed in the international arena against any actor, but primarily when it is used against officials from the United States and Israel.

The US government was never an adamant supporter of universal jurisdiction, but ever since international law began being deployed by individuals and groups to check certain practices utilized in the global war on terrorism it has adopted an oppositional stance. The United States opposed the 1998 passing of the Rome Statute that established the ICC (in 2002) as a permanent tribunal to prosecute individuals for genocide, crimes against humanity, and war crimes. It also pressured Belgium to change its domestic laws to limit the use of universal jurisdiction.[37] Despite this opposition, high-ranking government officials and CIA agents were still being held accountable for rendition practices in absentia in German and Italian national courts that exercise universal jurisdiction. Hence, in 2005, a 24-page Pentagon document commissioned by Donald Rumsfeld and entitled the "National Defense Strategy of the United States of America" warned that "Our strength as a nation state will continue to be challenged by those who employ a strategy of the weak using international fora, judicial processes, and terrorism."[38] The Bush administration thus associated legal threats to US state violence with terrorism.

The Israeli government has also been increasingly alarmed by the deployment of "lawfare." Already in 2001, Ariel Sharon, Israeli foreign minister at the time, was indicted by a Belgian court in relation to the well-known war crimes committed against Palestinian refugees in the Sabra and Chatila camps in Beirut in 1982.[39] Since then, news reports have suggested that scores of lawsuits have been submitted against Israeli politicians, high-ranking military officers, and heads of secret services in several states.[40] While none of these suits has actually led to a conviction, the Israeli government has assigned experts in international law to accompany combat military units and has advised former-politicians and military officers to refrain from traveling to certain European countries. In addition, government officials alongside staff members from NGOs and think tanks and a number of academics have spent time examining more closely the suits filed against Israelis.[41] Not surprisingly, they have found that the reports published by human rights NGOs are frequently cited as incriminating evidence.[42]

Writing for Bar Ilan University's Begin-Sadat Center for Strategic Studies (BESA Center), which characterizes itself as advancing a "realist, conservative, and Zionist agenda in the search for security and peace for Israel,"[43] Elizabeth Samson, an attorney specializing in international and constitutional law, contends that those who deploy lawfare "are not fighting an occupier or challenging a military incursion—they are fighting the forces of freedom, they are fighting the voice of reason, and they are attacking those who have the liberty to speak and act openly." The weapon that the enemy is using, Samson continues, "was created by our own hands—that is the rule of law, a weapon designed to subdue dictators and tyrants is now being misused to empower the very same, and being manipulated to subvert real justice and *indisputable truth*."[44] The enemy in this passage refers to the liberal human rights NGOs and the fear of lawfare is the fear of mirroring—between liberals and non-liberals—as well as the fear of a potential inversion of meaning ascribed to the history of violence.

Samson's outrage is informed by an accurate historical understanding of international law, which has been a tool of sovereign states and their imperialist endeavors ever since the 17th and 18th centuries.[45] From a historical perspective, then, the effort of human rights NGOs to use international law as a weapon against sovereign states, particularly dominant ones, is a form of illegitimate appropriation of law. It is an attempt to alter an existing idiom that confers privileges on powerful countries by granting them the moral high ground to define the legitimate or illegitimate deployment of violence. Law becomes lawfare, and human rights a menace, precisely when they are deployed against dominant states and their agents. It is then that law is accompanied with the suffix *-fare* and suddenly perceived to be—by sovereign states, parliaments and in this case think tanks like BESA and NGO Monitor—a violent force and a threat.[46] As a contemporary manifestation of what Edward Said called the "semiotic warfare" encompassing the Palestinian question, the attack against the threat of human rights lawfare must be understood as a semiotic struggle over the legitimacy of Israel's state violence, as well as over the meaning of human rights.[47]

Accordingly, NGO Monitor defines lawfare as a "strategy of using or misusing law as a substitute for traditional military means to achieve military objectives." Although NGO Monitor's Anne Herzberg acknowledges that Israel is not the only country that has been subject to nongovernmental human rights lawfare, it has been, she writes, "a primary target of these efforts."[48] Leading the lawfare campaign against Israel are what Herzberg calls "NGO superpowers" (e.g., Amnesty International and Human Rights Watch), who in cooperation with liberal Palestinian and Israeli human rights groups resort to universal jurisdiction to pursue litigation in European, North American, or Israeli national courts. While these NGOs claim to be part of the fight for human rights, the evidence shows, in Herzberg's opinion, "that the core motivation for this activity is to promote lawfare" in order to "punish Israel for carrying out anti-terror operations."[49] In other words, "anti-terror operations" are one of the referent objects of this securitization process; they are considered to be threatened by NGOs, which are accused of "misusing" human rights. Herzberg goes on to claim that

> NGO involvement begins well before the filing of any lawsuit. These organizations issue numerous press releases and lengthy "research reports" condemning Israeli anti-terror operations. Political NGOs also regularly submit written statements to UN committees and other international bodies. . . . Their reports are then adopted by the decision-making bodies of the UN such as the General Assembly, and underpin further condemnations and actions taken against Israel. Through this process, NGO statements become part of the official dossiers of cases at international legal institutions such as the International Court of Justice or the International Criminal Court, or part of the court record in domestic suits.[50]

NGO Monitor, the BESA Center, and other organizations and academics are employing the term *lawfare* to condemn the work of liberal human rights NGOs. Thus, the term, as mentioned, is not only descriptive, since it also frames the liberal human rights NGOs as a national security threat. In order to successfully constitute them as a threat, lawfare has to follow the "grammar of security," which constructs a plot that necessarily includes an existential national threat.[51] Moreover, for this discursive act to actually have an effect, it is not enough for it to appear in a couple of reports published by NGOs and think tanks. Rather, it has to capture the public imagination. Once the rationale informing the lawfare discourse is widely accepted, it then becomes logical for Israel to adopt exceptional methods to delegitimize the work of human rights NGOs and obstruct the supranational vernacularization of human rights. If, as we showed in the previous chapter, after Israel's establishment human rights served as a frame that helped legitimize domination and protect the state against a perpetual existential threat, over the past decade we witness an increasing attack against human rights by the state and its proxies because human rights activism has been striving to overcome the identification of the human with the national subject.

Existential Threats

While government officials criticized Israeli human rights organizations ever since they appeared on the political stage in the late 1980s, the effort to constitute them as a security threat gained momentum with the publication of the Goldstone Report.[52] A few hours after the report was published, NGO Monitor issued a press release characterizing it as an NGO "cut and paste" document.[53] The claim was that a considerable amount of the findings were based on reports and testimonies provided by biased human rights organizations, several of them Israeli. Joining NGO Monitor in this campaign was Im Tirtzu ("If you will it"),[54] a grassroots organization that was established in 2006 in order to renew, in its words, "Zionist discourse, Zionist thinking and Zionist ideology, to ensure the future of the Jewish nation and of the State of Israel." According to the organization's website, a "major portion of *Im Tirtzu's* efforts is devoted to combating the campaign of de-legitimization against the State of Israel."[55] Both NGO Monitor and Im Tirtzu used their considerable resources to attack Israeli human rights organizations and the New Israel Fund (NIF), the single largest donor to Israel's human rights community; hence the strategy was not only to delegitimize these organizations in the public's eyes by portraying them as a security threat to Israel, but also to create a wedge between the rights groups and their funding sources.

The organizations published long briefs claiming that Israeli human rights NGOs funded by the NIF served as the "building blocks" for the Goldstone Report.[56] Im Tirtzu calculated that 14 percent of the references in the UN report came from publications or testimonies of Israeli rights groups funded by the NIF.[57] NGO Monitor blamed Israeli rights organizations for lobbying the United States, the European Union, and other countries to legitimize the UN report and endorse its recommendations.[58] In this way the human rights organizations overstepped what the conservative groups consider the legitimate moral framework of human rights deployment, which inscribes human rights into the national Zionist agenda.

Following the publication of these briefs, *Im Tirtzu* initiated a magazine expose in the widely circulated *Ma'ariv* whose title on the front page read: "The Material from Which Goldstone Is Made," followed by the subtitle, "New research discloses how a group of Israeli leftist organizations were active partners in drafting the Goldstone Report, which defamed the IDF and the State." "[Israel's] reputation," the article explained, "is at an all-time low. Mounting international pressure, calls for boycotts and excommunication are increasing. All these were fueled by the Goldstone report, which was, in turn, fueled by Israeli sources. According to *Im Tirtzu*, the New Israel Fund provided money and financing for these sources."[59] Concomitantly, *Im Tirtzu* posted large, provocative—if not defamatory— billboard ads portraying the president of the NIF, former Knesset member Naomi Chazan, with a horn on her head.[60] The caption reads: "Naomi Goldstone-Chazan; Naomi Chazan's 'New Fund' Stands Behind the Goldstone Report." The campaign proved to be extremely successful. For several days, television and radio talk shows spent hours discussing whether or not the NIF and human rights organizations had betrayed their country and Zionism.

Simultaneously, NGO Monitor targeted policymakers, embassies, international newspapers, donors, and other groups. Between October 2009 and May 2011, the conservative watch group published 16 briefs and 11 opinion articles in leading newspapers, sent representatives to appear in several television and radio talk shows, and issued numerous press releases about the Goldstone Report's reliance on evidence provided by human rights NGOs. The campaign culminated in the publication of an edited volume called *The Goldstone Report Reconsidered*, which featured chapters by former Israeli ambassador to the UN, Dore Gold, and Harvard Professor Alan Dershowitz.[61] In this volume, Gerald Steinberg describes the UN report as an existential threat to Israel, arguing that it constitutes "*a major threat to the existence of Israel as the nation state of the Jewish people, and its sovereign equality among the nations.*"[62] To reiterate, *Israel as the nation-state of the Jewish people* is threatened by the "politicized NGOs." Despite the fact that these Israeli liberal human rights organizations never challenged the foundation of the Jewish state, and that in the past the government had often presented their existence as evidence of Israel's thriving democracy, after the appearance of the Goldstone Report these organizations became a major existential threat. The threat of human rights then becomes the threat to the Zionist project, a threat that the state compares to terrorism.

Legal Terrorism

Campaigns launched by civil society organizations normally aim to shape public opinion and to put pressure on policymakers and legislators. In this particular case, however, the policymakers and legislators did not need much convincing. Within two days of the Goldstone Report's publication the Israeli Ministry of Foreign Affairs responded, claiming that it "ties the hands of democratic countries fighting terror worldwide; calls into question the legitimacy of national legal systems and investigations; [and] promotes criminal proceedings against forces confronting terrorism in foreign states and tries to expand the jurisdiction of the ICC beyond its Statute."[63] Three months later, Israel's deputy foreign minister, Danny Ayalon, used a lawfare metaphor to describe the situation, claiming that "today the trenches are in Geneva in the Council of Human Rights, or in New York in the General Assembly, or in the Security Council, or in the Hague, the ICJ."[64] To mark Human Rights Day in 2010, Ayalon denounced the human rights misappropriations by liberal NGOs, and in a joint press conference held with representatives from NGO Monitor, he claimed that the "international human rights day has been transformed into terror rights day."[65]

Foreign minister Avigdor Lieberman's party, Yisrael Beiteinu, went on to propose creating national committees of inquiry to investigate human rights groups that delegitimize Israel and abet terror.[66] Although Prime Minister Benjamin Netanyahu ended up not supporting the initiative, he told the cabinet that while the law establishing such committees was important, "we have to act cautiously and wisely . . . and prevent further delegitimization of Israel."[67] The notion that Israeli rights groups support terrorism was, however, taken up by the Israeli colonel in charge of the military's international law department, who averred that war crimes charges brought abroad against Israeli soldiers and officers involved in Operation Cast Lead were nothing but "legal terrorism."[68]

The reports, policy briefs, press releases, and governmental statements that were put out by the Israeli Ministry of Foreign Affairs, the military, NGOs, think tanks, and public intellectuals rapidly coalesced into a doctrine about lawfare and how it constitutes a national threat. By November 2010, the Ministry of Foreign Affairs published a long report entitled "The Campaign to Defame Israel," where it asserted that "The strategy to delegitimize Israel using legal frameworks, and exploiting both international and national legal forums, was adopted following numerous failed military attempts to destroy the Jewish state."[69] The ministry proceeded to explain that lawfare had been used by individuals and groups who filed criminal and civil lawsuits in national and international legal forums against prominent military and government figures for alleged violations of international law. "The number of law suits that have been filed against Israeli officials has grown exponentially in recent years. . . . This form of lawfare does not simply impede Israeli travel plans" but aims "to intimidate officials from acting out of fear of prosecution, and in fact impacts foreign relations, strains international ties, and serves to delegitimize the Jewish state. . . . It must be recognized that just as German military theorist Carl von Clausewitz states that 'war is . . . a continuation of political activity by other means,' so too, lawfare is a continuation of terrorist activity by other means."[70]

The ministry's logic is straightforward: lawfare is a form of terrorism; human rights NGOs are lawfare enablers; hence, human rights NGOs are part of the terrorism network. International law, it should be stressed, is not criticized per se, but, on the contrary, what is debated is the legitimacy of its uses. The conflict is over its appropriation and its "correct" application. International law is thus conceived to be a weapon of war only when it is deployed in a certain way by specific actors, suggesting that lawfare denotes the illegitimate use of international law against states that consider themselves liberal and not simply its deployment in the global arena. According to this framework, international humanitarian and human rights law is legitimately mobilized, with broad international consensus, to invade and occupy a UN member state like Afghanistan (as seen in Amnesty International's campaign discussed in the introduction), but it becomes a form of legal terrorism when it is enforced against human rights violations perpetrated by a powerful state.

Insofar as international law is terrorism by other means, the implementation of exceptional measures against human rights organizations becomes necessary. And indeed, the Israeli legislature did not hesitate to pick up the gauntlet. In January 2011, the Knesset voted overwhelmingly (41 versus 16) in favor of establishing a panel of inquiry to probe sources of funding for rights groups accused of "delegitimizing" the Israeli military, resembling the inquiries President Bush had introduced to probe the funding of presumed terrorist organizations.[71] MK Fania Kirshenbaum (of the extreme-right party Yisrael Beiteinu), who submitted the proposal, accused human rights organizations of being "behind the indictments lodged against Israeli officers and officials around the world," while the coalition whip from the Likud said that "NGOs sometimes cooperate with foreign bodies that use them to infiltrate messages or acts opposed to Israeli interests."[72]

The proposal to create a panel of inquiry was just part of the legislative effort to clamp down on the production and international dissemination of liberal NGO knowledge. From 2009 to 2013, Israeli legislators introduced a spate of 30 antidemocratic bills that have either been approved or are still being discussed in subcommittees, and while only one touches directly on human rights organizations, many of them aim to limit freedom of expression.[73] Thus, paradoxically, the lawfare espoused by human rights organizations is countered with another form of lawfare, this time employed and mirrored by the Israeli legislator. One of the differences is that the legislator does not merely utilize existing laws to fight the threat of human rights, but also has the power to create new laws that can be used in this fray. The juridical framework becomes the site for criticizing the state or protecting it, while laws are the weapons in this war.

The most pertinent bill is a proposed amendment to the Israeli Associations Law and the Israeli Income Tax Ordinance that would prohibit foreign public funding of Israeli organizations that, inter alia, "support indictment of elected officials and IDF soldiers in international courts; call for refusal to serve in the IDF and support a boycott of the State of Israel or its citizens."[74] While this bill received widespread support in the Knesset, it was, nonetheless, shelved in November 2011 because of domestic and international pressure and is currently being reformulated.[75] The fact, however, that a majority of Knesset members supported such a move rendered the proposed bill an ever lurking threat.

Not surprisingly, the campaigns launched to muzzle human rights NGOs have engendered growing public animosity toward them. Although it is difficult to determine the precise effect of such campaigns, over the past decade there has been an identifiable and pronounced shift in the attitude of Israelis toward human rights organizations by about 30 percentage points. By 2011, only 21 percent of Israeli Jews had a favorable attitude toward Israeli human rights organizations focusing on Palestinian rights, while the proportion of respondents with an unfavorable attitude toward these organizations was 53 percent. The change in public perceptions suggests that the securitizing efforts succeeded and that a significant audience had accepted the designation of human rights organizations as a security threat.[76]

The Nomos of the State

Not long after the campaigns against "legal terrorism" were launched, the main liberal Zionist donor organization, the NIF, changed its funding guidelines and stopped channeling donations to two organizations it had worked with in the past.[77] With headquarters in the United States, and offices in Canada, Europe, Australia, and Israel, the NIF is the single largest donor to liberal human rights organizations in Israel, and has raised more than $200 million over the years almost solely from Jewish donors outside country. It provides assistance to numerous liberal NGOs like the Association for Civil Rights in Israel and B'Tselem in an attempt to enhance "equality of social and political rights to all its inhabitants, without regard to religion, race, gender or national identity." The organization describes itself as being "widely credited with building Israel's progressive civil society from scratch," and as "a leading advocate for democratic values [that] builds coalitions, empowers activists and often takes the initiative in setting the public agenda."[78]

While the conservative campaign against the NIF led the donor organization to introduce a series of new policies and guidelines for its grantees, it simultaneously stimulated a surge in donations from liberal Jews who had been outraged by the attack on human rights NGOs and freedom of expression in Israel.[79] Here, however, we are interested in how Im Tirtzu's and NGO Monitor's campaign impacted NIF to change its policy regarding universal jurisdiction. In its new guidelines it wrote:

> As the leading organization advancing democracy in Israel, the New Israel Fund strongly believes that our job is to work within Israel to ensure democratic accountability. With a free press, involved citizenry, a strong and independent judiciary, and a track record of officially constituted commissions and committees of inquiry, there are internal means to hold Israeli leaders accountable to the law, and we work to strengthen all those institutions. We therefore firmly oppose attempts to prosecute Israeli officials in foreign courts as an inherent principle of our dedication to Israeli democracy.[80]

Making explicit an issue that had until now been left vague, NIF stresses that although it does not oppose the application of international law, it believes that international law should only be applied against Israeli government and military officials tried in Israeli courts. This view is based on the widely accepted notion that universal jurisdiction is, as Human Right Watch states, a "reserve tool" in the fight against impunity, "to be applied where the justice system of the country that was home to the violations is unable or unwilling to do so."[81] This principle, known as subsidiarity, implies that courts within the state are able and willing to prosecute military and government officials for crimes and consequently should have the priority in exercising jurisdiction over the crimes. The problem with this principle, according to HRW, is that subsidiarity runs the risk of ignoring or widening the impunity gap that may exist in the state where the crimes occurred.

Legal scholars have shown that in the past four decades, in almost all of its judgments relating to the Occupied Territories, "especially those dealing with questions of principle . . . [the Israeli High Court of Justice] has decided in favor of the authorities, often on the basis of dubious legal arguments,"[82] and has never held government or military officials accountable for contravening international law. The upshot is that Israeli human rights organizations that wish to receive support from the NIF cannot directly submit evidence to courts abroad and have to be extremely careful when displaying any other kind of active or even vocal support for universal jurisdiction. Moreover, the fact that the donor made the decision in the weeks following the campaign against it underscores the campaign's impact.

It seems that liberal political actors like the NIF are not aware or prefer to ignore the paradox of human rights. In fact, the logic underlying the NIF policy change consists in reinforcing the role of the very state that is accused of violating human rights as the arbiter of those human rights violations themselves. The NIF conceives human rights to be a legitimate tool of the struggle for justice—which deserves to be funded—but only insofar as the institutional body responsible for implementing justice is the state. In this way, the legitimacy of mobilizing human rights is restricted to the Israeli High Court, which has a long record of legitimizing colonial violence and granting impunity to its perpetrators. The normative axiom about the state's role as the ultimate arbiter is extremely similar to the position held by the Israeli government and groups that supposedly sit on the opposite side of the Israeli political arena, like NGO Monitor and Im Tirtzu. In other words, the principle of subsidiarity which NIF decided to subscribe to following Im Tirtzu's and NGO Monitor's assault can be understood as a sign of convergence among these actors; for all of them human rights are bound by and inscribed in the *nomos of the state*.

Pillar of Cloud: Balancing Testimonies

Comparing the response of B'Tselem, the Israeli Information Center for Human Rights in the Occupied Territories, to the November 2012 attack on Gaza, dubbed by Israel as Operation Pillar of Cloud, with its response to Cast Lead, which took place about three years earlier, is revealing since it underscores how the securitization process affected liberal human rights NGOs. Established in February 1989 by a group of liberal Knesset members, academics, attorneys, and journalists, B'Tselem is currently one of the most prominent Israeli human rights NGOs. It endeavors to document and educate the Israeli public and policymakers about human rights violations in the OPT, "combat the phenomenon of denial prevalent among the Israeli public, and help create a human rights culture in Israel." As an Israeli human rights organization, "B'Tselem acts primarily to change Israeli policy in the Occupied Territories and ensure that its government, which rules the Occupied Territories, protects the human rights of residents there and complies with its obligations under international law." Thus, according to its mandate, B'Tselem focuses more on violations perpetrated by the Israeli government than on violations carried out by Palestinians.[83]

B'Tselem's response to Pillar of Cloud underscores the impact of the attack on liberal human rights NGOs. This military operation began following an escalation of clashes between Israel and Palestinians in Gaza. The two sides had reportedly entered negotiations (through Egyptian mediation) that abruptly ended on November 12 when Ahmad Jabari, the chief of Hamas's military wing, was assassinated by an Israeli air strike just hours after having received the draft of a ceasefire agreement.[84] Hamas retaliated by launching rockets on Israel's southern towns and cities, and on November 14 Israel responded with a full-blown military campaign. According to the United Nations, during an eight-day period Israel carried out over 1,500 air strikes on Gaza, as well as strikes from the sea and mortar shells from the border. After targeting training sites belonging to Hamas's Izz Al-Din Al-Qassam Brigades and other military sites, the Israeli air force struck at police stations, buildings housing civilian ministries, and other governmental structures. In the final days, Palestinian residential buildings and other civilian areas were also targeted.

Media offices, hospitals, and schools were also damaged, resulting in a significant increase in civilian casualties. All told, 174 Palestinians were killed in Gaza, at least 168 of them by the Israeli military, of whom 67 are believed to be militants and 101 civilians, including 33 children and 13 women. Hundreds of Palestinians were injured.[85] Palestinian armed groups fired hundreds of mortar shells, rockets, and long-range Grad rockets at Israeli targets. For the first time, a number of rockets reached Tel Aviv and Jerusalem. Six Israelis, including four civilians, were killed, and over two hundred were reportedly injured.[86]

During the 2008–2009 military operation in Gaza, the major Israeli human rights groups created an ad hoc coalition with a website, sent numerous letters to Israeli decision-makers, filed petitions to the High Court of Justice,[87] published a series of ads in Israeli newspapers, and sent a letter to the editors of all Israeli media outlets protesting the unbalanced coverage of the operation. Very little of this was repeated in Pillar of Cloud. Referring to the reaction of human rights organizations during Pillar of Cloud, one practitioner said, with obvious self-criticism, that "it's like someone in a state of shock, the blow is not as hard as before so she doesn't feel it anymore."[88] Still we would expect the difference in scope and magnitude between the two military operations to lead to a "reduction" in the response rather than a change in the strategy adopted by liberal human rights groups. It is precisely the strategic change that interests us here.

Analyzing how B'Tselem responded to the November 2012 military operation underscores the extent of this change. There was a conspicuous decline in its advocacy, limited to one relatively long press release calling on the government to protect civilians and not to repeat the mistakes of Cast Lead. In addition, the rights group published testimonies of events on its website without offering concrete analysis with respect to alleged breaches of international law carried out by Israel (except for an attack on the media offices in Gaza).[89] B'Tselem's most explicit condemnation was, however, directed against Hamas. Hamas and other groups operating in the Gaza Strip, the rights group explained, violated international law, which imposes "restrictions on combatants with regard to permissible targets, weapons and circumstances for carrying out attacks. Their violations include deliberately launching rockets at Israeli civilians and Israeli communities; firing from within civilian Palestinian neighborhoods, thereby jeopardizing the lives of the local residents; and concealing ammunition and arms in civilian buildings. Deciding whether the Israeli military has violated IHL provisions," the NGO continued, "is not as simple."[90] Thus, in addition to B'Tselem's limited response during this military operation, the only actor actually blamed for carrying out war crimes was Hamas. This despite the fact that there was no real comparison in terms of fatalities (172 Palestinians vs. six Israelis), and that the disparity of injured and the damage to civilian infrastructure was just as noticeable.[91] While we return to this point in the next chapter, since it sheds light on the relation between international human rights and humanitarian law, military technology, and the state, here we are interested more in B'Tselem's change of monitoring, documentation, and interpretation of violations of international law.

In terms of testimonies, a notable change can be discerned in B'Tselem's approach and framework of investigation. While in Cast Lead it published 30 testimonies, all of them taken from Palestinians from Gaza, in Pillar of Cloud it published 12 testimonies, four of which were testimonies provided by Israelis who had been subject to rocket attacks (strategic change). In other words, there was a concerted attempt by B'Tselem to create some kind of *balance* or *symmetry* between Israel and Palestinian armed resistance groups. So much so, that one of the testimonies provided by B'Tselem was taken from three children from a Kibbutz located not far from the Gaza Strip who had experienced rocket attacks in 2006, six years before Pillar of Cloud.[92] Also, the rights NGO added a disclaimer alongside the testimonies taken from residents of Gaza, stating, "With the current military campaign ongoing, B'Tselem is taking testimony from Gaza residents, mainly by telephone. B'Tselem verifies, to the best of its ability, the reliability and precision of the information reported; nevertheless, in these circumstances, reports may be incomplete or contain errors. Given the urgency of informing the public about events in Gaza, B'Tselem has decided to publish the information now available. When the military campaign ends, B'Tselem will supplement these reports as needed." Significantly, this disclaimer was not published next to testimonies posted during Cast Lead, despite very similar circumstances.

Without doubt, the disclaimer can be attributed to cautiousness due to the attacks waged by conservative groups against B'Tselem, but wittingly or not, it questions the truthfulness of the testimonies and positions the witnesses as partial so as to underscore the ostensible objectivity of the organization. On one level, this liberal postethnic stance situates Pillar of Cloud as both devoid of power relations and even outside of politics—therefore the balance—and simultaneously within politics—therefore the disclaimer. On another level, B'Tselem itself is politicized, because if the organization's self-proclaimed mandate is Israel's rights-abusive policies, why suddenly does it strive to create some kind of balance that necessitates broadening its mandate to the violations carried out by Palestinians?

B'Tselem's balance and its so-called apolitical position became instrumental in the characterization of the dominated group as an actor that deploys violence in an ethical way as it is inscribed in and sanctioned by international law: Israel—in B'Tselem's report published in the aftermath of Pillar of Cloud—is *suspected* of violating international law, while Hamas is *accused* of carrying out war crimes. In this way the liberal human rights group reproduces and reinforces the existing political asymmetry between the dominant and dominated. The insertion of symmetry in an asymmetric situation, to put it differently, amounts to the suspension of history, which is a well-known colonial mechanism of validation and justification of domination.

* * *

We have come full circle. The assault against human rights organizations that we described in the first part of this chapter is clearly informed by Edmund Burke's famous claim (when writing about the French Revolution) that there is no such thing as the abstract rights of men, only the rights of Englishmen.[93] For those leading the campaign against liberal human rights organizations in Israel the threat of human rights emerges from their ostensible universality. In order to dissipate this threat they have to reassert the theoretical and empirical claim that rights are borne solely by those who are part of the nation. Insofar as human rights are never really external to the state, but rather tend to be integrated within the state as part of its governing apparatus, then, at least partially, they reflect the state's rationality.

In Israel-Palestine, nationhood corresponds with settler colonial domination, and any form of human rights-inspired protection of the Palestinian native—even when this protection is innocuous, since it does not tackle the issue of the state's colonial nature—is perceived by the dominant as threatening the state's ethnocratic character. Accordingly, the charge that liberal NGOs are politicizing human rights is in fact an accusation that they are adopting human rights beyond the boundaries of Jewish Israeliness in order to protect non-Jews. It is at this point that human rights are compared to a terrorist threat, a ticking bomb. We, however, have tried to show that this opposition, made up of the state on one side and "threatening" human rights on the other, is tenuous. In this sense, the title of this chapter uses the notion of threat as a euphemism. To be sure, human rights are often deployed in an effort to shape the state by determining its practices, but they cannot have a concrete manifestation that is in some way external to the state.[94] The state remains the central political forum within which human rights are vernacularized. While actors of different stripes may try to use human rights in radically different ways, still the existence of the state as an immanent political organization responsible for enforcing human rights is sanctified by all of them. Our claim, in other words, is that the threat of human rights to state power is actually contingent upon human rights being already bound by the state.

Struggles like the one we described in this chapter are the manifestation of a certain *economy of human rights*, by which we mean the way human rights meanings and practices are produced, shared, and circulated in specific historical contexts and political forums; the way in which human rights groups are defined as legitimate and illegitimate representatives of "true human rights"; the way in which certain human rights practices are promoted and allowed and others repressed and banned for being "politicized" and posing a "national security threat"; the way in which international law is understood to be related to the context in which it is deployed; the way in which victims and perpetrators of human rights violations are identified; the situations in which the deployment of human rights is appropriate or inappropriate. The central feature regulating these processes involves the allocation of rights to certain groups and the exclusion of others, which in contexts of extreme political violence can resort to the legitimation of killing and dispossession. In this sense, the economy of human rights is also an economy of domination.

CHAPTER 3

The Human Right to Kill

It turns out that the American military is by far the world's largest human-rights train-ing institution. Across the globe, engagement with the U.S. military—purchasing our weapons, participating in joint exercises with our forces—comes with training in inter-national norms and regulatory practices of humanitarian law and human rights.

—David Kennedy

Prominent Harvard law professor David Kennedy describes the human rights training programs run by the US military in recent decades as courses in which the message is clear: "This," he says, "is not some humanitarian add-on—a way of being nice or reducing military muscle. We stressed that internalizing humanitarian law and human rights is a way to make the military more effective. . . . We asserted, with some justification, that it is simply not possible to *use* the sophisticated weapons one purchases or to coordinate with the international military operations in which they would be used without an internal military culture with parallel rules of operation and engagement."[1] An expert on the relation between international humanitarian and human rights law and war, Kennedy has gained a considerable amount of experience and public recognition working with numerous human rights organizations as well as with the US military and other armed forces.[2] Already in 1996, he traveled to Senegal as a civilian instructor with the Naval Jus-tice School "to train members of the Senegalese military in the laws of war and human rights." At the time, he notes, "the training program was operating in fifty-three countries, from Albania to Zimbabwe." De-scribing the message conveyed to the trainees in these countries, he writes: "We insisted, humanitarian law will make your military more effective—will make your use of force something you can sustain and proudly stand behind."[3]

Kennedy's ongoing reference to a "we," whereby the well-known law professor simultaneously portrays and considers himself as part of the military machine waging civilized wars, is not an oversight. To be sure, Kennedy, who called one of his books *The Dark Sides of Virtue*, is aware of the uncomfortable complicity between those who are trained to kill and those who are trained to defend human rights. But this complicity—the fundamental and recurrent convergence of human rights and violent forms of domination—is a conundrum that needs to be further interrogated beyond the questions that Kennedy asks in his pragmatist effort to make the international human rights movement more coherent and effective. Human rights, we maintain, are frequently used by the state, by conservative, and even by liberal human rights organizations to "'civilize' forms of killing as well as to attribute rational objectives [and justifications] to the very act of killing."[4]

The "unprecedented public scrutiny" that military forces have been subjected to in recent years triggered a pedagogic process in which men and women in uniform started learning through multiple ad hoc education programs the philosophical and moral foundations of the deployment of violence.[5] International human rights and humanitarian law occupy a prominent position in these programs. As we pointed out in the introduction, human rights classes are often mandatory in the US military, while the government trains each year approximately 100,000 foreign police and soldiers from more than 150 countries.[6] The education and professionalization of the military under the auspice of human rights is often described using aseptic language, as "essential to leadership skills in the armed forces."[7] The interesting issue for us is not so much that human rights professionals train soldiers, but rather that human rights NGOs and militaries converge with respect to the use of human rights as an epistemic and moral framework for judging the significance of killing within a given context. Kennedy maintains in his book that in order to participate in the international military profession, one has "to learn its new humanitarian vocabulary. We had no idea, of course, what it meant in *their* culture [i.e., of militaries of other countries] for violence to be legitimate, effective, something one could stand behind proudly. But they had learned something of what that meant in the culture of global humanitarian and military professionalism."[8] What stands out in Kennedy's description of the US military's training program is that human rights and military professionalism are not part of antithetical spheres informed by an opposing ethos, but are or have become part of the same political culture that aims to produce a specific ethics of violence. We are interested in analyzing this convergence and what it tells us about human rights appropriations in the contemporary world.

Not unlike its American counterpart, the Israeli military also emphasizes its concern with human rights and humanitarianism. On its official blog it describes, for example, how over the years "the IDF's humanitarian aid has served as a source of relief for people all over the world." The spokesperson notes that an IDF rescue delegation just returned (November 2013) from 12 days in the Philippines, assisting civilians in Bogo City whose lives were uprooted by Typhoon Haiyan. "Upon arrival," the spokesperson continues, "IDF doctors immediately set up a field hospital, where they treated over 2,600 patients, performed 60 surgeries, delivered 36 babies, and worked on repairing schools damaged by the storm." A certain kind of know-how developed in the military—for example, swiftly reaching unsafe places, setting up a makeshift hospital with doctors and medics that have experience working in difficult conditions—is utilized to mitigate humanitarian catastrophe. The blogs' readers are then referred to a map (figure 3.1) in order "to discover the long history of IDF aid delegations all around the world."[9] The poster, entitled IDF Without Borders, mirrors the motto of Doctors Without Borders, perhaps the most prominent humanitarian organization in the world. The Israeli military, which for years has been an instrument of domination in the OPT, is thus cast within a moral framework of global humanitarianism.

In this chapter, we show how the Israeli military, government officials, security think tanks and liberal human rights NGOs all concur that humanitarian and human rights law should be the framework for judging the morality of war, and therefore all of these actors use these bodies of law to advance their objectives. This, as we show, led to an institutional change in the military, where the international legal departments have grown and their political status within the military has risen. Focusing on the concept of human shields, we show how international humanitarian and human rights law is used by Israel to legitimize and justify the killing of Palestinian civilians. We go on to demonstrate that liberal human rights NGOs adopt international law in a similar way and therefore they too use human rights to rationalize the deployment of sovereign violence against the dominated.

MORAL KILLING

Considering that attempts to regulate war are "as old as war itself," this convergence between killing and humanitarian aid is the culmination of a

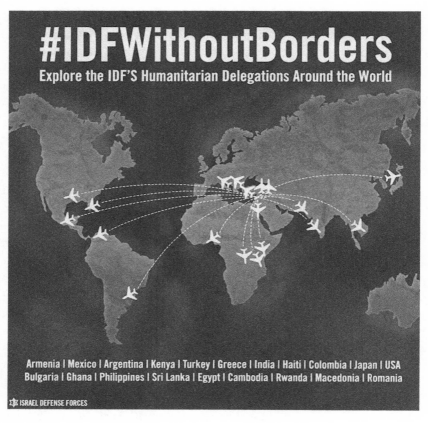

Figure 3.1.
IDF Without Borders echoes the name of the famous humanitarian organization Doctors Without Borders.
Source: Israel Defense Forces Official Blog.

long process.[10] While many scholars trace the emergence of modern laws of war and IHL back to Francisco de Vitoria's *De Indis Noviter Inventis* and *De Jure Bellis Hispanorum in Barbaros* (1532) and Hugo Grotius's *On the Law of War and Peace* (1625), it nonetheless took a few centuries before the different ideas pertaining to the regulation of wars were formulated in international declarations and conventions, beginning with the 1856 Paris Declaration Respecting Maritime Law and the 1868 St. Petersburg Declaration, which was drafted because "the progress of civilization should have the effect of alleviating as much as possible the calamities of war."[11] Later, the 1899 and 1907 Hague Conventions were published, followed by numerous treaties including the Four Geneva Conventions of 1949, whose goal has been to develop agreed-upon rules among states with respect to more humane ways of fighting.

Over the past decades legal experts, munitions experts, medical doctors, philosophers, statisticians, and, more recently, human rights professionals have been working together to continuously develop additional treaties and ethical codes to regulate and refine the methods and means of warfare, and, purportedly, to protect civilians as well as combatants in armed conflict.[12] Simultaneously, leading academic institutions and think tanks have been organizing conferences and workshops that bring together these diverse experts and thus have helped to produce a shared space where a common culture of ethical warfare can develop. A paradigmatic example is the Carr Center for Human Rights Policy at Harvard, which helped the US military revise its counterinsurgency field manual. Following vocal criticism, Sarah Sewall, the Center's faculty director who wrote an introduction to the manual and had previously been a Pentagon official, explained that faculty members were trying to instill institutional change within the military.[13] This convergence between human rights discourse (informed by the imperative to protect civilians) and forms of legal killing is constantly deepening, for, as Kennedy describes in his books, militaries the world over are inviting human rights experts to give talks and offer advice about what is permissible and impermissible in contemporary warfare. In this way they not only regulate the forms of killing, but also offer the state itself protection from accusations that its way of killing violated international law.

Israel is, of course, no exception.[14] Working together with the Israeli military, philosophy professor Asa Kasher of Tel-Aviv University formulated guidelines outlining when it is ethical to "assassinate in fighting terror." The right to assassinate, according to Kasher, is informed by the obligation of the state to protect the human rights of its citizens, including the right to life.[15] Put differently, assassinations are carried out within the framework of human rights (i.e., morally permissible) when they satisfy two forms of protection mentioned in chapter 1, the protection of the citizens by the state and the protection of the state itself. Human rights serve as the justification for killing and thus transform killing into a right.

One of the patent manifestations of this convergence is the widespread phenomenon of bringing experts in international humanitarian and human rights law into the war room and bestowing upon these lawyers the authority to make decisions that directly affect combat. Once considered obstacles to the war effort, "lawyers have been integrated into strategic and tactical decisions, and even accompany troops into battle."[16] It appears that the 1991 Gulf War was a watershed in this respect, with 200 lawyers being brought in to work in the US Army's theater of operations, ensuring that military "decisions were impacted by legal considerations at every level."[17]

In Israel this has also become common practice. Following the 2014 war in Gaza, one of Israel's first conclusions was that the IDF's international legal department had to be further enlarged. In a 2013 magazine interview, Zvi Hauser, Israel's former cabinet secretary and longtime aide to Prime Minister Benjamin Netanyahu, revealed the level of influence lawyers with expertise in international law have in the Israeli decision-making process. He described in detail a meeting in the days preceding the attempt of the *Mavi Marmara*, an unarmed ship manned by mostly Turkish citizens, to break Israel's military siege on the Gaza Strip in order to provide humanitarian aid to its Palestinian residents.

> In contrast to others, I said: Wait a minute, why shouldn't we allow this unarmed ship to enter Gaza? I did not anticipate the nine [Turkish citizens that would be] killed, but I didn't understand why we had to play the bad-guy part for which we were cast by the Turks in that bad movie. I know the prime minister. I saw in his eyes that he grasped the situation. Netanyahu likes to hear out-of-the-box ideas. But the jurists in the meeting argued that from the legal aspect, as long as a closure was in effect, Israel was obliged to enforce it. End of discussion. The political decision-makers don't think they can make a decision that is contrary to the imperative of the judicial level.[18]

The humanitarian maritime convoy was stopped by Israeli combat units, which, according to Israeli legal experts, abided by international law when they killed the nine civilians who were on the *Mavi Marmara*. This process whereby experts in international humanitarian and human rights law influence decisions that bear directly on combat has not been unidirectional, but rather reciprocal. Parallel to the military's incorporation of a humanitarian logic, human rights NGOs have been utilizing military know-how and military rationales to advance their goals. As Eyal Weizman points out, human rights NGOs have also begun integrating military theory and knowledge into their work, using, for example, munitions experts to gather evidence about the kind of bombs utilized to demolish houses in the Gaza Strip.[19]

From a slightly different perspective, Amnesty International USA's executive director, Suzanne Nossel, launched the campaign against NATO's imminent withdrawal from Afghanistan, claiming that military force helps to protect women's rights. In the introduction we did not mention that Nossel was hired by the Obama administration as the deputy assistant secretary of state for international organization affairs and from there she moved on to Amnesty International. This relocation is interesting because it reveals that Amnesty and the State Department occupy social spaces that are not all that distant from each other.[20] Nossel's move from the State Department to Amnesty underscores that there is a certain level of convergence between the dispositions, ideas, and actions of the state and those of human rights NGOs. In the first case then the human rights organization hires a munitions expert as an authority on violence, while in the second case the human rights organization hires a State Department official who encourages the deployment of violence as a way of protecting human rights. It is accordingly not only the military that mobilizes a humanitarian vocabulary of international law and uses it as a strategic asset, but also human rights organizations that use the military vocabulary, knowledge, and logic to protect human rights.

This discursive and practical proximity underscores that a culture of *ethical violence* is coalescing; one in which human rights, humanitarianism, and domination are intricately tied. The extent of this propinquity makes it, at times, difficult to understand if human rights and humanitarianism are regulating violence or whether violence is determining the parameters of human rights. The convergence between human rights and militarism has, as Kennedy's book intimates, the potential to produce three vital processes in which (1) humanitarian and human rights law renders violence legitimate; (2) these two bodies of law can make violence more effective; and finally, (3) they help transform violence into "something you can sustain and proudly stand behind," to quote Kennedy.[21] Human rights, in other words, are not the other side of killing, and killing is not necessarily the other side of human rights.

THE SOVEREIGN RIGHT TO KILL

The notion that the sovereign has the right to kill is intricately tied to the creation of the modern state. According to Thomas Hobbes, the state is that entity whose political legitimacy resides in its capacity to prevent the indiscriminate recourse to the natural right of every person to kill any other person.

> And because the condition of Man . . . is a condition of Warre of every one against every one; in which case every one is governed by his own Reason; and there is nothing he can make use of, that may not be a help unto him, in preserving his life against his enemyes; It followeth, that in such a condition, every man has a Right to every thing; even to one anothers body. And therefore, as long as this naturall Right of every man to every thing endureth, there can be no security to any man, (how strong or wise soever he be,) of living out the time, which Nature ordinarily alloweth men to live.[22]

The way to overcome the unbearable situation deriving from the natural right to kill accorded to every human being in the state of nature (and thus in effect constituting a universal human right to kill) was to introduce the social contract. Humans, Hobbes tells his readers, must "lay down this right to all things" and transfer it to a sovereign, thereby abandoning the state of nature and achieving—by entering a social contract—the condition of civil humanity under the protection of the state. The social contract, in other words, is an institution that was created to overcome the universal and natural right of every person to kill every other person; it congregates all rights within a sovereign body and thus institutionalizes various sorts of rights—including, crucially, the right to kill. This is one of the pillars of the modern social contract theory; law encompasses the sovereign administration of violence, which is based on the prior transferring of the right to kill from the individual to the sovereign.

Among the responsibilities bestowed on the sovereign through the social contract is the task for ensuring "the Peace and Defence of them all."[23] In order to carry out this responsibility the sovereign must become the sole bearer of the right to kill. Thus, the universal natural right of every human to kill is bequeathed upon the sovereign alone. This capacity to dictate who may live and who must die is, as Achille Mbembe reminds us, the "ultimate expression of sovereignty" and "its fundamental attribute"[24] since, as Foucault notes, "it is at the moment when the sovereign can kill that he exercises his right over life."[25]

Hobbes goes on to claim that the sovereign responsibility for ensuring peace—which means, in this context, putting an end to the natural human right to kill by assuming sole authority over the right to kill—comes with the right to determine the means to accomplish this goal. The sovereign is "Judge both of the meanes of Peace and Defence; and also of the hindrances, and disturbances of the same; and to do whatsoever he shall think necessary to be done, both beforehand, for the preserving of Peace and Security, by prevention of discord at home and Hostility from abroad; and, when Peace and Security are lost, for the recovery of the same."[26]

Hobbes is not only referring here to what Max Weber later called the state's monopoly over the legitimate use of violence, but even more importantly to the sovereign right to judge what the appropriate means and ends of violence are, which also includes judging the meaning ascribed to events.[27] In other words, the anarchy characterizing the state of nature, which the social contract aims to overcome by transferring all rights to the sovereign, is also an epistemological anarchy; there is no agreement on the definition of words and concepts, and each person within the state of nature has, as it were, a private language. This, to be sure, leads to disagreement and strife and prevents the creation of a political community. Consequently, if the sovereign is to establish peace and create stability, he or she must have the authority to determine the meaning of words—including the sense of violence—in public language.

A vital part of this role is the production of a specific moral economy of violence, made up of an array of doctrines, norms, and social practices that allow human beings to make sense of violence. The moral economy of violence is both a reflection of sovereign power and a form of power in and of itself. It is the power to define and determine the rational deployment of violence, the power to distinguish between violence's moral and immoral utilization. Hobbes tells us that the sovereign is "to be Judge of what Opinions and Doctrines are averse, and what conducing to Peace."[28] This can only be done if the sovereign controls the meaning of words and the significance ascribed to events, including the way the deployment of violence is framed. In this way, Hobbes connects the sovereign right to kill to the sovereign decision of when it is right to kill as well as the best way to describe the killing, thus establishing the sovereign's role as the producer of a moral economy of killing, as the fabricator of ethical violence. The transfer of the natural human right to kill to the sovereign produces a new order—incarnated in the modern state—whereby the sovereign determines which forms of violence are morally acceptable and under what circumstances it is legitimate to use them. In *On the Postcolony*, Mbembe describes a similar process when he notes that the founding violence in the colony is always presented as necessary for peace.[29]

It is within the context of the production of a moral economy of violence that the *human right to kill* has emerged. This human right does not denote a natural right of every person to kill every other person as it did in the state of nature, but rather the idea that human rights can serve as a moral justification and validation of the sovereign right to kill. The sovereign never gave up his right to kill, and he has always had to justify the killing by controlling the meaning of words in public language. It is only in the past two decades, however, that human rights are being mobilized to justify sovereign violence, whether in Afghanistan, Iraq, or Palestine. Because of the rise of human rights discourse as the new lingua franca of global moral speak, Hobbes's sovereign, which is currently identified with the state executive, legislative, and judicial apparatus, is framing its deployment of violence as an "act of state" that sticks to human rights standards. If once the civilizing mission was deployed to underscore the moral superiority of colonial democracies, currently universal human rights serve a similar purpose for liberal democracies. In other words, human rights acquire a civilizational function in the contemporary liberal era.

Moral killing coincides with human rights in two major ways. First, killing has to be carried out in a way that does not breach international humanitarian and human rights law. This imperative has become categorical. Second, killing should be used to advance human rights. This imperative is not categorical, but it bolsters the moral claims attributed to the act of killing. Hence, it is not only that the sovereign state emerged following World War II as the organizational entity responsible for guaranteeing and protecting human rights, as we pointed out in chapter 1, but that the act of protection itself has to be carried out in a way that accords with human rights and, if at all possible, advances human rights. Hence, the importance of the military human rights training programs.

David Kennedy highlights the novelty of using the lexicon of human rights to frame killing when he contends that the "emergence of a powerful legal vocabulary for articulating humanitarian ethics in the context of war is a real achievement of the intervening years." International humanitarian law has, in other words, reached a new stage in its development due to its interlacing with human rights law and is constantly used by liberal regimes to legitimize their wars. Kennedy says this, even though he is aware that "compliance with international law 'legitimates'. It means, of course, that killing, maiming, humiliating, wounding people is legally privileged, authorized, permitted, and justified."[30] Put differently, those trained to kill are also trained in human rights precisely because human rights have, over the past several decades, become a yardstick for conferring meaning to events and practices of political violence. Militaries are allowed to kill only when the act does not violate a human right, only when killing and human rights coincide, when killing can be carried out according to human rights and humanitarian regulations. To become morally sound, civilized, and legitimate, sovereign violence has to be framed as corresponding with the standards of the new human rights regime and transmuted into a discourse of human rights.

The use of human rights to validate and legitimate domination can be seen very clearly, for instance, through the discourse surrounding human shields. Offering a concise genealogy of the way human shields have been invoked in Israel/Palestine reveals how the "insistence on legality of action," as Laleh Khalili points out, "goes hand in hand with the will to improve that is inherent to liberal imperial invasions, occupations, and confinements." "If," Khalili continues, "our intent is to better the condition of living of the 'lesser' people (by making a gift of our civilization, or development, or modernization, or democracy), then what happens in the process matters little, even if what happens in the process is cruelty, torture, or indefinite confinement. A virtuous intent to improve is one of the strongest characteristics of liberal [warfare] and is what distinguishes it from its illiberal kin."[31]

Khalili's analysis of liberal warfare and the desire to frame its deployment of violence as legal and therefore ethical helps explain why the discourse of human shields is prominent within the Israeli context, but nearly absent in relation to regimes that—at least at this point in time— do not claim to adhere to liberal humanitarian and human rights principles. Moreover, human shielding provides a concrete example of how the liberal logic of contemporary warfare operates. Therefore, analyzing how it has been deployed during Israel's 2014 Gaza war provides us with some insight into the subtle ways liberal ethics helps to shape violence, and violence helps to shape liberal ethics.

HUMAN SHIELDS

Human shielding refers to the use of persons protected by international humanitarian law, such as prisoners of war or civilians, to deter attacks on combatants or military sites.[32] Placing civilians on train tracks, in airports, or in any site that is considered to be a legitimate enemy target in order to prevent the latter from striking is illegal according to IHL. Along similar lines, carrying out military operations from within civilian spaces, particularly schools, hospitals, religious sites, and even civilian neighborhoods and industrial areas is considered illegal because of the inevitable transformation of the noncombatant populations into human shields. Article 28 of the Fourth Geneva Convention states that "The presence of a protected person may not be used to render certain points or areas immune from military operations."[33] The 1977 Additional Protocol I to the Convention explains in article 51(7) that

> The presence or movement of the civilian population or individual civilians shall not be used to render certain points or areas immune from military operations, in particular in attempts to shield military objectives from attacks or to shield, favor or impede military operations. The Parties to the conflict shall not direct the movement of the civilian population or individual civilians in order to attempt to shield military objectives from attacks or to shield military operations.[34]

More recently, the 1998 Rome Statute of the International Criminal Court characterized the use of human shields as a war crime.[35] The significance of human shield clauses in international law cannot be overstated considering that urban settings are rapidly becoming the most prominent arenas of contemporary warfare. Urban areas, as Stephen Graham proposes, "have become the lightning conductors for our planet's political violence," while "warfare strongly shapes quotidian urban life."[36] The dramatic increase in urban warfare entails that civilians inevitably occupy the front lines of the fighting. Insofar as this is the case, then practically all fighting within cities involves warfare practices that, according to IHL, include the use of human shields.

Civilians have often been at the forefront of violence in Israel/Palestine. Yet it was only in the midst of the second Intifada that several liberal human rights NGOs decided to use IHL clauses pertaining to human shields to criticize practices deployed by the Israeli military. In a report entitled *Human Shield*, the Israeli human rights organization B'Tselem describes how, during the 2002 military operation Defensive Shield, Israeli soldiers would randomly take Palestinian civilians and force them to enter buildings suspected of being booby-trapped, made them remove suspicious objects from roads, stand inside houses where soldiers had set up military positions, and walk in front of soldiers to shield them from gunfire.[37] Just a few months earlier, HRW had published a similar report, *In a Dark Hour*, which documented how within the same military operation the IDF routinely coerced Palestinian civilians into performing life-endangering acts that assisted its military operations.[38] These liberal human rights organizations condemned Israel for violating the fundamental principle of civilian immunity inscribed in IHL. They noted that the Fourth Geneva Convention explicitly forbids the use of the civilian population to aid the military objectives of the occupying army as well as the forced use of local residents as a means toward military advantage or for the securing of intelligence. Invoking article 28 and the Additional Protocol, they emphasized that this prohibition includes the use of civilians as human shields.

In an attempt to stop this form of state violence, seven liberal Israeli human rights NGOs submitted a petition against the prime minister, the minister of defense, and the Israeli military, asking the High Court of Justice to ban the use of human shields.[39] In 2005, the court reached a decision. Citing Jean Pictet, who wrote the official commentary on the Fourth Geneva Convention, Chief Justice Aharon Barak characterized the use of people as human shields as a "cruel and barbaric" act. He noted that "a basic principle, which passes as a common thread running through all of the law of belligerent occupation, is the prohibition of use of protected residents as a part of the war effort of the occupying army."[40] In addition, he claimed that according to humanitarian law, everything possible must be done to separate the civilian population from military activity; this rule, in turn, indicates that local residents are not to be brought—even with their consent—into a combat zone because the notion of consent is meaningless within a situation of inequality between the occupying force and the local resident.[41] In this instance and unlike the B'Tselem's report cited in the previous chapter, the High Court of Justice took into account the asymmetrical context in which violence was being deployed and ruled that people cannot be used as shields. Humanitarian law was, in other words, used by the court to protect civilians against the demands of "military necessity."

One year after the High Court ruling, other Israeli political actors began appropriating the term human shield while giving it a slightly different meaning. The Intelligence and Terrorism Information Center (ITIC), a conservative Israeli think tank whose offices are located in the Ministry of Defense, published a lengthy report about Hezbollah's use of Lebanese civilians as human shields during the 2006 Lebanon War.[42] In this report, the arguments originally made by Israeli and international human rights organizations against the IDF, and which were validated by the High Court of Justice, were slightly reframed. Appropriating the same logic advanced by the human rights NGOs, the anti-terrorism think-tank accused Israel's enemies of human shielding. In so doing, the think-tank transformed the prohibition of using human shields into a legal and ethical justification for military necessity. It reasoned that Hezbollah's violation served to legitimize Israel's killing of Lebanese civilians, pointing out that the "exploitation" of a civilian population is "considered a war crime and gross violation of international laws governing armed conflict." The same think tank went on to argue that "the IDF's air strikes and ground attacks against Hezbollah targets located in population centers were carried out in accordance with international law, which does not grant immunity to a terrorist organization deliberately hiding behind civilians, using them as human shields."[43] Hence, the use of human shields is not only a violation, but, within contemporary asymmetric urban wars, can also help validate the ethical claim that the death of "untargeted civilians" is merely collateral—and thus legitimate—damage.

A few years later, in the aftermath of the Israeli military campaign in Gaza called Cast Lead (winter 2008–2009), the same conservative think tank published a report entitled *Evidence of the Use of the Civilian Population as Human Shields*.[44] In this and other reports released in subsequent months, the ITIC provided a series of images and testimonies as evidence of how Hamas and other militant groups had used homes, schools, and mosques for military-operational purposes.[45] ITIC's descriptions help corroborate Eyal Weizman's claim that cities are not simply the site, but the very medium, of warfare as urban spheres increasingly become primary theatres of violence.[46] Hence, alongside the convergences we have been describing within urban warfare the noncombatant and combatant as well as civilian and military edifices overlap. This became evident during the 2014 Gaza war, where human shielding became a central trope in Israel's semiotic warfare, as it strived to provide moral justification for killing hundreds of civilians.[47] An analysis of a series of posters disseminated by the Israeli military on its Twitter account, Facebook, and blogs during Protective Edge provides an unparalleled illustration of how Israel strived to provide legal and moral justification for the killing of hundreds of civilians.

PROTECTIVE EDGE

The poster "Where Do Gaza Terrorists Hide Their Weapons?" (figure 3.2) is a paradigmatic example, where the subtext does the speaking: houses, mosques, schools, and hospitals are legitimate targets because they are presumed to be weapon depositories. This is also the message in "When Is a House a Home?" (figure 3.3), which simply zooms in on one of the images in the previous poster, showing how Palestinians presumably hide rockets in civilian homes. The logic is straightforward: insofar as Hamas hides weapons in houses (illegitimate), Israel can bomb them as if they were military targets (legitimate). Within this framework, a single function (hiding weapons) out of many existing functions (home, shelter, intimacy, etc.) determines the status of an urban site (in our case the house), so that the edifice's form loses its traditional signification.

Giorgio Agamben's analysis of sovereignty helps to understand the discursive operation of the Israeli army. In *Homo Sacer*, Agamben defines sovereign power as the power to determine and administer the threshold between private and public life. In this case, the Israeli army defines the function of a house and the forms of life taking place within it by claiming that the armed resistance in Gaza distorted its traditional function and created an exceptional situation. This exceptional situation sanctions the deployment of lethal violence—albeit in conformity with international law—against those civilians who occupy the space where normally private life takes place. In this way, the notion of human shielding erases any distinction between private and public life, thereby transforming private life into bare dispensable life.[48]

Figure 3.2.
Where do Gaza terrorists hide their weapons?
Source: Israel Defense Forces.

The overlapping of civilian and military functions in urban warfare alongside the resignification of the urban architectural structures (as well as subjects) creates new challenges for international law and the sovereign articulation of ethical violence. Accordingly, the question posed in figure 3.3, "When does it become a legitimate military target?" should be understood as merely rhetorical. The answer the IDF expects is "All houses in Gaza can be legitimate targets since all houses are potentially non-homes." In this way, the IDF resolves the ethical dilemma of bombing civilian sites.

Israel's warfare is, however, not only about the resignification of architectural structures, but also about the transformation of human beings

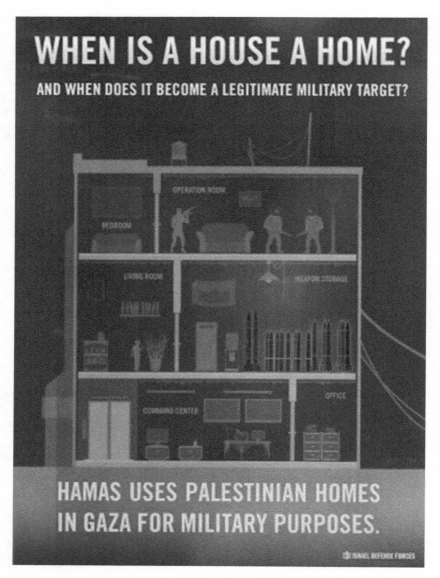

Figure 3.3.
When is a house and home?
Source: Israel Defense Forces.

into collateral damage, subjects who can be killed without violating international law. The legitimization for its indiscriminate bombing is premised upon a profound moral disjuncture between Israelis and Palestinians. According to the poster, "Israel uses weapons to protect its civilians. Hamas uses civilians to protect its weapons" (figure 3.4). Palestinians are depicted

Figure 3.4.
Israel uses weapons to protect its civilians. Hamas uses civilians to protect its weapons.
Source: Israel Defense Forces.

as barbarians who ignore the elementary grammar of international law. This trope was also reiterated by the renowned intellectual Elie Wiesel, who during Protective Edge published—in collaboration with the US-based This World: The Values Network—an advertisement in *The Guardian* entitled "Jews Rejected Child Sacrifice 3,500 Years Ago. Now It's Hamas' Turn." The thinly veiled racist statement included an analogy between Hamas and the SS brigades: "In my own lifetime," Wiesel wrote, "I have seen Jewish children thrown into the fire. And now I have seen Muslim children used as human shields."[49] The equation between Palestinians and Nazis is explicit.

This is also the subtext of the poster featuring Israel's chief of staff saying: "Even as we carry out strikes, we remember that there are civilians in Gaza. Hamas has turned them into hostages" (figure 3.5). Again, the logic is clear. All civilians in Gaza are being held hostage by Hamas, a practice that is considered a war crime and a gross violation of international law governing armed conflict. This, then, provides legal and moral justification

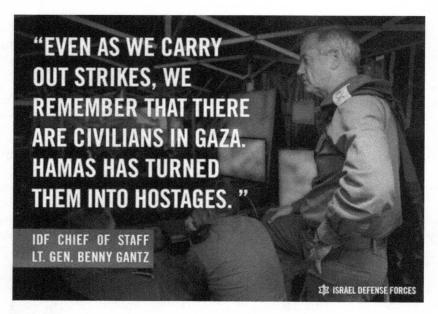

Figure 3.5.
Even as we carry out strikes, we remember that there are civilians in Gaza. Hamas has
turned them into hostages.
Source: Israel Defense Forces.

against the accusation that Israel is the one killing civilians. Presumed
human rights violations carried out by Palestinians against Palestinians—
taking hostages and human shielding—thus become the legitimization of
lethal and indiscriminate violence on the part of the occupying force.

Hence, the use of human shields is not only a violation. In contemporary asymmetric urban wars, accusing the enemy of using human shields
helps validate the claim that the death of "untargeted civilians" is merely
collateral damage. When all civilians are potential human shields, when
each and every civilian can become a hostage of the enemy, then all enemy
civilians become killable. In order for all this to be convincing, the Israeli
military depicts the asymmetric context in which it unleashes its violence
against a whole population as symmetric. This symmetric representation
is carried out, for instance, through the poster that proclaims, "Some
bomb shelters shelter people, some shelter bombs" (figure 3.6). Here a radically disproportionate situation is presented as if it were balanced. The
residents of Gaza are bombed by cutting-edge F-16 fighter jets and drones,
yet they do not have bomb shelters, and they have nowhere to flee. Israel's
residents are bombed mostly by makeshift rockets, many of which have
been intercepted by Iron Dome missiles.[50] The majority of the population

Figure 3.6.
Some bomb shelters shelter people, some shelter bombs.
Source: Israel Defense Forces.

in Israel has access to shelters and can flee out of the rocket's range, but the radically disproportionate power differential between a besieged population confined to an enclave and its besiegers is depicted as if the two camps were equal and enjoyed the same juridical status.

These powerful images, spread by the Israeli military through social media, attempt to transform the very presence of civilians as suspect in the areas it bombards, regardless of the fact that these areas are urban centers. For Palestinians living in Gaza, simply spending time in their own homes, frequenting a mosque, going to a hospital, or to school became a dangerous enterprise since any one of these architectural edifices could become a target at any moment. One can no longer safely assume that the existence of masses of human bodies in civilian spaces can serve as defense against the lethal capacity of liberal high-tech states.

Human shielding does not provide a last resort and a protection against the killing of vulnerable persons, as the phrase would seem to suggest. On the contrary, the deployment of the phrase human shielding allows the inclusion of the shield within the category of those human beings that can be killed in accordance with international law. Similar to Agamben's *homo sacer*, a human shield is a person who can be killed without it being a crime. However, unlike *homo sacer*, a human shield is not outside the law. Indeed, the condition of possibility of becoming a human shield is that one *is not* a homo sacer, but instead the person is recognized as a civilian situated within the law and a bearer of rights.

PALESTINIAN TESTIMONIES

Let us go back in time to Israel's operation Cast Lead in order to expose yet another dimension of the human right to kill. After the winter 2008-2009 war on Gaza, in addition to a series of images that were disseminated as evidence demonstrating that Palestinian "terrorist organizations" violated the Fourth Geneva Convention and its Additional Protocol by hiding weapons in residential houses and mosques and launching rockets from sites located near schools, mosques, and UN facilities, the ITIC and Ministry of Foreign Affairs cited testimonies provided by Palestinians about how Hamas had exploited civilians as human shields. Nawaf Feisal Attar, a Palestinian from Gaza who had been detained on January 11, 2009, said during interrogations that Hamas "regularly launched rockets from civilian houses and agricultural areas despite the objections of the owners, who feared their houses and fields would be destroyed by the IDF. However, he said, local opposition was limited because the Palestinian population did not dare argue with Hamas operatives, who would shoot their legs or even kill them, claiming they were collaborators."[51] Mirroring B'Tselem, which uses testimonies gathered from Palestinians in the Gaza Strip, the Intelligence and Terrorism Information Center and the Ministry of Foreign Affairs also invoke Palestinian testimonies. Crucially, however, when B'Tselem posts a testimony, it is meant to serve as evidence of human rights violations, while the testimonies cited in these reports have two additional functions.

Testimonies like the one given by Nawaf Attar are simultaneously an accusation and a defense. As an accusation, they have a function similar to the testimonies provided by B'Tselem. The victim remains the same (Palestinian population), but the perpetrator is new; namely, they supposedly provide evidence of Hamas's violation of international law. But the testimonies also function as a defense, since the descriptions of Hamas's violations are meant to provide legal and moral justification for the accusation that Israel kills civilians. Human rights violations carried out by Palestinians against Palestinians thus become the legitimization of violence. If in the previous chapter we described how the Israeli government and think tanks have launched a campaign against human rights NGOs that subject the Israeli-Palestinian conflict to legal oversight, here we see that simultaneously the government and other think tanks invoke IHL to justify state violence against civilians. This underscores yet again two central claims: that in and of itself international law is neither inherently just nor unjust and its value is determined by its use; and that liberal regimes use international law to frame their violence as ethical.

Hamas, as Nawaf Attar testifies, is immoral because it shoots the legs and kills fellow nationals, while Israel's ethical superiority is established by the statement that Palestinians "knew" Israel would not bomb a school even though Hamas has no qualms about launching military operations from educational facilities. In this way the sovereign uses the voice of a Palestinian prisoner to produce a framework of ethical violence, whereby the immorality of the colonized corroborate the morality of the colonizer and its adherence to IHL. It is also through these processes that the sovereign right to kill is uttered and presented as coinciding with human rights. Taken together, then, these testimonies are used to create an ethics of violence framing the civilizational distinction between colonizer and colonized.

The testimonies cited by ITIC and the Ministry of Foreign Affairs mirror those published by liberal human rights NGOs in that they too are used as a form of legal evidence employed to reveal the truth about an existing human rights violation. The think tank and ministry did not, however, gather the testimonies themselves, but rather used testimonies that were obtained by the Israeli Security Agency, the secret services known as the Shabak. Mimicking B'Tselem, the Shabak also posted the testimonies on its website, explaining that during Operation Cast Lead IDF forces arrested dozens of Hamas and Islamic Jihad activists.[52]

Interrogations by the Shabak have a long history and have usually been associated with uncovering "ticking bombs" and "terrorist networks" and not so much with human rights violations. Hence, it seems that interrogations are being marshaled by the Shabak to do certain kinds of evidentiary work that they had not done in the past. In this case, the interrogators, who may have received human rights training, extracted testimonies about a violation of humanitarian law: the illegal use of Palestinians as human shields by other Palestinians. The Shabak tells us that all the testimonies posted on the website provided evidence that "Hamas used mosques, public institutions including schools, and the houses of activists for weapon storage; as well as the fact that rocket launchings were carried out from these locations and from densely populated areas, on the assumption that Israel would avoid targeting such areas."[53] These testimonies serve to justify Israeli bombing of densely populated neighborhoods so as to underscore its ethical use of violence. Thus, the human rights of the dominated are deployed as a way of legitimizing the violence carried out by the dominant.

TESTIMONIES AND VIOLATIONS

Reconstructing the process leading to the production of these testimonies uncovers yet another dimension of how the sovereign right to kill is framed as part of a human rights discourse. B'Tselem, like many human rights NGOs, has "fieldworkers" whose job is to go out in the field and find people who can and are willing to provide testimonies. The fieldworkers choose people who witnessed events in which human rights violations occurred.[54] They then interview these people, record their testimonies, and use them both to make the "truth of inhumanity present" and as a form of legal evidence.[55] Once the testimonies have served their purpose they are filed in the organization's archive, and can be accessed at a later date if the need arises.

The Shabak, by contrast, interrogates the witnesses often using physical and psychological violence to obtain a "confession," which can later be used as testimony and serve as evidence. Raji Abed-Rabbo, born in 1987, single, a resident of Jabalya and an Islamic Jihad activist, was arrested by the IDF during Operation Cast Lead and interrogated on January 12, 2009. During his interrogation, Abed-Rabbo revealed that "Hamas military activists frequently bury explosive charges in streets, near mosques and in orchards. . . . He also said that senior Hamas members took over a very large bunker under Al-Shifa Hospital, where they were hiding out."[56] The "outcome" of the interrogation was posted on the Shabak's website as the testimony of a witness.

There are, no doubt, significant differences between the testimonies collected by B'Tselem and those gathered by the secret services, particularly in terms of how and under what circumstances they were assembled. Raji Abed-Rabbo, whose testimony appears on the Shabak website, provided another testimony to two liberal human rights NGOs, which later published part of it in a report called *Exposed: The Treatment of Palestinian Detainees during Operation "Cast Lead."* In this second testimony, he describes how on January 6, 2009, he was in his home together with

15 family members when they were ordered by Israeli soldiers to leave their home before it was bombarded. Over the next three days he and his brother Rami were held by the military and used as human shields; the soldiers instructed them to walk in the street in front of the force as they aimed their weapons toward them. The brothers were then made to enter houses in the neighborhood before the soldiers, often through windows and balconies. Raji's brother Rami notes that "The soldiers, after we would exit the house, would send a dog and after it exited they would check a mechanism hanging around its neck and only then enter[ed] the house and set up there."[57] When they were not serving as human shields, their hands were tied behind their back and they were barely fed.

In the one example of Raji, there are multiple layers of shielding. During the Gaza offensive, Raji served as a human shield to protect Israeli soldiers from booby traps and Hamas militants. Raji then provides testimony to the Shabak about how Hamas uses human shields, and his testimony serves as a shield to protect military and government officials from lawfare carried out by the UN Fact Finding Mission and numerous local and international NGOs. Raji and his brother, it is important to stress, are not the only ones who appear on both the Shabak and liberal human rights NGOs websites. In many ways, Shabak's mirroring of human rights NGOs has further effects, since certain liberal organizations may locate those interrogated by the Shabak and publish new testimonies, not so much to contradict the first testimonies, but to expose what is missing from them, including vivid descriptions of numerous human rights violations carried out by the military and Shabak. So while the Shabak mirrors strategies of human rights NGOs, these NGOs reappropriate these same strategies to expose the Shabak. These mirroring tactics are complex because the form constituting quotidian human rights work preserves its shape—collecting testimonies, fieldworkers, and so on—while the content not only changes but in many respects is inverted. In the next chapter we analyze a series of human rights inversions and discuss their significance in the context of legal struggles over land, while here we focus on what is missing from the testimonies extracted by the Shabak to reveal other dimensions of how human right are used to rationalize killing.

Husam As'ad Attar, another Palestinian whose testimony appears on the Shabak website, confessed about his involvement "in the placement of an explosive charge detonated against IDF forces on the fifth day of fighting" and admitted "his awareness of tunnels intended to serve for the kidnapping of soldiers."[58] In the testimony that he gave later to two Israeli liberal human rights NGOs, he describes parts of an interrogation after his arrest.

I was taken to a trailer with two interrogators behind a desk and soldiers around them. One of the soldiers said his name was "Mukhtar" [the head of a village or a community] and that he was there to beat me. At the beginning they interrogated me while I was still standing, and afterwards they ordered me to squat on my knees and look at the floor. Throughout the interrogation they asked if I knew where the abducted soldier Gilad Shalit was. After about an hour and a half they took me outside. "Mukhtar" and five soldiers began to spit on me, kick me, slap me and punch me all over my body, mostly in my upper body. Afterwards they put me in a small pit and threatened to shoot me and said, "we want your mother to suffer because of you."[59]

Husam Attar's first testimony, as it turns out, was given while being tortured. His body and mind had to be violated while he provided evidence of another human rights violation (Hamas's use of human shields), evidence that was used to justify the killing of civilians and as a shield against the lawfare campaigns. To be sure, the basic human rights of the Palestinians whose testimonies appear on the Shabak website as evidence of human rights violations were violated; first when their body served as a shield to protect soldiers carrying out urban warfare and later when it was physically and mentally broken. This, we believe, is neither coincidental nor in any way unique. The pilot who justifies bombing urban edifices by referring to human rights is doing much the same thing. Hence, hegemony produces the convergence between human rights and killing, which is, in effect, the reconceptualization of the sovereign right to kill as a human right.

"FIGHT IT RIGHT"

Not only have the Israeli government and its think tanks formulated sovereign acts of killing as a human right, but liberal human rights NGOs that analyze conflict and warfare have followed suit, framing state violence within the sphere that human rights deems permissible. As we show below, the use of human rights as a discursive mechanism to justify domination is not merely the prerogative of the state. As it turns out, the hegemonic practices that produce convergences between the state and liberal human rights NGOs enhance an agreed upon conception of ethical violence.

According to the UN, during the 2012 Operation Pillar of Cloud 174 Palestinians were killed in Gaza, at least 168 of them by the Israeli military, of whom 67 are believed to be militants and 101 civilians, including

33 children and 13 women.[60] Palestinians killed six Israelis, four of whom were civilians.[61] Analyzing the circumstances in which these people were killed, the Israeli human rights NGO B'Tselem invokes international humanitarian law:

> Even when the target of an attack is legitimate, the combatants must, as far as possible, adopt various precautionary measures to prevent harm to civilians. Therefore, the law permits the use only of precise weapons capable of distinguishing military from civilian targets. Furthermore, the provisions stipulate that the civilian population in the area must be given prior warning, as far as circumstances permit, to enable them to protect themselves. In any case, if projected harm to civilians significantly outweighs anticipated military benefit, attacks must not be carried out.[62]

B'Tselem concludes that Hamas and other groups operating in the Gaza Strip "violated these provisions." Their violations include deliberately "launching rockets at Israeli civilians and Israeli communities; firing from within civilian Palestinian neighborhoods, thereby jeopardizing the lives of the local residents; and concealing ammunition and arms in civilian buildings." Hence, according to B'Tselem, the Palestinian militants breached the principle of discrimination—between combatants and non-combatants—in two ways: by deliberately targeting Israeli civilians and by using the local population as human shields, thus also violating the human rights of Palestinians. Because Hamas did not "fight it right" (to use a phrase developed by the ICRC), it committed, according to the liberal human rights NGO, war crimes.

At least in relation to these two accusations the human rights organization is in full agreement with the Israeli government and its think tanks. This convergence deepens when the rights group notes that "deciding whether the Israeli military has violated IHL provisions is not as simple." It is not simple, in B'Tselem's view, because

> Statements by Israeli officials assert the military's commitment to abide by IHL provisions. In addition, published Israeli summaries of the campaign emphasize that the military went to great lengths in order to prevent harm to the civilian population in Gaza. Similarly, an ISA announcement stated that "during the attacks an effort was made to prevent injury to the innocent, and to minimize as far as possible any injury to uninvolved civilians." This approach is also evident in an article posted on the IDF spokesperson's website after the campaign, entitled "How did the IDF minimize harm to Palestinian civilians during Operation Pillar of Defense?"[63]

B'Tselem also notes that in the above-mentioned article (taken from the same IDF blog in which the posters we analyzed were posted) the IDF "explains how the military minimized harm to non-involved civilians through the use of its technological capabilities that enabled the use of 'pinpoint surgical strikes' and the option to abort missions in real-time if it discovered that noninvolved civilians were on-site." Precision, however, is not judged by its effect, only by the inherent components of the weapon deployed. In other words, Israel's use of advanced technological weapons that can be guided and directed with relatively high level of precision protected it from violating international law, irrespective of the actual number of civilian fatalities. We notice not only how ethical violence is intricately tied to the type of weapons used, but also that the liberal human rights NGO appropriates the connection between ethics and hi-tech weapons.[64]

B'Tselem goes on to cite the IDF blog, noting that the commanding military officers were given legal advice prior to and during the campaign, underscoring the IDF's claim that its "forces operate in accordance with international law, including all restrictions it imposes." Hence, the practice of providing the military with legal advice in and of itself serves to protect it from violations. Finally, the rights group accentuates the IDF's decision to include a representative of the District Civil Liaison Office, which coordinates between the civilian population in Gaza and the military, in all meetings related to the fighting, because this representative "communicates the humanitarian needs of the population."[65]

In line with IHL doctrine, B'Tselem intimates that without intent to deliberately kill, no violations occurred.[66] It is important to note, however, that "pinpoint surgical strikes," "precision bombs," and the "ability to abort attacks" signify the possibility to devise a perimeter for intentions and not necessarily a reduction in human fatalities. B'Tselem takes at face value Israel's declared precautions published on the IDF blog and ascribes to them a more significant value than it does to the actual effect of the violence—87 Palestinian civilian deaths as opposed to four Israeli civilian deaths, not to mention the long-term lethal effect of bombing Palestinian civilian infrastructure. Laleh Khalili underscores this point when she writes that "What matters in the end is how virtuous our intent was, how precisely we targeted the guilty, what clean instruments of killing and confinement we used."[67] Since intent becomes the primary criterion for judgment, numbers (in this case the number of fatalities), which on other occasions are so important to both the state and liberal human rights NGOs in determining an ethics, have no impact on the morality of violence. In this way the human rights NGO helps buttress the position that

Israeli "fought the war right" and that the killing of Palestinians was carried out in a humanitarian way.[68] Humanism, as Grégoire Chamayou notes, can be the bearer of murderous policies.[69]

A HUMANITARIAN SHIELD

While the evidence B'Tselem relies on to substantiate its legal position—namely, statements made by the Shabak and IDF—is questionable and reflects the increasing permeability between human rights violators and human rights defenders, it should also be stressed that the human rights NGO is reiterating the dominant interpretation of IHL. As we noted, the illegality of using human shields is spelled out in IHL, so that article 51(7) from Additional Protocol I, for example, can be interpreted as a legal and moral protection for the sovereign right to kill. To reiterate, according to the article, "The presence or movement of the civilian population or individual civilians shall not be used to render certain points or areas immune from military operations."[70]

Scholars of different stripes agree that the principle of proportionality—which requires belligerents to refrain from causing damage disproportionate to the military advantage to be gained—remains prevalent in cases of human shielding, but as Yoram Dinstein claims, the "actual test of excessive injury to civilians must be relaxed. That is to say, the appraisal whether civilian casualties are excessive in relation to the military advantage anticipated *must make allowances for the fact that*—if an attempt is made to shield military objectives with civilians—*civilian casualties will be higher than usual*."[71] The United Kingdom's Manual of the Law of Armed Conflict adopts a similar position, noting that "if the defenders put civilians or civilian objects at risk by placing military objectives in their midst or by placing civilians in or near military objectives, this is a factor to be taken into account in favour of the attackers in considering the legality of attacks on those objectives."[72] And the US Air Force maintains that in such cases, "otherwise lawful targets shielded with protected civilians may be attacked, and the protected civilians may be considered as collateral damage, provided that the collateral damage is not excessive compared to the concrete and direct military advantage anticipated by the attack."[73] Hence, according to international law the human shielding clause permits the killing of civilians.

This is not only the view of the high-tech militaries and their agents, but is basically the position adopted by humanitarian and human rights organizations. The International Committee of the Red Cross notes in a manual entitled *Fight It Right* that the "attacking commander is required to do his best to protect [civilian shields] but he is entitled to take the defending commander's actions into account when considering the rule of proportionality."[74] The convergence between B'Tselem, ICRC, and militaries of different countries can be understood, using Gramsci's terms, as the manifestation of a historic bloc composed of ostensibly conflicting actors that both reflects and reproduces the hegemony of liberal regimes. They would all concur that Israel "fought the war right": it used "precise hi-tech weapons" and took the "necessary precautions" when launching the assault. Thus, humanitarian law not only frames Israel's war as ethical, but also serves as a shield, protecting the pilots, drone operators, and those who sent them on their missions from legal suits in courts that exercise universal jurisdiction.

COLONIAL LEGACIES

The notion that international law helps rationalize the violence deployed by the dominant is not new. Different scholars remind us that in the colonial era domination tended to be in compliance with IHL.[75] This was so not least because the term civilian is one of the key concepts that helps determine the legitimacy and illegitimacy of violence in IHL, and during colonialism only the citizens of colonial powers were recognized as civilians since civilianhood was couched along racial lines.[76] When colonial states killed the colonized they did it without violating international law precisely because colonial subjects were considered outside IHL's sphere of application.[77] Only during the process of decolonization the category of civilian was extended to the ex-colonized, who became civilians and as such human beings protected under international law. Within this postcolonial context, whereby civilianhood has been universalized, warfare and international law have been facing new ethical dilemmas. A new tension emerged between, on the one hand, the desire of liberal states to frame their wars and violence within international law and, on the other hand, the wide scale killing of civilians in contemporary wars. This, again, can be witnessed when examining the contemporary legal and ethical debates on the deployment of the category of human shield.

Writing for the *Israel Yearbook on Human Rights*, Michael Schmitt notes that human shielding has become "endemic in contemporary conflict, taking place across the legal spectrum of conflict" from the Iraq-Iran war and the two Gulf wars to Somalia, Liberia, Sierra Leone, and Chechnya.[78] The extended use of shielding, Schmitt explains, is in great part due to the dramatic asymmetry characterizing many of today's conflicts: "Confronted with overwhelming technological superiority, weaker parties have embraced shielding as a 'method of warfare' designed to counter attacks against which they cannot effectively defend using the weaponry and forces at their disposal. The tactic presumes that the prospect of killing civilian shields may dissuade an attacker from striking."[79] The human body has thus become the last defense of the weak against the lethal capacity of the high-tech states.[80]

This observation about the asymmetry of current warfare needs to be considered alongside the asymmetry characterizing international law in its various vernacularizations. The capacity to carry out "surgical strikes," for example, opens, according to Thomas Smith, a legal divide between technological haves and have-nots. Smith notes that while aerial bombings—the main form of violence used in Cast Lead, Pillar of Cloud, and Protective Edge—are subject to the general rules of armed conflict, no laws govern air attacks per se. Bomber altitudes have not been codified; certain types of ordnance have not been proscribed for aerial attacks in urban settings; rules for identifying targets from the air do not exist.[81] One should add that international law is totally silent on the terrorizing effect of prolonged aerial strikes; in the shadows of President Obama's drone wars, whole populations live under permanent terror, regardless of the number of people actually killed. Hence, international law is applicable when condemning atrocities carried out face-to-face like the ones perpetrated in Syria, Rwanda, and Sudan, or when Israel's infantry enters Gaza. By contrast, high-tech violence, particularly when it is carried out from the air, is shielded from prosecution. We notice then that IHL creates a humanitarian shield for violence also by restricting the view of violence.

The crux of the matter, though, is that the weapons gap characterizing many instances of modern urban warfare reinscribes the long-standing gap that existed in international law between colonizer and colonized. If in the past international law sided with the state against nonstate colonized actors, currently, after some of those colonized achieved statehood, international law favors the high-tech states (usually the colonizers of old) over the low-tech states (usually the ex-colonized). When high-tech states bomb cities of low-tech states with precise weapons, their technological superiority enables them not to breach international law. Not unlike the historical omission of the colonized, the current silence regarding high-tech violence is central to an understanding of the character and nature of international law and its role in producing ethical violence. Humanitarian law is structured to favor the dominant—namely, those who have the power to define and determine the criteria for its application in given historical and geographical contexts.

In this process, it is important to stress, the dominated *is not* completely excluded from human rights. On the contrary, the state, its military, and courts, as well as its human rights NGOs, must acknowledge and condemn the human rights track record of the dominated in order to enhance the human right to dominate. This was clearly seen in the testimonies gathered by the Shabak, which invoked the violations carried out against Palestinians (by Palestinians) in order to justify Israel's bombing of urban centers. The human right to dominate is deployed within a relationship that ultimately defines who the subject of human rights is and who can be subjected to legitimate killing.

CHAPTER 4

The Human Right to Colonize

The successes of history belong to those who are capable of seizing these rules, to replace those who had used them, to disguise themselves so as to pervert them, invert
their meaning, and redirect them against those who had initially imposed them; controlling this complex mechanism, they will make it function so as to overcome the
rulers through their own rules.

—Michel Foucault

*O*n the Perversion of Justice, a glossy booklet published in 2010 by the
Israeli NGO Regavim (National Land Protection Trust), describes the
alleged deficiencies of "law enforcement" in Israel, particularly in relation
to the execution of demolition orders against Palestinian "illegal building."
One of several new Jewish settler human rights organizations, Regavim's
mandate is "to protect national lands and properties" and prevent Palestinians "from taking over the country's territorial resources." The booklet's
authors analyze an array of legal cases brought before the Israeli High
Court of Justice, and argue that the court "sees the Judea and Samaria regions [the biblical names for the West Bank] as 'occupied territory' and not
parts of the Homeland . . . sees the State of Israel as an 'occupying power'
and not as a nation returning to its land . . . and sees the Palestinians as an
'occupied and oppressed people' instead of an enemy that desires to destroy us and expel us from our ancestral home."[1] The "lack of law enforcement" and the "discrimination in favor of Palestinians" are, in Regavim's
view, placing the foundations of the Israeli state and the democratic principle of "legal equality" at risk by fostering the dispossession of Jews.

The report proceeds to catalog instances of "differential treatment" by
the High Court of Justice, while criticizing several liberal Israeli NGOs

that have been urging the court to abide by international law and oppose the expropriation of Palestinian land and the construction of Jewish settlements. Disregarding the fact that Israel's High Court of Justice has consistently legalized and reinforced Israel's colonial project, Regavim goes on to argue that Israel's judicial system has been perverted because it tolerates Palestinian construction in the West Bank, while simultaneously persecuting Jewish settlers for building in their homeland.[2] Reminding its readers that "equality guards government from arbitrariness" and "is a basic value in democratic societies," Regavim inverts the historical trajectory of Israeli dispossession: Jewish settlers are victims of discrimination, while the colonized Palestinians are the "invaders" and "silent conquerors" of Israeli national lands as well as the perpetrators of human rights violations against Jewish citizens of Israel.

To better understand the complex processes that have driven Regavim and other conservative organizations to marshal the language of human rights in order to legitimize Israel's colonial practices, in this chapter we analyze the historical conditions that allowed for the institutional emergence of these new human rights NGOs, the networks they have created, and the legal-political practices they have adopted and developed in order to achieve their goals. The recent appearance of settler human rights NGOs—a new type of actor that in spite of its specificities aligns ideologically with the conservative organizations we dealt with in the second and third chapter—sheds light on social, political, and institutional transformations within the culture of human rights in Israel/Palestine. These organizations came into being by adopting a threefold strategy. First, they have appropriated the language of human rights, translating and vernacularizing it into a specific colonial dialect. Second, they have been mirroring the techniques and strategies of liberal human rights NGOs. Finally, they have been trying to invert the way the asymmetry of power on the ground between colonizer and colonized is being framed by transforming the settler into the native and the indigenous into the invader.

The analysis of this new political force can help explicate further the way in which human rights language becomes the weapon of the strong. Not unlike other forms of the human right to dominate, the human right to colonize cannot be reduced to a cynical perversion of justice by Israeli conservative NGOs. Rather, this appropriation and resignification of human rights occurs through a form of mirroring of liberal human rights NGOs that aims to invert the meaning of colonization and transform it into a just act so as to legitimize the existing political regime. Despite their denunciation of the government for its "perversions," the goal of these conservative human rights NGOs is *not* to overcome the rulers—to borrow Foucault's words—but to enhance the historical mechanism through which the processes of dispossession have been taking place in Israel/Palestine. The paradox of human rights continues to reproduce itself, in a new form, in our colonial present.[3]

SENSITIVE SOULS

In 1993, at the wake of the so-called Olso peace process, Israeli prime minister Yitzhak Rabin believed that the creation of a Palestinian Authority responsible for administering the daily lives of Palestinians in the OPT would stifle the mounting criticism directed against Israel.[4] In his view, this would end the involvement of the High Court of Justice and Israeli human rights organizations in the conflict. "I hope," he said, "that we will find a [Palestinian] partner who will be responsible for the internal problems in Gaza . . . without the High Court of Justice, without B'Tselem and without all kinds of sensitive souls."[5]

Rabin's peace equation was straightforward: if Palestinians would be responsible for administering themselves, Israel would no longer be legally responsible for human rights violations taking place in the OPT. This would render the activities of institutions like the High Court of Justice and human rights organizations such as B'Tselem—actors that he described as "sensitive souls" embodying humanitarian compassion for the Palestinians—unnecessary. Rabin's declaration can be seen as a precursor to the Israeli debate on the "threat of human rights" (see chapter 2), since it seems that his aspiration was to purge what he already conceived of as the dangerous efforts to frame Israel's occupation as a human rights issue; he hoped Oslo's two-state framework would deflect the human rights criticism by establishing a new juridical structure regulating the relationship between Israelis and Palestinians.

Two years later, Rabin was assassinated by an Israeli settler. He therefore could not have known that over the successive decades—during and after the failure of the peace process—there would be an exponential increase in both Israeli and Palestinian human rights activity. Indeed, Rabin could not have foreseen that human rights would become the dominant lexicon deployed by different and often conflicting actors and that the human rights discourse would mushroom in the most unthinkable corners of the Israeli-Palestinian political arena. Obviously, Rabin could not have predicted that by 2010, fifteen years after his assassination, a different conservative group of "sensitive souls" would establish several human rights NGOs—Regavim, the Legal Forum for the Land of Israel, and Yesha for Human Rights—and that these NGOs would deploy the vocabulary of human rights in a petition to the High Court of Justice, asking the court to cancel the conviction of Margalit Har-Shefi, the woman who in 1998 was found guilty of failing to prevent her friend Yigal Amir from assassinating Rabin.[6]

JEWISH OUTPOSTS

Yesha for Human Rights, one of the NGOs petitioning in favor of Margalit Har-Shefi's release, was founded in 2002 by Orit Strook. Strook is a Jewish settler who in 1982 was evacuated from a settlement in the Sinai and currently lives in a Jewish settlement inside the Palestinian city of Hebron, located in the occupied West Bank.[7] She was one of the key figures who initiated the new wave of settler human rights activism by creating the first settler human rights NGO after the Israeli army evacuated a Jewish family from an outpost near Hebron during the second Palestinian Intifada. In order to understand how and why settlers began creating human rights organizations, however, it is important to zoom out and examine what was happening on the ground with respect to settlements during the Oslo years (1993–2000).

In 1996, in the midst of the Oslo peace process, Israel promised the US administration that it would stop building new settlements in the OPT. But while the Israeli government was carrying out negotiations with Palestinians, it encouraged approximately 50,000 Jewish citizens to move from Israel to the occupied West Bank and Gaza Strip. Practically all of the Oslo settlers moved into new neighborhoods that were built by expanding existing settlements. Simultaneously, the Israeli government actively supported the settler movement by establishing scores of "illegal outposts"— outside the boundaries of existing settlements—providing electricity and water to these new settlements, and constructing roads that would allow the settlers to reach them.[8]

By 2001, five years after the United States' prohibition on new settlements, the settlers had built more than 60 new "illegal outposts" on expropriated Palestinian land.[9] The Israeli government frequently depicted the Jewish settlers as defiant or unruly citizens, even as it transferred millions of dollars to support their "recalcitrant" behavior, primarily because this allowed the state—when criticized—to claim that it is a democracy made up of a vibrant civil society that has many voices. In this way it could deflect external pressure and absolve itself of responsibility by attributing the expropriation of Palestinian land to illegal initiatives carried out by "extremist" settler groups. In fact, however, the "illegal outposts" are not really illegal (since Israeli law regulates and very often condones them) and are not really outposts; they are simply settlements.

During the surge of so-called outpost building, Israel's police and military carried out symbolic acts of law enforcement in which settlers who were residing in the new outposts were evicted. Parallel to this process of settlement expansion and very sporadic law enforcement—often during periods when there was increasing international pressure to restart the peace process—the Israeli military carried out massive house demolitions against Palestinians, a practice on which many Israeli and Palestinian human rights NGOs focused their advocacy.[10] It is within this legal and political landscape of settler dispossession of Palestinian land and government demolitions of Palestinian homes that Yesha for Human Rights, the organization founded by Orit Strook, started its activities. Strook is a pioneer in the sense that she initiated an institutional change within the context of human rights in Israel/Palestine. This was the first time settlers created an NGO whose goal was to defend the human rights of settlers—the human right not to be evacuated from the settlements and to continue to colonize Palestinian land. The ultimate objective of this institutional change is to reframe the way the colonization project is conceived.

Yesha for Human Rights' official mandate is to struggle against human rights violations carried out by the police and the military on those rare occasions when they enforce the law against settler outposts or when they prevent settlers from carrying out vigilante activities.[11] The rights group operates under the auspice of the Yesha Council, the umbrella organization of the municipal councils that are responsible for administering Israeli settlements in the occupied West Bank and previously the Gaza Strip (Yesha is the Hebrew acronym for Judea, Samaria, and Gaza). Since its foundation in 2002, Yesha for Human Rights has filed numerous petitions to Israeli courts against "police discrimination and brutality" toward settlers especially in relation to the evacuations of Jewish outposts, while blaming state institutions for undermining solidarity among Israeli Jews.[12]

Over the years, Yesha for Human Rights alongside other similar settler human rights NGOs has retooled human rights and produced an unprecedented rhetoric depicting Israel as a "democracy at risk" and the settlers as victims of an orchestrated program of state-sponsored ethnic cleansing. In many ways this settler appropriation of human rights is a reaction to the relative success of liberal human right NGOs in reframing the Israeli-Palestinian conflict and in inverting the identity of victim and perpetrator (see chapter 1). The objective of these new settler organizations is to reassert Jewish victimhood and frame morally and legally the Palestinians as culprits. Indeed, Strook and her allies appropriated the human rights discourse precisely because it has this power to shape narratives of justice and injustice, equality and inequality, and constantly reshape the signification of the dialectic between victims and perpetrators.

GOVERNMENTAL PERVERSIONS

A pronounced increase in Israeli settler human rights activism can be detected following the 2005 and 2006 evacuations of settlers carried out by the Israeli government (figure 4.1). In August 2005, Prime Minister Ariel Sharon decided to disengage from Gaza.[13] About 8,500 settlers living in 21 Jewish settlements within the Gaza Strip were evacuated alongside a few hundred settlers from four settlements in the northern part of the West Bank. The military troops stationed in the Strip were also redeployed, but Israel nonetheless maintained first a closure, and after Hamas took over the Gaza Strip it implemented a full-blown military siege on the region in order to continue to control the Palestinian territory and population even after the "disengagement."[14]

Following the evacuation of Jews from Gaza, the Ariel Center for Policy Research, a settler think tank, published articles condemning the Israeli government while defining the withdrawal as "ethnic cleansing," "deportation," and "Jewish self-hatred." One of the articles in *Nativ*, the think tank's journal, characterized Sharon's government as "A regime lacking basic respect for universal human rights—the rights to life and property, to freedom of conscience, expression, and assembly, the right to fair and impartial justice and to equality under the law—such a regime is no longer a democracy."[15] The notion that the disengagement abrogated the settlers' *universal* human rights was a pervasive trope informing the rhetoric of conservative organizations.

Yesha for Human Rights—in collaboration with two other organizations—prepared a report entitled *Israeli Government Violations of Disengagement Opponents' Civil Rights*.[16] After several years of submitting lawsuits in various Israeli courts against outpost evacuations, the settler human rights NGO capitalized on its experience and began a wider advocacy campaign against the "potential disintegration" of the Jewish polity. Denouncing what it conceived of as the suspension of the law and the breach of the national-Jewish contract on which Israel's sovereignty is

Figure 4.1.
Clashes between Jewish settlers and Israeli soldiers during the evacuation of Kfar Darom, Gaza Strip, August 18, 2005.
Source: Wikicommons.

founded, the report condemns the government's "extensive violations" of the human rights of those who had opposed the disengagement.[17]

As in the case of the human right to kill (chapter 3), the human right to colonize constitutes a specific translation of human rights into a local idiom, within the context of colonial domination. And like the human right to kill, the human right to colonize is inspired by and reproduces the techniques and methods of global and local human rights advocacy. It mirrors the most widespread forms of evidence production and legal argumentation utilized by mainstream liberal human rights organizations. Similar to standard human rights advocacy reports, *Israeli Government Violations* lists hundreds of incidents of pretrial detentions of protestors during the 2005 Israeli disengagement from Gaza, underscoring the unwarranted restrictions on the "freedom of movement" and "on the liberty of defendants."[18] Providing testimonies of many witnesses, the report's authors analyze a series of cases of "extended detention and police brutality towards minors," "false arrests, violation of prisoners' rights and due process," as well as the "suppression of legal dissent."[19]

In addition to its critique of how the police treated the evacuees, *Israeli Government Violations* targets two other state institutions that have historically played a crucial role in upholding Israel's colonial enterprise: the judicial system and the General Security Service also known as the Shabak. Scrutinizing a set of legal cases in which the High Court of Justice and district courts adopted the notion of "ideological crime" (*avaryanut idiologit*) in their decisions against the antidisengagement protestors, the report accuses the judicial system of equating settler "civil disobedience" with "insurrection" and "sedition." It also accuses the government of perverting the Shabak "from its brief to counter armed conspiracy against the state, to investigating ordinary crimes and nonviolent civil disobedience connected with disengagement." The report concludes by blaming the law enforcement and judicial system for a "moral failure," and while questioning Israel's democratic character, the authors demand a public enquiry "into the nature of these bodies, how their personnel are appointed, and the legal culture cultivated within them."[20] These words could just as easily have been taken out of a report published by B'Tselem or any other liberal human rights NGO.

Mirroring other aspects of the work carried out by liberal human rights NGOs, including the legal vocabulary and investigative techniques, the contributors to *Israeli Government Violations* meticulously reconstruct the systemic character of human rights violations against Israeli Jews who opposed the disengagement in order to defuse the theory of the rotten apples. "The phenomena documented in this report did not occur in a vacuum, were not the acts of rogue cops, rogue prosecutors or rogue judges, but were," according to the report's authors, "the consequence of the policy of Israel's law enforcement and judicial system."[21] The responsibility for the evacuation from the Gaza Strip, for the trauma that it produced, and for its related human rights violations is national in scope and involves the whole state apparatus, according to the report.

The human rights rhetoric reproduced and developed by Yesha for Human Rights in the context of its struggle to maintain the Jewish settlements and outposts and against the evacuation from Gaza had three closely knit objectives. First, the appropriation of human rights was instrumental in the battle against "governmental perversion" of the Zionist project. Second, this new idiom was deployed to fortify settler colonialism, by labeling any potential governmental evacuation of settlements as a human rights violation—this despite the fact that the evacuation of the settlements in Gaza did not signify the demise of the government-led settler national project, but rather its rearticulation and reinforcement outside of the Gaza Strip. In fact, the disengagement from Gaza corresponded with an increase of settlement construction in the occupied West Bank. Finally, the appropriation of human rights aimed to reconstitute the settler as the victim.

The ostensible divergence between settler human rights NGOs and the state during the evacuation from Gaza actually conceals a fundamental affinity between the two. To be sure, the settler NGOs characterize the policies initiated by the government (i.e., evacuations) as a perversion of justice, but their ultimate aim is to stop the "derailing" of the state in order to make good on its original ethnocratic Jewish contract. In order to better understand this intimate bond between the state and conservative NGOs it is important to examine the work of other settler human rights NGOs that joined Yesha for Human Rights after a government-led evacuation of Jewish houses in the West Bank.

REGAVIM AND THE "AMONA POGROM"

Ari Briggs, the international relations director of the settler NGO Regavim, describes the motivations behind the 2005 creation of his organization as follows:

> We understood that there was a serious issue with the misuse of the legal system for political goals. . . . [The liberal human rights NGOs could not achieve their objectives] through a democratically elected government. . . . So they were able to advance their goals through the courts, through the bureaucracy, and through the media. And that's where Regavim fills in the vacuum. These left-wing organizations that were not well represented in the elected bodies, the democratic elected bodies in the Knesset, in the parliament, they were using other means as lawfare. We need to work to see some equality, and not a perversion of justice.[22]

The perversion of justice, which Regavim also mentions in the booklet cited at the beginning of this chapter, not only refers to the government's discrimination against Israeli Jews when carrying out evacuations, but also denotes the attempt on the part of a few liberal Israeli NGOs to subvert—through legal action and human rights advocacy—the democratic processes that should be determined in parliamentary elections. The "perverse" recourse to Israeli law by liberal NGOs following the electoral failures of liberal parties is identified by Regavim as a crucial motivation for the NGO's creation.

Not unlike the institutional transformations we described in previous chapters, the creation of this NGO was also a reaction to the entrenchment of human rights discourse worldwide and the emergence of human rights activism amongst Israeli liberals—which Briggs describes as undemocratic lawfare. Instead of rejecting the human rights discourse and strategies, the new conservative organizations entered the field of human rights activism by developing their own human rights idiom. The dynamics leading to the 2006 evacuation of some settlers from the West Bank settlement of Amona, a year after the evacuation of Gaza's colonies, are vital for understanding this process of responsive vernacularization.

One of the key actors of the Amona evacuation is Peace Now, a liberal Israeli NGO founded in 1978 by a group of reserve military officers. The group eventually turned into a grassroots organization whose aim was to pressure Israel to reach peace with Arab countries, while trying to mobilize the Israeli public against Jewish settlements in the OPT, arguing that they are the major obstacle to reaching a two-state solution with the Palestinians. In 1996, the organization began "Settlement Watch," a project that monitors the expansion of settlements, using international humanitarian law to campaign against them. By 2002, one year after the eruption of the second Intifada, Peace Now had lost most of its public support, and consequently shifted its focus from grassroots mobilization to advocacy and litigation.[23] That year, it filed a petition to the Israeli High Court of Justice demanding that the government "enforce the law" and dismantle 90 illegal outposts. In 2005, the court decided in Peace Now's favor, but the (characteristic) decision culminated in issuing a demolition order for nine houses in the West Bank outpost of Amona.

In February 2006, violent clashes took place in Amona between the military and police in charge of carrying out the evacuation order issued by the High Court of Justice and the settlers. Thousands of settlers, mostly from the settler youth movement, joined the outpost's inhabitants and tried to prevent the evacuation. Settler activists and right-wing members of parliament formed a human chain around the outpost, while others used the building rooftops as a garrison of sorts. Clashes between 5,000 soldiers and 3,000 settlers resulted in several hundred injuries and arrests, and massive local and international media coverage. For the settler movement and their new human rights NGOs, Amona confirmed the "persecution" that began in Gaza. The "expulsion" carried out in 2005 was considered the beginning of a chain of unjust and discriminatory acts, including the discriminatory application of the law against Jews. SOS Israel, an NGO that was founded in 2003 in order to "to oppose and fight the political accords with the Arabs [Palestinians] that include land or security concessions," went so far as to baptize the evacuation as the "Amona pogrom," thus evoking the history of anti-Semitism in order to frame the settlers as victims of egregious abuse committed by the Jewish state.[24]

Dror Etkes, a former staff member of Peace Now and initiator of its Settlement Watch project, explains why Amona was a turning point for many of the actors involved in the promotion of Israel's settlement activity.

[Amona] was the biggest clash ever between Israeli settlers and [the military]. . . . It was bigger than the disengagement [from Gaza], and actually it was a counterreaction, or if you want a reaction to the disengagement from Gaza. It was an attempt of a new generation, a new leadership generation [of settlers] in the West Bank, to say, "Hey! We are not going to run this scene as the Yesha Council did in Gaza! Here we are, and we are going to show what our position is. We are going to fight with you." The context was totally different. . . . The outpost was not dismantled. The only thing that was demolished were nine houses. This is the only time in which Israel demolished [settler] houses in the West Bank. But the context was not political redeployment; the context was law enforcement in the West Bank.[25]

According to Etkes, the evacuation of houses in Amona served to show that Israel could enforce the law in the OPT. Law enforcement or lack thereof thus becomes a fundamental point of convergence between opposing political actors. Indeed, *discriminatory law enforcement* is one of the common mantras used by both settler and liberal human rights NGOs to advance their advocacy goals in Israel/Palestine.[26] As we show below, the condition of possibility of this convergence is the mutual agreement between politically opposing NGOs on fundamental assumptions. Amona became a site where liberal and settler human rights language overlapped and was used by the opposing political camps to frame the events in radically different ways. Both camps invoked the human rights vocabulary to criticize the government's policies vis-à-vis the settlers.

The idea that human rights can be appropriated by the settlers to defend their right to colonize rapidly crystallized, transforming into a rhetoric whose central effect—for the purpose of our analysis—is the creation of a convergence between conflicting actors. In other words, after the 2005 and 2006 settlement evacuations, liberal human rights activists advocating for the rights of the occupied Palestinians suddenly found themselves in the same discursive field with representatives of settler NGOs advocating for the human rights of the occupiers. It also engendered an organizational and institutional change, which is unique in the history of settler colonialism, whereby settlers established human rights NGOs to advocate colonization. The settlers staffing these NGOs have issued hundreds of press releases; they have sent representatives to television and radio talk shows, lobbied in the Knesset, presented their ideas in parliamentary committees, and spent time on university campuses to rally the student body around their cause. The mirroring of criticism against discriminatory law enforcement as well as the mimicking of legal and advocacy techniques produced debates about the legitimate appropriation and vernacularization of human rights among politically opposing NGOs. Rapidly, however, the idea that the settlers' human rights were being infringed upon became common sense among different circles in Israeli society.

PALESTINIAN OUTPOSTS

Inverting the relationship between oppressors and oppressed is a key feature characterizing the work carried out by settler human rights NGOs. The transformation of dispossession into a human right is a vital part of the moral economy of settler colonialism. It is grounded in an inversion that transforms Palestinians into invaders and their physical presence into a colonial outpost. This inversion takes place through the production of a human rights idiom that is dependent on the historical erasure of the colonized and the reconstruction of a specific settler history and geography. Simultaneously, the human right to colonize is claimed within the framework of a series of convergences and strategic mirrorings.

We have already pointed out that both liberal and conservative human rights NGOs share certain juridical assumptions about the authority of the law, the court's decisive role as the arbiter of disagreement, and what constitutes adequate language to discuss evidence, such as the legal vocabulary of human rights. These convergences include an agreement on the appropriate techniques for gathering data, what constitutes valid data, and, consequently, what constitutes evidence. Both liberal and conservative NGOs use the evidence of human rights abuses to generate meanings and allocate guilt and innocence. Such convergences suggest that human rights lawyers, activists, and different kinds of experts ultimately concur about several assumptions, thus producing an alignment among organizations of different political stripes regarding what constitutes juridical and technological truth. We defined the concrete manifestation of this alignment in the political arena—namely the deployment of the same strategies by different organizations—as mirroring.

Meir Deutsch, one of Regavim's founders, begins to reveal these convergences and mirrorings when he recounts his service in the Israeli military. As a soldier he navigated in southern Israel and "came across a lot of illegal" Palestinian Bedouin houses. This experience, he explains, was decisive because he realized that when it comes to Palestinian "illegal building" the State of Israel "does not enforce the law."[27] Deutsch co-founded Regavim in order to fill a void he believed existed in relation to law enforcement within the geographical region where he had navigated as a soldier. The knowledge he acquired during his military service was thus transferred into the nongovernmental universe of human rights activism. "Military navigating"—a skill the majority of Israelis who serve in combat units acquire during their military service—is transferred to the nongovernmental sphere and becomes a specific form of, so to speak, human rights navigating.

Regavim monitors Palestinians by mapping the areas in which they reside, often using Geographic Information System (GIS), a technology on which government agencies in the OPT rely for, inter alia, surveying "illegal" construction and agriculture development, and even bombing (figure 4.2). The strategic use of the same techniques—from GIS and aerial photos to legal petitions—by state institutions (the military, Civil Administration, and Shabak) and human rights NGOs with similar or different political objectives (from Regavim to B'Tselem) within a given historical framework is what we have called mirroring. Mirroring can occur, we maintain, because several fundamental assumptions that drive the work of different organizations and institutions have converged.

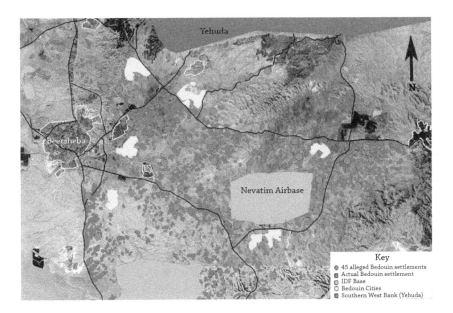

Figure 4.2.
GIS image produced by Regavim of "Bedouin settlements".
Source: Regavim.

Another manifestation of such convergences is an overlapping of actors from different organizations. When this overlapping takes place in organizations aiming to advance the same political objectives it seems almost natural, as in the case of the main spokesperson for Regavim, who was also a supervisor within a financial department of a settlement regional council, and is himself a settler living in one of the outposts.[28] The relationship between the Civil Administration (the military's administrative body in the OPT) and the settler human rights NGO Regavim is, at least partially, a convergence of this kind, based on shared political objectives and operational goals. The movement of people from one organization to another helps explain the osmosis of technical instruments as well as the strategies among actors that are symbiotically related in their political agenda—in this instance, the preservation of the state's settler nature. But it also epitomizes the kind of exchanges taking place between the state and nongovernmental human rights actors. The movement is bidirectional, from the state to the nongovernmental world and vice versa, and includes both conservative and liberal NGOs with seemingly opposing political agendas.[29]

Dror Etkes, the founder of Peace Now's Settlement Watch project, reveals some of the points of convergence his organization has had with the Civil Administration, and how the two organizations mirror each other. "It's been four or five years since I started using GIS," he says.

> I was able to get information from the Civil Administration, based on the Freedom of Information Act. . . . The official layer [of my GIS data] is from the Civil Administration. And then there is a lot of mapping that I am doing by myself. But the legal foundations of the petitions are basically relying on information from the Civil Administration. That's why the Civil Administration cannot come to court and say that the information is not accurate. It's all based on their information.[30]

Etkes reveals that the Civil Administration and Peace Now utilize nearly identical techniques of monitoring, data gathering, and data mining. These techniques serve as the premises whereby actors with radically different political objectives mirror each other's strategies. Describing Regavim's petitions to the High Court of Justice, Dror Etkes underscores how convergences and mirroring manifest themselves in the legal arena: "It's a copy-paste of our petitions. I am not a lawyer and I am not the one writing the petitions but they were copy-pasting parts of the petitions, changing names."[31] This copy-paste is not merely a mirroring of a human rights strategy, but also denotes a convergence of beliefs about what constitutes a valid technique, what is legitimate evidence, and about what, in Etkes's words, are "the legal foundations of the petitions." It is precisely these convergences based on the common idea of law enforcement and the procedures that it entails that enable both Peace Now and Regavim's lawyers to translate the same data and cartographic evidence into legal petitions against the "lack of law enforcement," and to ask the court to instruct the Civil Administration to stop the violation of human rights.

Hence, different organizations mirror each other in the legal petitions because they agree about the techniques of producing evidence and about the importance of using human rights language. The deployment of the same practices is, in other words, due to a shared recognition that certain types of forensic evidence are valid and constitute the source of legitimization of human rights claims, but also due to a shared recognition among them about the authority that derives from the law (albeit in different ways) and about the court's role as the arbiter of disagreement.[32] The same courts that in their rulings have helped legitimize Israel's policies of dispossession and have created a false symmetry between colonizer and colonized[33] are exactly the physical and epistemic spaces in which the political and legal meanings of the pictures, videos, aerial photos, topographical plans, and maps utilized by different parties are contested.

This osmosis is not the manifestation of a political pathology, but rather the incarnation of a political trajectory resulting from the proximity between the State and human rights organizations. The numerous variables informing this proximity constitute a kaleidoscope of shared practices that encompass multiple actors who populate the battlefield of human rights in Israel/Palestine.[34] Indeed, different actors often driven by diverging political objectives converge within the space of the *praxis* and struggle over the expropriation of land, illegal building, agricultural restrictions and numerous other forms of dispossession. In this kind of multiple convergences, political actors like Peace Now, Regavim and the Civil Administration meet.

It is therefore not surprising that like the military and the Civil Administration, the majority of local and international human rights NGOs involved in legal cases of land expropriation, "illegal building," and agricultural restrictions have been increasingly expanding their research units through the creation of pools of experts in the field of satellite and monitoring technologies as well as planning and topographical measurement. The hard drives of these social actors have progressively become the sites where human rights struggles take their embryonic shape. This convergence between social actors—with diverging political positions—that apply symmetrical practical operations to the same settler colonial events and situations is one of the foundational elements informing human rights claims and the legal struggles in Israeli courts.

Within this context of convergence and mirroring, settler colonial NGOs like Regavim invert the historical asymmetry in which they operate and produce the framework of justice they rely on. The inversion—such as the indigenous being transformed into a settler and vice versa—is the political product of the mirroring, as intimated by a legal expert at Bimkom, a liberal Israeli human rights organization supporting Palestinian building through planning and legal advocacy:

> [Regavim] are basically using the same language . . . a mirror picture of what [liberal human rights organization are] using. . . . What is striking is that . . . for example, they have a petition [pertaining to the West Bank village of] Yitma, about an unauthorized outpost. [Regavim's] petition is against [Palestinian] houses and they call these houses "illegal Palestinian outposts." . . . They are taking the petitions [of "leftist" organizations] and they are reversing everything.[35]

In the human rights struggles waged by settler NGOs, mirroring becomes inverting: Jewish settlements become Palestinian settlements; "illegal Jewish construction" becomes "illegal Palestinian construction"; Palestinian villages become "Palestinian outposts," transforming Palestinian presence and existence into a kind of illegal occupation. Human rights become a weapon for further indigenous displacement.

THE HUMAN RIGHT TO DISPLACE

The human right to colonize—a notion we have coined in order to understand the intermingling of the human rights rhetoric deployed by conservative NGOs on the one hand, and settler colonial practices of dispossession on the other—is informed by two interdependent moral imperatives: the protection of the settlements based on the idea that the evacuations of Jewish settlers are a human rights infringement; and the displacement of Palestinians based on the conception of expulsion as an act of justice. The geographic and historical displacement of the indigenous and the protection of the settlements and their new inhabitants are pillars of this settler moral economy.

Settler human rights NGOs like Regavim have been developing these two imperatives—protection and displacement—of colonization since their establishment. Protecting Jewish settlement construction and its expansion while promoting the enforcement of demolitions of Palestinian buildings and the eviction of their owners are two sides of the same ethos through which settler organizations mobilize human rights. In its petitions to the High Court of Justice, lobbying campaigns in the Knesset, and advocacy among the Israeli public, Regavim's representatives and lawyers—and its twin NGO Legal Forum for the Land of Israel—use the notions of law enforcement and discrimination in order to advocate for the demolition of Palestinian houses and the restriction of Palestinian construction in Israel/Palestine.[36] The translation of human rights by these settler human rights NGOs is based on an imaginative geography whereby the OPT, Israel, and the occupied Golan Heights are part of a single space. According to these colonial NGOs, the very presence of Palestinians constitutes a threat to the human rights of Israeli Jews since their presence embodies a historical narrative that the colonial project— not unlike other instances of settler colonialism—must displace and replace if it is to succeed.[37] What is specific to this displacement is the emergence of human rights NGOs that frame settling as a human right and the native's presence as a threat to the human rights of the settler.

The displacement of the indigenous and the protection of the settler are constitutive elements of a settler colonial moral economy. By moral economy we mean, following Didier Fassin, "the production, dissemination, circulation and use of emotions and values, norms and obligations in the social space [which] characterize a particular historical moment and in some cases a specific group."[38] Insofar as a moral economy "underline[s] the permanent work of adopting, redefining and contesting norms and values" and constitutes also a certain judgment on history as well as a process of production of a specific sense of what is just and unjust,[39] then in our case, enhancing the practices of displacement of the indigenous is experienced as and given the value of an act of justice. The corollary of this moral economy is that indigenous presence in itself is transformed into an immanent manifestation of injustice, while his or her displacement (followed by replacement) is conceived of as justice.[40] In this vertiginous inversion, human rights are not only mobilized as the "weapons of the strong" rather than in a framework of a "moral economy of the weak," but also coincide within the same universe of meaning and values of settler colonialism.[41]

Key to this link between justice and displacement is the inscription of human rights practices within a specific notion of sovereignty as expressed by Regavim's motto: "Sovereignty is not a theoretical issue. When it is not enforced, it no longer exists." This motto sustains a specific ethnoracial social contract informing the very foundation of Israel's sovereignty. As Ari Briggs puts it: "The loss of sovereignty in certain areas in this country is amazing. . . . The whole idea of national lands and why to protect national lands . . . why? Because national lands is an issue of sovereignty."[42] When Briggs speaks about "certain areas," he means those areas with Palestinian presence, and when he refers to "national land" he means Jewish land. In this way, Briggs articulates human rights along very specific ethnic lines, dividing settlers and indigenous populations. Hence, Regavim's struggle for equality actually coincides with the protection of a settler colonial sovereignty based on a geopolitical map of Israel without Palestinians and where ultimately Palestinian presence in itself is conceived of as a form of discrimination against Jews. The human right to colonize is concomitantly a human right not to have settlements dismantled and a human right to displace Palestinians wherever they are in order to produce ethnoterritorial purity.

Regavim's vernacularization of human rights builds on a political fact: that the Green Line demarcating pre-1967 Israel from the territories it had occupied in the 1967 war has never constituted a barrier against Israel's policies of domination toward Palestinians. In a certain sense, this is a recent rearticulation of Israel's paradoxical relation to human rights (explicated in chapter 1). Thus, alongside petitions asking the High Court of Justice to instruct the state to demolish Palestinian schools, mosques, and houses in the West Bank because they were built without the permits required by the occupying administration, the settler human rights NGO has also filed petitions against what it calls "Druze illegal construction" on the occupied Golan Heights and against "illegal" Palestinian Bedouin building in Israel's southern region called the Negev.[43] While attacking the government, the organization's lawyers unwittingly expose that the rule of law in Israel is constructed to protect a widespread policy of—implemented or pending—Palestinian displacement, from the Jordan River to the Mediterranean Sea. When Regavim criticizes the government for, so to speak, not displacing enough, it concomitantly unveils and tries to reinforce the nature of the state whose condition of possibility is the displacement of the indigenous. The alleged opposition toward the government, is thus revealed as a mere chimera, since Regavim uses human rights based petitions to force the government to abide by the state's founding logic. Like the Greek mythological creature, Regavim constitutes one of the many limbs of the same colonial body.

The human rights techniques performed by Regavim in court in order to facilitate the displacement of Palestinians are based on different interconnected practices. In some of its petitions the organization operates using a law enforcement argument. "Riding" on existing demolition orders against Palestinian construction issued by the High Court of Justice, Regavim monitors which of these orders is still pending and then petitions the court, asking it to pressure the Israeli government to implement the orders. The cases are constructed with the help of Regavim's "area managers" who monitor—also through aerial photos and satellite technology—those places with the highest percentage of Palestinian inhabitants and identify the houses on which there are pending demolition orders.[44] The monitoring and surveillance of Palestinian life and construction is then translated into the legal human rights language of the petitions.[45]

In other circumstances, Regavim does not build on pending legal orders, but submits its own petitions for demolitions and law enforcement. In one such petition, the language of human rights intertwined with the international rhetoric of environmental protection. In a *Jerusalem Post* op-ed discussing a Palestinian charcoal production plant in the West Bank, Regavim's international relations director, Ari Briggs, explained that "The massive amounts of air pollution released into the environment during the production of the charcoal has ruined the lives of many [Jewish] families whose only wish was to live in the pastoral northern Sharon region [located in pre-1967 Israel]." Briggs goes on to criticize the Israeli government and the High Court of Justice, accusing them of inaction against the "illegal" Palestinian production of charcoal, and rebukes the Israeli Ministry of Environment for not intervening in a situation that he defines as an "environmental emergency" and that according to him could "poison our [Israeli Jewish] children."[46]

Hence, the human right to colonize sometimes assumes the shape of and can be articulated as an environmental question. Indeed, protection from environmental hazards has become part of Regavim's strategy against what it defines as the Palestinian "building intifada." In the petitions and advocacy campaigns, Regavim and other settler human rights NGOs frequently link human rights language to other forms of legitimization, such as landscape, environment, and security, in order to facilitate and justify dispossession.[47]

THE INDIGENOUS INVADERS

In a campaign against the "Silent Conquest," Regavim describes how the Jewish people are "being robbed of the Land of Israel" "ever so quietly, without the roar of battle and clamor of war." "On this battlefield," the organization explains, "cement mixers have replaced tanks, plows replace cannons and innocent-looking civilians replace uniformed soldiers…. Acre after acre, house after house, buying, squatting, illegally cultivating the soil that is not theirs, sometimes with guile, other times with violence, with huge sums of money and firmly backed by anti-Zionist organizations in Israel and abroad—Israel is losing its hold on the Jewish people's lands."[48]

Regavim's campaign constructs a reality rooted in settler erasures. By displacing Palestinian history and geography and replacing it with a Zionist imaginary, the NGO produces a series of inversions in order to legitimize its claims of justice (figure 4.3). A prime example is epitomized by the NGO's attacks against the Palestinian Bedouin of Israel. This case is particularly relevant because it reveals that the human right to colonize is essentially about dehumanization and continued colonization of all Palestinian inhabitants in Israel/Palestine.

At least 60,000 (out of 210,000) Palestinian Bedouin in the Negev live in villages currently classified as "unrecognized" by the Israeli government. Regavim refers to these villages as "outposts," but, unlike Jewish outposts in the West Bank, Israeli law forbids the Bedouin to connect to the electricity grid or the water and sewage systems.[49] Construction regulations are harshly enforced, and in 2011 alone about 1,000 Bedouin homes and animal pens—usually referred to by the government as mere "structures"—were demolished. There are no paved roads, and signposts to the villages from main roads are removed by government authorities. The villages are not shown on official maps. As a matter of official and administrative geography, the places inhabited by these citizens of Israel who live under constant threat of dispossession do not exist.

In 2009, Benjamin Netanyahu appointed his planning policy chief, Ehud Prawer, to try, yet again, to solve the "unrecognized Bedouin problem." Prawer's main task was to relocate those Palestinian Bedouin who had refused to sign over their property rights and continued living in the unrecognized villages.[50] The government argues that because these people live in small villages scattered across a large area, it is not possible to provide them with basic services and therefore its goal is to concentrate them in a few townships.

Regavim maintains that Israel has until now "offered the Bedouins 'carrots'—but completely lacked a 'stick'," claiming also that through their "criminal activity" the Bedouin are colonizing the land, threatening to "put an end to the Jewish future of the Southern region."[51] The very existence of Palestinian Bedouin in the area constitutes a form of colonialism and an existential threat to the state. In this way, the organization's human rights discourse shapes a very particular meaning of indigenousness and

Figure 4.3.
Poster of a conference organized by Regavim in order to counter what it calls Israel's
"Silent surrender".
Source: Regavim.

completely inverts the history of settler-colonial dispossession to which the Jewish state has subjected Palestinians of the Negev and elsewhere.

Citing Prime Minister David Ben-Gurion's famous declaration that "The Negev is the test of the nation in Israel," Regavim offers a four-stage solution to counter this threat, which includes curbing "illegal Bedouin construction," preparing the population for removal, and then evacuating all the "illegal populations" and transferring their residents to legal settlements. Finally, the government must prepare for "the day after" and not allow "matters to return to their original state." "Original state" refers to the existing situation, which in Regavim's view is characterized by the invasion of Jewish space by Palestinian "illegal populations." According to this narration, space is, by definition, Jewish and therefore non-Jewish presence is a form of contamination—and the stake of Ben-Gurion's test.

In a 2014 report entitled *The Truth about the Negev Bedouin*, Regavim claim that the Palestinian Bedouin do "not fulfill the world's accepted criteria for being considered indigenous" and that discrimination against them by the State of Israel is a myth.[52] The NGO refers to the work of three scholars (one of whom is an attorney at the Israeli Ministry of Justice) who define Palestinian claims of indigenousness as a "fabrication of history," thus revealing that settler human rights discourses emerged in a fertile environment developed and disseminated also by members of the Israeli academia.[53]

Palestinian Bedouin have been depicted and treated as invaders in the Israeli public sphere for several years. Responding to a petition submitted to the High Court of Justice against the evacuation of unrecognized Bedouin villages from land near the southern town of Arad, the town's deputy mayor told journalists that the claims of the "insolent invaders" are "disingenuous."[54] Numerous articles have used the term *invader* when describing Bedouin activity in southern Israel, while a popular news website notes that the Bedouin have begun invading the country's central region.[55] Even in *Ha'aretz*, in an opinion piece supporting the High Court of Justice's ruling against the government's practice of spraying poison on "illegal Bedouin agricultural fields," the author refers to the Bedouin using the same term.[56]

Crafting the indigenous presence as invasion and couching the settler as native are two interrelated discursive operations that are made possible by the ambivalent nature of colonial power. As Homi Bhabha explained in his analysis of mimicry, in a colonial relationship not only the colonized desires to mimic the colonizer, but the colonizer at times desires to mimic the colonized.[57] Mimicry entails reciprocity. Not unlike other forms of settler colonialism, in the Israeli case colonial power is exerted also through the colonizer's desire of appropriating the position of the native, of "going native." The articulation of this desire through the human rights discourse expresses a desire for becoming native, but does so in a very specific way: the colonizer's nativeness can, so to speak, be achieved only through a twofold process, beginning with the dispossession of the colonized and followed by protecting the colonizer from a presumed invasion carried out by the colonized. Through this mimetic process the colonized native is transformed into a colonizer and a human rights violator. Accordingly, in order for the colonizer to go native the historical and moral relationship between colonizer and colonized must be inverted.

But since every inversion depends on a prior recognition of the relationship of domination that is inverted, the nature of the relationship between the colonized and colonizer is unveiled. In a context in which Palestinians have been systematically alienated from history and geography, the constitution of the Palestinian native as an illegal subject whose lineaments are that of the foreign invader serves as the condition of possibility for the human right to colonize. In other words, the inversion exposes the ultimate political objective of the settler human rights NGOs, and, by extension, the colonial logic of the state.

The moral economy in which all this is being played out is thus grounded in a specific idea of the state: the Jewish *and* democratic State of Israel. Both the liberal and conservative NGOs demand that the state—from a presumed position of opposition—abide by their moral frame. The liberal NGOs are trying to rectify the "excesses" arising from the state's Jewish character, aspiring to make the government adhere to their conception of liberal democracy and universalist principles, but without challenging the notion of a Jewish state in which the dispossession and dehumanization of the Palestinians is rooted, whereas the conservative NGOs are "pushing" the government to adhere to its ethnocratic commitments to the Jewish polity on which the state is founded. In this way, dispossessing the non-Jews is elevated to an act of self-defense and, ultimately, justice.

JUST LIKE ROSA PARKS

It is difficult to calculate the exact political impact of the human rights work of organizations like Regavim and Yesha for Human Rights, but some examples can provide a sense of their influence within Israel's public sphere. In a 2011 interview, Orit Strook from the settler NGO Yesha for Human Rights explained that nine years after her organization's foundation, their activities and legal cases had produced some significant effects within the Israeli human rights field and among state institutions. "Tracking down police officers who mistreat citizens," she explained, "is one of the activities on which we spend a great deal of time. About 2% of cases filed by the Ministry of Internal Affairs end up generating an indictment, while about a third of the complaints we file do. . . . Today, police, the courts, and the Knesset have learned that the [Jewish] residents of Yesha [namely, the OPT] are Israelis with rights. That's a big change from just a few years ago." According to Strook, Yesha for Human Rights now receives the recognition it deserves: "Nowadays, we are invited to all Knesset deliberations on human rights."[58]

Strook was not exaggerating. The notion of the settler as the subject of human rights permeated Israeli society and became part of numerous discussions in the Israeli parliament. In February 2008, fourteen Knesset members from seven parties sent a letter to defense minister Ehud Barak protesting the discriminatory enforcement of the law against settlers.[59] Along similar lines, in a meeting with the minister of public security, one MK inquired "why the police refrains from enforcing public order in the Jerusalem neighborhood Simon the Righteous [Palestinian Sheikh Jarrah, located in occupied East Jerusalem], when [Israeli] anarchists, leftists and local Arabs harass the Jewish residents [settlers] in the neighborhood, who returned to Jewish homes by court order?"[60] And during a meeting of the Knesset Constitution, Law and Judicial Committee discussing issues of law enforcement in Israel, another MK from the religious party Shas said:

> When we are told that there is discrimination, so to speak, for the benefit of the settlers—it's really not like that. Those who have recently toured the settlements can see illegal construction, villas like those in Savion [one of Israeli's richest suburbs], that Arab residents, the Palestinian residents, are building, and I have not heard of a single demolition order there. . . . Yesterday at 12:00 p.m. we received a message that a number of [military] vehicles were sent to dismantle [Jewish] settlements. The feeling of the people [settlers] who sleep in fear every night, [because of the concern that they will be] disassembled and taken away—that is the biggest discrimination, because it is to give them, on the one hand, a sense that they are residents who the State of Israel sent there, and, on the other hand, they are constantly under threat of demolition and displacement and expulsion from there.[61]

One notices how the human rights vocabulary adopted by the settler organizations following the 2005 and 2006 evacuations is being cited and utilized by members of the Knesset of different political stripes. In numerous parliamentary discussions law enforcement is presented as discriminatory: there is too much of it when it comes to the settlers, and too little with respect to Palestinians.

Since they define the situation they want to repair as one of democratic emergency, the new conservative NGOs do not limit their initiatives to legal and parliamentary activism but also aim to introduce wider policy change at the governmental level. In 2012, for instance, Regavim passed information to the Levy Commission, which had been established by Prime Minister Netanyahu's cabinet in order to examine the legal status of Israeli settlements in the West Bank and to provide the government with recommendations about how to deal with the settlements from the perspective of international law. Regavim's international relations director noted:

> We worked very closely with the Levy Commission. We provided them with details about land use in the West Bank. So we prepared a big report for them and spent many days in session with them, unlike many other [liberal human rights] organizations that were invited to testify, but refused to meet the committee.[62]

After consulting different Israeli governmental and nongovernmental bodies, the Levy Commission, headed by retired Supreme Court judge Edmund Levy, argued in favor of legalizing the existing Israeli settlements and outposts, "simplifying" the settling procedures, and extending Israel's district court system to the West Bank for resolving future "land disputes."[63] In this way the Levy Commission hoped to guarantee the ongoing expropriation of Palestinian land for the benefit of Israel's settlement project. After years of denouncing the government for persecuting settlers, it seems that the efforts of the new conservative human rights NGOs have managed to enhance the common objective linking them with the state: legalizing settler colonialism and dispossession.

Parallel to the parliamentary incorporation of the human rights discourse mobilized by the settler NGOs, the new language of human rights circulates with increasing frequency in the Israeli media. "Statistics Show Police Discrimination against Yesha Jews," reads a headline of one conservative news site, while "Blatant Anti-Jewish Policy in Yesha," reads the title of another.[64] But mainstream outlets also have been increasingly hosting debates about settler human rights, thus wittingly and unwittingly facilitating the inversion of liberal human rights discourse by both producing and justifying the human right to colonize. One opinion piece in Israel's most popular newspaper, *Yedioth Ahronoth*, discusses the necessity of rearticulating Zionism within a human rights framework, claiming that the use of biblical scriptures for justifying the colonial project is no longer sufficient.[65] Another article decries the persecution of Jewish settlers by Palestinian "land thieves" and "land grabbers" in the West Bank, while a third rejects the notion of "illegal settlements," mentioning a conference organized by the Legal Forum for the Land of Israel (another conservative human rights NGO created in 2004, on the eve of the disengagement) for members of the press and representatives of the UN "on the legal status of Judea and Samaria." The list of articles like these goes on and on.[66]

Significantly, the discourse of the human right to colonize has even entered—albeit in a more limited way—liberal arenas like the Israeli broadsheet *Ha'aretz*, whose editorial line is generally one critical of the Israeli occupation. In 2009, during the so-called settlement freeze—a (never fully implemented) measure forced on Israel by the first Obama administration in order to reignite the negotiations between Israelis and Palestinians—*Ha'aretz* hosted an article written by a settler who argued that the freeze on construction in the settlements was a measure of state discrimination comparable to racial discrimination in the United States.[67]

"My family and friends were outlawed," the settler wrote. "We woke up one morning to the humming of drones in the sky, taking pictures of us and the situation on the ground. It is forbidden to build. Not even a store-room. Not a kennel. In certain places, it is even forbidden to add an air conditioner." The author was referring to the techniques of surveillance normally deployed by the Israeli military, security forces, and Civil Administration (the military's administrative body in the OPT) in order to monitor and control Palestinian life in the West Bank. Alluding to the international archive of human and civil rights icons, the author concludes: "This is humiliating, insulting and outrageous. A person with a manual cement mixer in Samaria can change history. . . . Sometimes the man in the field can be a lot stronger than the great leaders. Just like Rosa Parks."[68]

Within the framework of settler appropriation of human rights, the construction of settlements becomes an act of civil disobedience against the government and the evacuation of settlements one of racial discrimination. It is crucial to note, however, that those striving to mobilize the human rights history of African American struggles against government-sanctioned racism are formally directing their criticism against the Israeli government, but are actually the government's allies. Indeed, their aim is to reform the state (in both the courts and parliament) by correcting some of the government's policies. In this sense too they are mirroring liberal NGOs.[69] The genealogy of the human right to colonize is thus not linear, because the critique of the government through the appropriation of the human rights discourse often corresponds with the desire to incarnate the state.

CONCLUSION

What Remains of Human Rights?

For in its afterlife—which could not be called that if it were not a transformation and a renewal of something living—the original undergoes a change. Even words with fixed meaning can undergo a maturing process.

           —Walter Benjamin

In a 2014 interview about the possibility of a two-state solution between Israelis and Palestinians, Prime Minister Benjamin Netanyahu claimed that Palestinians conceive their own state in the West Bank as an act of ethnic cleansing: "they say no Jew can live there, it has to be Jew free, ethnic cleansing."[1] In this way, Israel's premier intimated that any dismantlement of Jewish settlements in the West Bank and their relocation to pre-1967 Israel would entail an act of "ethnic cleansing." This apocalyptic description of decolonization as ethnic cleansing reflects a specific moral economy of settler colonialism whereby unsettling is equated with injustice. It highlights also a convergence between state and nonstate actors who have been adopting the moral and epistemic framework of what we have called the human right to dominate. Similar to the settler NGOs we described in the previous chapter, Israel's premier inverts the facts that Israel's colonial project has produced on the ground. He is unwilling to acknowledge that Palestinians were ethnically cleansed in 1948 and 1967 and that they continue to live under the constant threat of displacement.[2] Not unlike Regavim and other similar organizations, he depicts disengagement from the occupied territory that had constituted 22 percent of Mandatory Palestine as an egregious violation of the rights of Jewish settlers who at the behest of the state colonized this land after it was captured in the 1967 war. Netanyahu's utterance thus encapsulates many of this book's arguments about the intricate relation between human rights and domination.

Not long after Netanyahu gave this interview, the conservative Israeli human rights NGO Shurat HaDin requested the International Criminal Court (ICC) to open an investigation against Palestinian president Mahmoud Abbas for war crimes and crimes against humanity.[3] These two events are intricately tied. By invoking the phrase ethnic cleansing of Jews, Netanyahu mobilizes a concept that is deeply ingrained in Jewish collective memory and constitutes a red line for international human rights advocates. At the same time, he reiterates the idea of settler human rights: the human rights of a dominant ethnic group instituted on the basis of expulsion and subjugation. In this way, he helps constitute the settler as the primal subject of human rights and intimates that the state's role is to secure the rights of this group. Shurat HaDin's appeal to the ICC helps bolster this logic. It transforms the one whose rights have been violated into the perpetrator of human rights abuse, the dominated into the dominant and the dominant into the dominated. Together, Netanyahu and Shurat HaDin translate within the context of Israel/Palestine the global discourse of human rights in a specific way and use it to advance domination.

We began this book by tracing this relationship between human rights and domination back to the post–World War II human rights regime. The nation-state, which had been the agent responsible for perpetrating crimes against humanity in the colonies and in Europe, was elevated to become the protector of human rights. In this way, the human rights regime also empowered the state and granted it recognition, protection, and legitimacy. Despite the assumptions of many human rights textbooks, we have shown that the universal discourse of human rights is in no way antithetical to the state. Rather, this discourse helps legitimize the state—even in its settler colonial form—as the founding political entity of the global order. Hence, the idea that human rights are fundamentally external to the state, threatening it from outside, is erroneous.

In many ways, we have tried to further articulate Hannah Arendt's critique of human rights, but from a twenty-first-century perspective where the discourse of human rights has become much more popular and widespread. In *The Origins of Totalitarianism*, she observed that "the rights of man, supposedly inalienable, proved to be unenforceable—even in countries whose constitutions were based on them—whenever people appeared who were no longer citizens of any sovereign state."[4] Arendt's assertion that the separation between the sovereign state and the human leads to a condition of rightlessness is still poignant.[5] Here, we are less interested in how Arendt tries to salvage human rights and wish to continue focusing on the impact of the sovereign state on human rights.[6] While human rights need the state in order to be enforced, the sovereign state is always less than universal and consequently frames human rights and vernacularizes them to advance its particular policies, which as we have shown throughout this book coincide, at times, with rightlessness and domination.

We accordingly problematized the widely accepted "hydraulic model" of human rights, which conceives human rights as a counterhegemonic tool of collective or individual emancipation from state violence and associates the promotion of human rights with empowerment of the weak. In this concluding chapter, we are interested in inquiring what remains of human rights. After the convergences, the mirroring, and the inversions that we have described, can human rights still be deployed as a counterhegemonic and counterdominant discourse? Do human rights, to paraphrase Walter Benjamin, conserve a liberating afterlife once they have been appropriated as a tool that enhances domination?[7]

We think they do. Paradoxically the conditions that have transformed human rights into instruments of domination are also the conditions that ensure their own afterlife. We do not subscribe to the simplistic inference that because human rights equal domination, we should abandon them. Insofar as human rights are unstable signifiers that are always translated and retranslated, human rights can always have an afterlife after their entanglement with domination becomes manifest. They can always be reappropriated and resignified to counter domination and produce anew the subject of human rights. They can always be redefined in a new way that mobilizes people to struggle for emancipatory projects.

As we have shown throughout this book, there are different ways of doing things with human rights, but very often the ways human rights are used in global and local politics share common traits. We highlighted the similarities among those actors who do things with human rights, especially when they claim that they are doing different things than their political opponents. Therefore, our perspective is not a radically relativist conception of human rights, whereby human rights appropriations are incommensurable. On the contrary, the difficult epistemological task of any political theory that deals with human rights' ability to frame both justice and injustice is to understand the affinities among different appropriations, both when they challenge and when they reinforce domination. In the previous chapters, we have shown how human rights can become a discourse functional to domination. We now turn to briefly explore how human rights can be given an afterlife and reconstituted as counterdomination.

This book can be read as a critique of a certain impoverishment of human rights. One of the main characteristics of the contemporary human rights regime is its subordination to its own legal and methodological framework. Kenneth Roth, the executive director of Human Rights Watch (HRW) for over two decades, underscores this point when he writes that "the international human rights movement, in my view, has no choice but to rest on a positive-law justification for its work."[8] Roth does not seem to be aware that the human rights/international law nexus is related to the same knotted relationship between human rights and the state that we have highlighted in this book. Indeed, the post–World War II human rights regime became intricately tied to the state primarily through the different legal instruments that this regime has produced. Notwithstanding the numerous inspiring clauses within these legal instruments, it is vital to keep in mind that the state is an ever-present specter within them.

Yet it is not simply the relationship to the state that hinders human rights from becoming counterhegemonic, but also the way law-centered human rights activism is conceived and operates. This can be readily seen in the work of HRW, which is probably the best-funded human rights organizations in the world, boasting an annual budget of over $50 million and a staff of close to 300 people. Its headquarters are located in the Empire State Building (with all the irony this entails), adjacent to corporations such as Walgreen, Bank of America, and LinkedIn, as well as several prominent law firms. This spatial proximity unveils a broader one, one that has to do with the impoverished version of the politics of human rights HRW has adopted.

HRW normally does not pursue direct litigation in courts. Nevertheless, the organization invokes human rights and humanitarian law in its advocacy campaigns (and, at times, files amicus briefs). These campaigns are often spurred through publication of reports about social wrongs. In an article defending HRW's limited focus on economic and social rights, Roth explains that the issues the organization deals with are determined by its methodology, rather than, for instance, by the gravity of abuse. "The essence of that methodology," he explains, "is not the ability to mobilize people in the streets, to engage in litigation, to press for broad national plans, or to provide technical assistance. Rather, the core of our methodology is our ability to investigate, expose, and shame."

The organization explicitly rejects popular participation into the politics of human rights. HRW, its director explains, can address only issues where the nature of the violation, violator, and remedy is clear, and this is most possible when one can "identify arbitrary or discriminatory governmental conduct that causes or substantially contributes to a . . . violation."[9] Arbitrary and discriminatory conduct, it should be emphasized, is another way of saying that the conduct is not in accordance with international humanitarian and human rights law. HRW, in other words, focuses primarily on those cases where it can detect lack of application, erroneous application, or discriminatory application of the law. But as we have shown throughout this book, the problem is that in various global contexts of violence the human right to dominate takes precisely the shape of a debate around the adequate enforcement of the law.

While Roth, in his article, responds to commentators who have criticized HRW for not addressing certain types of social wrongs, we are more interested here in examining what happens to human rights once they become subservient to a legalistic methodology of this kind. A clear example is a 2013 report on US drone attacks, where HRW examines six unacknowledged US military attacks (four by drones, one by cruise missile, and one by either a drone or warplane) against alleged al-Qaeda members in Yemen. Eighty-two people, of whom at least 57 civilians, were killed in these six attacks—and this is a mere sample of the 81 attacks in Yemen that are part of what has recently been called the drone wars and that also include hundreds of targeted killings in Pakistan and Somalia. According to HRW, "each of the airstrikes bears the hallmarks of a so-called targeted killing, the deliberate killing by a government of a known individual under color of law."[10]

The report begins with a description of five men assassinated near a mosque in Khashamir, a village in southeast Yemen. Citing Yemen's Defense Ministry, HRW notes that three of the men were members of al-Qaeda, and two others were "respected members of their community." The report describes Salim Bin Ali Jaber, a cleric and father of seven, who had long preached against al-Qaeda's violent methods, and Walid bin Ali Jaber, one of the village's few police officers, while the three men who are accused of being al-Qaeda operatives remain nameless. Zooming out, HRW argues that two of the six attacks examined in the report "were in clear violation of international humanitarian law—the laws of war—because they struck only civilians or used indiscriminate weapons. The other four cases may have violated the laws of war because the individual attacked was not a lawful military target or the attack caused disproportionate civilian harm, determinations that require further investigation. In several of these cases, the US also did not take all feasible precautions to minimize harm to civilians, as the laws of war require."[11]

These opening sentences of HRW's 98-page report on drone attacks already provide a clear indication of how the reduction of human rights to a legalist discourse has led to their impoverishment. According to the liberal human rights NGO, the fact that the United States carries out drone attacks in Yemen is not a violation of human rights, except when the drones strike "only civilians" or use "indiscriminate weapons." If, in other words, the United States uses discriminate weapons, takes all the "necessary precautions," and kills many civilians while targeting militants, then the "deliberate killing by a government" in another country halfway across the globe is not a violation. In line with international law, HRW goes on to discuss whether the "terrorist suspects" are in fact "valid military targets"; it analyzes whether the situation in Yemen can be characterized as passing the "threshold of armed conflict"; it examines the assassinations' adherence to US policies of targeted killing; and although it acknowledges the lawfulness of some of the attacks, it criticizes the US government for not offering compensation to families whose members were killed as civilian bystanders. "The governments of the United States and Yemen should," according to HRW's key recommendation, "immediately take measures to reduce civilian casualties from targeted killings in Yemen and to ensure these strikes comply with international law." Hence, the best human rights can do when it is subservient to legal discourse is to call for a reduction of civilian casualties, the provision of economic compensation, and guarantees that all future targeted killings comply with the law.

While the narrow legalist framework invoked in this HRW report may be slightly more blatant than others, the report does reflect the general approach of most liberal human rights NGOs. Such reports underscore what happens to human rights after they have been hijacked by the law and become a prism for debating the legality or illegality of violence, without raising questions about the morality and legitimacy of the law itself. HRW's worldview is problematized from within when it positively cites Faisal Bin Ali Jaber, a relative of the cleric and policeman killed in Khashamir, as saying, "We are caught between a drone on one side and Al-Qaeda on the other." The human rights organization fails to acknowledge that for Ali Jaber the drone attacks are tantamount to al-Qaeda's acts of terrorism. This oversight results from the dictates of international law that HRW doggedly follows. Regardless of the thousands of civilians killed during the drone wars and the terrorizing impact these wars have had on hundreds of thousands of civilians, insofar as drones are armed with discriminate weapons and do not intend to kill civilians, the US drone wars are not, in HRW's view or Amnesty International's view, a terrorist act.[12] This is the rule of the law in the era of the human right to kill. The law that enables the dominant to kill is preserved and even reinforced by those who claim to struggle for human rights. When human rights denunciations are articulated in a way that complies with the sovereign right to kill, human rights easily become a discourse that rationalizes killing.

Human rights law, as mentioned, operates both through direct litigation and through legalistic advocacy. Both these strategies can sometimes challenge unjust social structures. Usually, however, the social criticism they advance is confined to mitigating the structure's excesses without contesting the structure itself. The invocation of human rights law, as we mentioned in chapter 1, often translates the violation into a "case," classifying, separating, and insulating it and thus covering up its structural foundations. The "case" approach often renders each infringement an isolated issue with its own cause and rationality. This elides the common causes and reasons that underlie seemingly disparate violations.[13] Going beyond the case and demanding the destruction of oppressive structures, not to mention the dismantlement of the regime that carries out the violations, is perceived, especially when the abuse is carried out by a liberal state, as a political instrumentalization of human rights. In Israel/Palestine, for example, demolitions of Palestinian homes are often considered legally separate from torture and administrative detention, as if each of these violations emanates from a distinct structure rather than from Israel's colonial project. Treating violations as "cases" covers up the intricate connections between diverse manifestations of domination. It divides those who were subjected to torture from those whose home was demolished. In this way, the broader apparatus of violation deployed by the dominant is ultimately preserved.[14]

The legalistic approach to human rights often negates and even subjugates certain forms of more radical politics and may end up supporting those kinds of politics that coincide with murderous foreign policies, such as the drone wars. This is because law is frequently blind to underlying asymmetries of power.[15] When legal advocacy does criticize such structures, the criticism is usually confined to correcting some of the structure's "dysfunctions," especially when the political structure is that of a liberal state. The deployment of human rights in accordance with the law thus produces the belief that there is an impartial system adjudicating between parties and correcting wrongs. It excludes the constitutive elements of the legal system from its critique. In this way, it helps silence resistance to social, economic, and political structures of domination rooted in and supported by the law. This, we believe, is one of the founding features leading to the impoverishment of human rights. In turn, it facilitates the development of the human right to dominate.[16]

REPRESENTATION, PROFESSIONALISM, AND THE SOCIAL DIVISION OF HUMAN RIGHTS LABOR

The legalistic impoverishment of human rights tends to be informed by a top-down approach: those who are violated and abused very often have no hand in their own emancipation.[17] In fact, the contemporary human rights regime functions also as a regime of representation in which human rights advocates operate as if they had a natural mandate from the wretched of the earth. The way NGOs practice human rights prevents human rights from becoming a popular language deployed by the people for their own—popular—mobilization. In this sense, human rights do not purport to be a tool of the masses, but only of those experts who represent the wronged population. But does HRW's report on drones really represent the population in Yemen? Does the human rights NGO, in other words, take into account what the Yemini people think when it drafts its recommendation that targeted killings can continue so long as they are carried out in accordance with international law?

Once an NGO adopts a strategy of direct litigation in courts or legalistic advocacy à la HRW and Amnesty International, it often misrepresents the "beneficiaries" and deepens the gap with those who have been wronged. This crisis of representation is informed by the antidemocratic ethos of many human rights NGOs. True, these organizations organize workshops on "participation." But participation cannot be "injected" into society from the top down. Legalism and the professionalization of human rights often widen the gap between human rights advocates and the populations they claim to represent.

Legalism is undoubtedly one of the main factors producing professional hierarchies. Legal experts and lawyers are among the key figures of human rights advocacy who claim a unique expertise. HRW's director, for example, begins his response to his organization's critics by asserting: "many who urge international groups to take on [economic, social, and cultural] rights have a fairly simplistic sense of how this is done."[18] However, when we speak of professionalization, we mean also a broader social transformation that took place during the last decades, whereby human rights organizations increasingly diversified the array of experts they rely upon: media consultants, forensic pathologists, archaeologists, anthropologists, social workers, psychologists, munition specialists, geographers, medical doctors, and different health specialists, as well as other kinds of professional figures. The paradox of this increasing professionalization of human rights is that it popularizes human rights discourse in a particular way. The mushrooming of human rights courses in medical schools, social work and education programs, MBA programs and business schools (to the extent that in some universities human rights themselves are now considered a discipline) parallels the process of the social production of a class of human rights experts often alienated from the people they purportedly represent.

The professionalization of human rights gave birth to a specific form of social and cultural capital. The employment of experts in human rights organizations helps make these organizations professional. Professionalism is, in turn, a capital that helps secure *economic capital*, since without it donors who are interested in satisfying certain standards, which are ultimately professional standards, would not invest in human rights NGOs. In general terms, most human rights activism is a manifestation of this interaction between professional and economic capitals. Professionalization not only helps NGOs access economic capital, but very often it opens doors in government offices and helps human rights NGOs garner the media's attention.[19] It provides human rights NGOs with *credit*, which Pierre Bourdieu defines as "the power granted to those who have obtained sufficient recognition to be in a position to impose recognition."[20] This recognition is a form of symbolic power that enables human rights NGOs to attract funds and "to impose upon minds a vision" of justice that is constituted through the framework of a professional vocabulary of human rights.[21] The credit becomes a form of epistemic power that frames and reproduces dominant human rights paradigms.

One of the main effects of the professionalization of human rights is the constitution of a social class authorized to define and utter legitimate human rights expressions and idioms. They ultimately shape the political field of human rights. In other words, the professionalization of human rights helps establish the norms and the conditions of access to the political field of human rights. And the reduction of human rights to a language owned and mastered by experts—regardless of whether they are liberal or conservative—renders it a discourse of representation. Belonging to the social class of the experts is a fundamental condition that provides access to the debate and confers the right to speak human rights. To be sure, as members of a profession human rights practitioners have to comply with a set of rules and regulations about "correct" utterances and conduct. These regulations end up delimiting the language and strategies that can be deployed by practitioners when they vernacularize human rights. Human rights practitioners and organizations only rarely take to the streets in an attempt to occupy public spaces, since this can result in an accusation of unprofessionalism and bias. Therefore, the spaces human rights practitioners occupy and make appearances in are professional spaces, conferences, seminars, and workshops in which they claim to speak on behalf of the earth's vulnerable people.[22]

To become a human rights professional, one also has to take on the "appearance of neutrality."[23] To be sure, human rights practitioners are aware that their reports and press releases have political implications, but they maintain their position is ostensibly neutral and determined by universal—that is, nonpolitical—considerations such as arbitrary and discriminatory application of the law.[24] The notion that political change can be achieved through the guise of political neutrality is a manifestation of the impoverishment produced by human rights professionalism, which often leads human rights NGOs and their practitioners to collaborate with and corroborate existing power structures. Through the trope of neutrality, human rights professionalism defines "the limits of the thinkable and unthinkable and so [contributes] to the maintenance of the social order from which it derives its power."[25] This becomes clear, for instance, in HRW's drone report. Instead of challenging drone wars tout court, human rights experts reinforce their legitimacy by restricting the discursive field to a legalistic-professional discussion about the kinds of weapons used, the number and ratio of civilian deaths, and compensation to their families. In this way, the possibility of a radical political opposition to such wars becomes part of the unthinkable: the power of the human rights expert and the power to wage drone wars reinforce each other.

LIBERATING HUMAN RIGHTS

Human rights vocabulary and strategies lose their critical edge because very often legalism and professionalism impoverish them in such a way that they become nonthreatening to structures of domination, or, as we have shown in this book, human rights become organic to domination. The crisis of human rights in places like Israel/Palestine is due to their appropriation and deployment as a nonthreat. Insofar as this is the case, the question we need to ask is how do we produce or reproduce the threat of human rights? How, in other words, can the relationship between human rights and domination be subverted so that the human rights language and strategies end up challenging and destabilizing domination? How do we reconnect contemporary human rights struggles to those emancipatory legacies—for example, anticolonialism, antiapartheid, antislavery—which have, for the most part, been erased by NGOized orthodoxy?

First, it is vital to appropriate human rights using a nonlegal perspective. If, as we have shown, international human rights and humanitarian law often enhances domination, then human rights should be deployed as a critique of law. This does not mean that human rights should be mobilized in a way that ignores the law. On the contrary, activists should appropriate human rights to target the law where and when it enhances domination. The issue seems banal, but ultimately it is not: did anticolonial activists and movements demand legal reform of the colonial systems, or did they demand their complete dismantlement? Did Nelson Mandela and the antiracist South African movement fight for legal reform within apartheid, or did they want to undo the system itself? Did they use the law to direct the antiapartheid struggle, or did they adopt strategies of violent sabotage that were illegal and were rejected by the premier human rights NGO, Amnesty International?[26] The different histories and experiences of dispossession have taught us that the demands for reforms and correction of the institutionalized excesses of oppressive legal regimes ended up reorganizing domination instead of dissolving it. If the use of the law confers legitimacy to the dominant, a short circuit has to be created, combining human rights with other political discourses and practices of emancipation in order to undo the law-legitimacy nexus. This seems to be a valid recommendation for all those contexts in which the adherence to the law (instead of an attack against the law) reproduces mechanisms of domination.

Second, if the professionalization led by HRW, Amnesty International, and numerous human rights NGOs has impoverished human rights, we need to begin thinking seriously about ways of deprofessionalizing human rights.[27] This entails broadening human rights beyond their legalistic interpretations and the professional culture. The issue is not merely one of overcoming those who have been crowned as human rights experts or priests, but one of trying to dissolve the boundaries in which the contemporary political field of human rights has crystallized. Insofar as the politics of human rights are currently shaped through the creation of privileged classes of intellectuals, which are bestowed with authority and allowed to speak more legitimately than others, even those who suffer most from violations, then these class differences should be abolished. This can be carried out through institutional change, either by completely reshaping NGOs in order to make them accountable to the people they claim to represent—namely, democratizing them—or by establishing totally different institutions, more aligned with grassroots social movements.

This leads us to a final consideration. As we have shown, human rights are appropriated in a political space that is not neutral, but rather an asymmetrical space informed by relationships of domination. Thus, the challenge is to develop forms of appropriation that can produce a resistance to domination. In a sort of negative ethics, human rights should always be measured in relation to domination: if a specific mobilization of human rights advances domination, then it should be rejected. It should be countered and abolished and taken as a point of departure for a new model of human rights appropriation.

The issue is simultaneously one of form and of substance. When in a given situation the existing forms of human rights mobilizations do not help undo domination, human rights activists should reconceptualize and reframe the struggle. This is what happened in Palestine with the birth of the boycott, divestment, and sanctions (BDS) movement in 2005. The movement adopts a human rights framework. But instead of deploying human rights to solve isolated legal cases in colonial courts, the BDS movement translates human rights in order to challenge the existing structure of domination. Unlike professional human rights NGOs, the BDS movement is a creation of Palestinian society. Its aim is to develop international solidarity and to mobilize international popular support. It deploys human rights alongside discourses of antiracist, anticolonial, and antiapartheid popular inclusion. The movement invokes human rights in a way that many professionals would reject. But it has managed to reframe the debate on Israel/Palestine and to establish a growing alliance among Palestinian, Israeli, and international political forces. In this new framework, human rights can be mobilized to advocate for liberation. They can help create new political communities based on justice, instead of oiling an unrecoverable apparatus of injustice.

NOTES

INTRODUCTION

1. Since the occupation of Afghanistan in late 2001 and until 2013 the number of US military fatalities topped 2,000 soldiers, while the number of fatalities of all the occupying forces amounted to over 3,000. The United Nations estimated that the number of Afghan civilians who had lost their lives in the six-year period 2006–2012 was 14,728. For military fatalities consult http://icasualties.org/oef/ as well as http://www.huffingtonpost.com/2012/09/30/afghanistan-war-death-toll_n_1926668.html (accessed April 24, 2014). For Afghans killed consult United Nations Assistance Mission in Afghanistan, *Annual Report 2012: Protection of Civilians in Armed Conflict* (Geneva: United Nations, 2013).

2. Ann Marie Clark, *Diplomacy of Conscience: Amnesty International and Changing Human Rights Norms* (Princeton, NJ: Princeton University Press, 2010).

3. Amnesty International framed the conference as a moment of reflection on how "to protect Afghan women's rights and freedoms in planning for the military exit." Amnesty International, "Former Secretary of State Madeleine Albright, Ambassador Melanne Verveer and Congresswoman Jan Schakowsky Join Amnesty International for 'Shadow Summit' Sunday to Bring Afghan Women's Voices to the Forefront of NATO Summit," http://www.amnestyusa.org/news/press-releases/former-secretary-of-state-madeleine-albright-ambassador-melanne-verveer-and-congresswoman-jan-schako (accessed April 24, 2014).

4. The campaign was criticized by many human rights practitioners, who demanded the resignation of Suzanne Nossel as Amnesty USA's executive director. Went 2 the Bridge, "Letter to Board of Directors, Amnesty International-USA," http://went2thebridge.blogspot.co.il/2012/07/letter-to-board-of-directors-amnesty.html (accessed April 24, 2014).

5. Talal Asad traces this logic back to the medieval Christian tradition, pointing out that for the Christian thinkers "love was not incompatible with violence: St. Augustine had, after all, taught that punishment meted out to redeem sinners must always be infused with love." Talal Asad, "Reflections on Violence, Law, and Humanitarianism," *Critical Inquiry* Online Features, March 9, 2013.

6. In this sense it is similar to the kind of aggressive feminism in support of post-9/11 wars described by Judith Butler. Judith Butler, *Precarious Life: The Powers of Mourning and Violence* (London: Verso, 2006); see also in this respect Anne Norton, *On the Muslim Question* (Princeton, NJ: Princeton University Press, 2013).

7. Frantz Fanon, *The Wretched of the Earth*, trans. Constance Farrington (New York: Grove Press, 1965).

8. Nelson Mandela, *Long Walk to Freedom: The Autobiography of Nelson Mandela* (New York: Hachette Digital, 2008), 612; see also Randall Williams, *The Divided World: Human Rights and Its Violence* (Minneapolis: University of Minnesota Press, 2010).

9. United Nations, General Assembly, "Importance of the Universal Realization of the Right of Peoples to Self Determination and of the Speedy Granting of Independence to Colonial Countries and Peoples for the Effective Guarantee and Observance of Human Rights," A/RES/3246 (XXIX), November 29, 1974.

10. It is as if Amnesty failed to learn from NATO's intervention in Kosovo, the first military campaign in history conducted in the name of human rights. Noam Chomsky, *The New Military Humanism: Lessons from Kosovo* (Monroe, ME: Common Courage Press, 1999); Costas Douzinas, "Humanity, Military Humanism and the New Moral Order," *Economy and Society* 32, no. 2 (2003), 159–183.

11. Arundhati Roy, *War Talk* (Boston: South End Press, 2003).

12. Suzanne Nossel, "Smart Power," *Foreign Affairs* 83, no. 2 (2004), 131–142.

13. Eyal Weizman, *The Least of All Possible Evils: Humanitarian Violence from Arendt to Gaza* (London: Verso Books, 2012).

14. Nossel, "Smart Power," 131–142.

15. David Chandler, *From Kosovo to Kabul and Beyond: Human Rights and International Intervention* (Ann Arbor, MI: Pluto, 2006); Annelise Riles, "Anthropology, Human Rights, and Legal Knowledge: Culture in the Iron Cage," *American Anthropologist* 108, no. 1 (2006), 52–65; Anne Orford, *Reading Humanitarian Intervention: Human Rights and the Use of Force in International Law* (Cambridge: Cambridge University Press, 2003); Costas Douzinas, *The End of Human Rights: Critical Legal Thought at the Turn of the Century* (Oxford: Hart, 2000); David Kennedy, *The Dark Sides of Virtue: Reassessing International Humanitarianism* (Princeton, NJ: Princeton University Press, 2011); Jean Bricmont, *Humanitarian Imperialism: Using Human Rights to Sell War* (Delhi: Aakar Books, 2007).

16. Nossel, "Smart Power," 131–142.

17. Samuel Moyn, *The Last Utopia: Human Rights in History* (Cambridge, MA: Harvard University Press, 2010); Barbara Keys, *Reclaiming American Virtue* (Cambridge, MA: Harvard University Press, 2014).

18. Clifford Bob, *The Global Right Wing and the Clash of World Politics* (Cambridge: Cambridge University Press, 2012).

19. It is not only in France that populist right movements justify anti-immigrant policies with alleged violations of the cultural and economic rights of the indigenous people; the justifications are also given in Germany, the Netherlands, and Scandinavia. Cas Mudde, *Populist Radical Right Parties in Europe* (Cambridge: Cambridge University Press, 2007).

20. CBS News, "Dutch Anti-Islam Speech in Ottawa Angers Muslims," CBS Canada, http://www.cbc.ca/news/canada/ottawa/dutch-anti-islam-speech-in-ottawa-angers-muslims-1.1040535 (accessed April 25, 2014); BBC News, "Netherlands Islam Freedom: Profile of Geert Wilders," http://www.bbc.com/news/world-europe-11443211 (accessed April 25, 2014).

21. Eran Shor, "Utilizing Rights and Wrongs: Right-Wing, the 'Right' Language, and Human Rights in the Gaza Disengagement," *Sociological Perspectives* 51, no. 4 (2008), 803–826.

22. Michael Ignatieff, *Human Rights as Politics and Idolatry* (Princeton, NJ: Princeton University Press, 2001), 53; Stephen Hopgood, *The Endtimes of Human Rights* (Ithaca, NY: Cornell University Press, 2013).

23. Douzinas, "Humanity."
24. Breitbart, "Human Rights Groups Support New Russian Law," http://www.breitbart.com/Big-Peace/2013/09/06/human-rights-groups-support-new-russian-law (accessed April 25, 2014).
25. World Congress of Families, "Home," http://worldcongress.org/ (accessed April 25, 2014). Italics added.
26. Steven P. Brown, *Trumping Religion: The New Christian Right, the Free Speech Clause, and the Courts* (Birmingham: University of Alabama Press, 2002); Bob, *Global Right Wing*; Rutherford Institute, "About US," https://www.rutherford.org/about/ (accessed April 25, 2014).
27. American Center for Law and Justice, "Our Mission," http://aclj.org/our-mission (accessed April 25, 2014).
28. Laura Van den Eynde, "An Empirical Look at the Amicus Curiae Practice of Human Rights NGOs before the European Court of Human Rights," *Netherlands Quarterly of Human Rights* 31, no. 3 (2013), 271–313.
29. Orford, *Reading Humanitarian Intervention*.
30. Kenneth Roth, "Defending Economic, Social and Cultural Rights: Practical Issues Faced by an International Human Rights Organization," *Human Rights Quarterly* 26, no. 1 (2004), 63–73.
31. Several scholars have highlighted the way the burka has come to symbolize women's oppression among both liberal and conservative thinkers and politicians. Lila Abu-Lughod, *Do Muslim Women Need Saving?* (Cambridge, MA: Harvard University Press, 2013); Charles Hirschkind and Saba Mahmood, "Feminism, the Taliban, and Politics of Counter-insurgency," *Anthropological Quarterly* 75, no. 2 (2002), 339–354; Deniz Kandiyoti, "Old Dilemmas or New Challenges? The Politics of Gender and Reconstruction in Afghanistan," *Development and Change* 38, no. 2 (2007), 169–199.
32. Alexandra Williams, "Switzerland Risks Muslim Backlash after Minarets Vote," http://www.telegraph.co.uk/news/worldnews/europe/switzerland/6685719/Switzerland-risks-Muslim-backlash-after-minarets-vote.html (accessed April 25, 2014); on the liberal politics of the veil in France see Joan Wallach Scott, *The Politics of the Veil* (Princeton, NJ: Princeton University Press, 2009). On the relationship between Islamophobia and the deployment of human rights discourses in order to advocate a discriminatory conception of gender equality consult Abu-Lughod, *Do Muslim Women Need Saving?*
33. Shoon Lio, Scott Melzer, and Ellen Reese, "Constructing Threat and Appropriating 'Civil Rights': Rhetorical Strategies of Gun Rights and English Only Leaders," *Symbolic Interaction* 31, no. 1 (2008), 5–31.
34. We use the term *framing* in the sense developed by David Snow and Robert Benford. Robert D. Benford and David A. Snow, "Framing Processes and Social Movements: An Overview and Assessment," *Annual Review of Sociology* 26, no. 1 (2000), 611–639; David A. Snow and Robert D. Benford, "Ideology, Frame Resonance, and Participant Mobilization," *International Social Movement Research* 1, no. 1 (1988), 197–217.
35. Duncan Kennedy, "The Critique of Rights in Critical Legal Studies," in *Left Legalism / Left Critique*, ed. Wendy Brown and Janet Halley (Durham, NC: Duke University Press, 2002), 185.
36. Asad, "Reflections on Violence."
37. Already in 1977, liberal president Jimmy Carter asked the Department of State to evaluate foreign policy with respect to whether and how it advances global

human rights. A few months later, the Department of State established the Bureau of Human Rights and Humanitarian Affairs and Carter issued Presidential Directive 30, which linked economic and military assistance to the human rights records of the recipients; countries with good or improving records would receive favorable consideration, while those nations with poor or deteriorating records would not. Needless to say, this directive was not really adhered to, but it did signify the infiltration of human rights language to policy decisions. President Ronald Reagan was not a great proponent of human rights language, and one of his first acts was to nominate Ernest Lefever—a man who had suggested that the promotion of human rights abroad should not be the responsibility of the United States—to be assistant secretary of state for human rights and humanitarian affairs. But the language of human rights was adopted in his second term and by later conservative administrations. Tamar Jacoby, "The Reagan Turnaround on Human Rights," *Foreign Affairs* 64 (Summer 1986), 1066–1086.

38. Fort Benning, "Who We Are," http://www.benning.army.mil/WhoWeAreFull.html (accessed April 25, 2014).

39. Fort Benning, "Human Rights Training Classes," http://www.benning.army.mil/tenant/whinsec/humanRightsClass.html (accessed April 25, 2014).

40. Amnesty International, *Military Training 101: Human Rights and Humanitarian Law* (London: Amnesty International, 2002).

41. Fort Benning, "The Human Rights Instructional Program," http://www.benning.army.mil/tenant/whinsec/humanRightsClass.html (accessed April 26, 2014).

42. Laleh Khalili, *Time in the Shadows: Confinement in Counterinsurgencies* (Palo Alto, CA: Stanford University Press, 2012).

43. One merely needs to examine human rights reports about armed conflicts and military occupations to see that they use the two bodies of law concomitantly. For a more academic discussion consult Hans-Joachim Heintze, "On the Relationship between Human Rights Law Protection and International Humanitarian Law," *International Review of the Red Cross* 86, no. 856 (2004), 789–814; Alexander Orakhelashvili, "The Interaction between Human Rights and Humanitarian Law: Fragmentation, Conflict, Parallelism, or Convergence?" *European Journal of International Law* 19, no. 1 (2008), 161–182.

44. Heintze, "On the Relationship," 789–814; See also in this respect Hopgood, *Endtimes of Human Rights*, particularly chapter 6.

45. In this way, we are also trying to do something different than Stephen Hopgood, who distinguishes between human rights and Human Rights. The noncapitalized human rights, he claims, are the "local and transnational networks of activists who bring publicity to abuses they and their communities face and who try to exert pressure on governments and the United Nations for action, often at tremendous personal cost." Capitalized Human Rights, by contrast, are the "global structure of laws, courts, norms and organizations that raise money, write reports, run international campaigns, open local offices, lobby governments, and claim to speak with singular authority in the name of humanity as a whole." The latter are, in a word, institutionalized human rights, and they are approaching their "endtimes" since they have become morally corrupt. While we follow Hopgood in claiming that human rights are experiencing a crisis, we do not accept his distinction, and, more importantly, we think the roots of the crisis are much deeper. Finally, we disagree with the notion of "endtimes,"

which supposes that historical processes have a concrete end. *Endtimes of Human Rights*, viii.

46. Classic examples of this paradigm include Thomas Risse, Stephen C. Ropp, and Kathryn Sikkink, *The Power of Human Rights: International Norms and Domestic Change* (Cambridge: Cambridge University Press, 1999); Margaret E. Keck and Kathryn Sikkink, *Activists beyond Borders: Advocacy Networks in International Politics* (Cambridge: Cambridge University Press, 1998); Jack Donnelly, *International Human Rights* (Boulder, CO: Westview Press, 2012); D. P. Forsythe, *Human Rights in International Relations* (Cambridge: Cambridge University Press, 2012); P. Alston and R. Goodman, *International Human Rights in Context: Law, Politics, Morals* (New York: Oxford University Press, 2007).

47. Michael Ignatieff, "The Attack on Human Rights," *Foreign Affairs* 80, no. 6. (2001), 109.

48. Donnelly, *International Human Rights*, 20–21.

49. Achille Mbembe reminds us that this phenomenon is not altogether new. Even slavery was conceived as a form of protection, whereby slavery was conceived as humanitarian violence deployed to protect a form of inferior humanity. Achille Mbembe, *Critique de la raison nègre* (Paris: La Découverte, 2013).

50. Keck and Sikkink, *Activists beyond Borders*; Risse, Ropp and Sikkink, *Power of Human Rights*.

51. Karl Marx, "On the Jewish Question," in *The Marx-Engels Reader*, ed. Robert C. Tucker (New York: W. W. Norton, 1978), 26–46; Neve Gordon, Jacinda Swanson, and Joseph Buttigieg, "Is the Struggle for Human Rights a Struggle for Emancipation?" *Rethinking Marxism* 12, no. 3 (2000), 1–22; L. Kolakowski, "Marxism and Human Rights," *Daedalus* 112, no. 4 (1983), 81–92.

52. Studies of this kind include primarily theorists of governmentality. Costas Douzinas, *Human Rights and Empire: The Political Philosophy of Cosmopolitanism* (London: Routledge, 2007); Giorgio Agamben, *Homo Sacer: Sovereign Power and Bare Life*, trans. Daniel Heller-Roazen (Stanford, CA: Stanford University Press, 1998); Michel Foucault, Graham Burchell, and Colin Gordon, *The Foucault Effect: Studies in Governmentality* (Chicago: University of Chicago Press, 1991); Wendy Brown, "'The Most We Can Hope for ...': Human Rights and the Politics of Fatalism," *South Atlantic Quarterly* 103, no. 2 (2004), 451–463.

53. Adamantia Pollis and Peter Schwab, "Human Rights: A Western Construct with Limited Applicability," in *Human Rights: Cultural and Ideological Perspectives*, ed. Adamantia Pollis, Peter Schwab, and Nigel Eltringham (New York: Praeger, 1979).

54. Bricmont, *Humanitarian Imperialism*; Danilo Zolo, *Terrorismo umanitario: Dalla Guerra del Golfo alla strage di Gaza* (Rome: Diabasis, 2009); Douzinas, *Human Rights and Empire*.

55. Makau Mutua, "Savages, Victims, and Saviors: The Metaphor of Human Rights," *Harvard International Law Journal* 42 (2001), 244.

56. Bricmont, *Humanitarian Imperialism*. On the notion of human rights as a weapon of the strong consult Raimundo Panikkar, "Is the Notion of Human Rights a Western Concept?" *Diogenes* 30, no. 120 (1982), 75–102; Pollis and Schwab, "Human Rights."

57. Grégoire Chamayou, *Manhunts: A Philosophical History* (Princeton, NJ: Princeton University Press, 2012).

58. Jacques Derrida, *Writing and Difference*, trans. Alan Bass (Chicago: University of Chicago Press, 1980).

59. Ian Balfour and Eduardo Cadava, "The Claims of Human Rights: An Introduction," *South Atlantic Quarterly* 103, no. 2 (2004), 277–296.
60. Hannah Arendt, *The Origins of Totalitarianism* (New York: Mariner Books, 1973).
61. Balfour and Cadava, "Claims of Human Rights."
62. M. Goodale, "Introduction to 'Anthropology and Human Rights in a New Key,'" *American Anthropologist* 108, no. 1 (2008), 1–8; Sally Engle Merry, "Transnational Human Rights and Local Activism: Mapping the Middle," *American Anthropologist* 108, no. 1 (2008), 38–51; Knut Dörmann, "The Legal Situation of 'Unlawful/Unprivileged Combatants'," *International Review—Red Cross* 85 (2003), 45–74.
63. Akira Iriye, Petra Goedde, and William I. Hitchcock, eds., *The Human Rights Revolution: An International History* (New York: Oxford University Press, 2012), 14–15; Merry, "Transnational Human Rights."
64. Walter Benjamin, "The Task of the Translator," in *Illuminations*, ed. Hannah Arendt, trans. Harry Zohn (New York: Schocken, 1968).
65. Mark Goodale, "Toward a Critical Anthropology of Human Rights," *Current Anthropology* 47, no. 3 (2006), 485–511; Goodale, "Introduction"; Merry, "Transnational Human Rights."
66. Douzinas, "Humanity."
67. Actually, the term *unlawful combatant* was first used in 1942, but only after 9/11 did it become prevalent. Lisa Hajjar, "International Humanitarian Law and 'Wars on Terror': A Comparative Analysis of Israeli and American Doctrines and Policies," *Journal of Palestine Studies* 36, no. 1 (2006), 21–42; Joseph P. Bialke, "Al-Qaeda and Taliban: Unlawful Combatant Detainees, Unlawful Belligerency, and the International Laws of Armed Conflict," *Air Force Law Review* 55 (2004), 1–85; Dörmann, "Legal Situation."
68. Michel Foucault, "Nietzsche, Genealogy, History," *Semiotexte* 3, no. 1 (1978), 78–94.
69. Joy Gordon, "The Concept of Human Rights: The History and Meaning of Its Politicization," *Brooklyn Journal of International Law* 23 (1997), 689–737.
70. Discussion with Morton Winston, March 21, 2013. Today, it is widely acknowledged that the historical emphasis of practically all the large human rights NGOs in the West on one group of rights and the complete de-emphasis on the other was a result of Cold War politics.
71. Michael Hardt and Antonio Negri, *Empire* (Cambridge, MA: Harvard University Press, 2001).
72. Iriye, Goedde and Hitchcock, *The Human Rights Revolution*, 14–15.
73. Henk Van Houtum and Freerk Boedeltje, "Europe's Shame: Death at the Borders of the EU," *Antipode* 41, no. 2 (2009), 226–230; Michael Grewcock, "Shooting the Passenger: Australia's War on Illicit Migrants," in *Human Trafficking*, ed. Maggy Lee (London: Routledge, 2007), 178–200; see also Jørgen Carling, "Migration Control and Migrant Fatalities at the Spanish-African Borders," *International Migration Review* 41, no. 2 (2007), 316–343; Thomas Spijkerboer, "The Human Costs of Border Control," *European Journal of Migration and Law* 9, no. 1 (2007), 127–139.
74. The idea that human rights are bound by the state is really no surprise to anyone interested in economic and social rights such as the rights to education and health, which are framed in terms of the state's obligations toward its citizens and residents.
75. Fatou Bensouda, "The Truth about the ICC and Gaza," *The Guardian*, August 29, 2014.

76. Even those thinkers who like Jürgen Habermas interpret universal human rights as the protection of individual autonomy within a constitutional framework of collective self-determination fail to disconnect human rights from the state. Jürgen Habermas, *Between Facts and Norms: Contributions to a Discourse Theory of Law and Democracy*, trans. William Rehg (Cambridge, MA: MIT Press, 1996); Jürgen Habermas, "Remarks on Legitimation through Human Rights," *Modern Schoolman* 75 (1998), 87–100.

77. Timothy Mitchell, "The Limits of the State: Beyond Statist Approaches and Their Critics," *American Political Science Review* 85, no. 1 (1991), 77–96.

78. Anne Orford points to a different and no less important effect when she argues that humanitarian interventions also operate to draw boundaries between "us" and "them" as a means of distancing the other and locating suffering and violence elsewhere. Orford, *Reading Humanitarian Intervention*, 82–125.

79. In December 2013, the right-wing organization Im Tirtzu organized a "Zionist Conference for Human Rights" in order to "break the [leftist] monopoly of human rights and promote a Zionist vision for human rights." "Zionists from Country's Minority Communities Speak Out for Israel, *Jerusalem Post*, December 18, 2013, http://www.jpost.com/National-News/Zionists-from-countrys-minority-communities-speak-out-for-Israel-335325.

80. We would like to thank Daniel Cohen for pointing us in this direction.

81. Mbembe, *Critique de la raison nègre*.

82. Antony Anghie, *Imperialism, Sovereignty and the Making of International Law* (Cambridge: Cambridge University Press, 2007).

83. Michael Mann, *The Dark Side of Democracy: Explaining Ethnic Cleansing* (Cambridge: Cambridge University Press, 2005). Michael Mann discusses the idea that sovereignty of the people, one of the central principles of democracy, is curbed and curtailed by and through the limitation of the people. He distinguishes between two different conceptions of peoples—stratified and organic—in order to underscore two fundamental ways through which the restriction is achieved. Mann maintains that if the people is conceived of as stratified, "then the state's main role is to mediate and conciliate among competing interest groups. This will tend to compromise differences, not try to eliminate or cleanse them. . . . Yet if the people is conceived of as organic, as one and indivisible, as ethnic, then its purity may be maintained by the suppression of deviant minorities, and this may lead to cleansing" (55). Mann argues that while both carry out exclusions, ethnic cleansing of a group that was excluded has taken place only in democracies where the conception of the people was organic. He contends that in northwestern European regimes the conception of the people was stratified and therefore they developed liberal forms of democracy; radically different interest groups and class conflict were accepted within the citizen body. By contrast, democratization struggles in central and eastern Europe pitted local ethnicity against minority populations and at times led to ethnic cleansing (69). The problem with Mann's analysis is that it does not take into account the colonial project. England and France, for example, are portrayed as countries that relate to the people as stratified and therefore do not underscore ethnicity, a portrayal that might be convincing if one ignores English and French colonialism. Once their colonial projects are taken into account, then Mann's analysis and conclusions need to be altered, since it appears that England and France did conceive "the people" as organic, but did so vis-à-vis the colonized populations. Taking colonialism into account allows us to see an

oversight in Mann's analysis and to complicate the relationship between democracy and the people. If for Mann democracy relates to the people either as stratified or organic, adding the colonial dimension reveals that the same democracy can simultaneously conceive the people as stratified in one context and organic in another.

84. Alice L. Conklin, "Colonialism and Human Rights, a Contradiction in Terms? The Case of France and West Africa, 1895–1914," *American Historical Review* 103, no. 2 (1998), 419–442.

85. Jacques Rancière, "Who Is the Subject of the Rights of Man?" *South Atlantic Quarterly* 103, no. 2 (2004), 297–310.

86. For a fascinating description of this process consult Cyril Lionel Robert James, *The Black Jacobins: Toussaint L'Ouverture and the San Domingo Revolution* (London: Penguin, 2001).

87. Edward Said, "Nationalism, Human Rights, and Interpretation," *Raritan* 12, no. 3 (1993), 26–51. Italics ours.

CHAPTER 1

1. Louis Henkin, *The Age of Rights* (New York: Columbia University Press, 1990); Raphael Lemkin, "Genocide as a Crime under International Law," *American Society of International Law* 41, no. 1 (1947), 145–151.

2. Anja Jetschke, *Human Rights and State Security: Indonesia and the Philippines* (Philadelphia: University of Pennsylvania Press, 2010).

3. Donnelly, *International Human Rights*, 27.

4. Aryeh Neier, "Misunderstanding Our Mission," Open Global Rights, https://www.opendemocracy.net/openglobalrights/aryeh-neier/misunderstanding-our-mission (accessed September 18, 2014).

5. Most human rights books accept this narrative, including Donnelly, *International Human Rights*; Risse, Ropp, and Sikkink, *Power of Human Rights*; Thomas Risse, Stephen C. Ropp, and Kathryn Sikkink, *The Persistent Power of Human Rights: From Commitment to Compliance* (Cambridge: Cambridge University Press, 2013); Keck and Sikkink, *Activists beyond Borders*; Beth A. Simmons, *Mobilizing for Human Rights: International Law in Domestic Politics* (Cambridge: Cambridge University Press, 2009).

6. Preamble to the Universal Declaration of Human Rights, Universal Declaration of Human Rights, 217A (III) sess., UN Doc. A/810, at 71 (December 10, 1948).

7. Ibid.

8. For a list of the core human rights treaties and the monitoring bodies consult United Nations, "Human Rights Treaty Bodies," http://www.ohchr.org/EN/HRBodies/Pages/TreatyBodies.aspx (accessed April 28, 2014).

9. As Samuel Moyn has shown, this node was all but unequivocal. Samuel Moyn, "Imperialism, Self-Determination, and the Rise of Human Rights," in Iriye, Goedde, and Hitchcock, *The Human Rights Revolution*, 159–178; see also Moyn, *The Last Utopia*.

10. Arendt, *The Origins of Totalitarianism*, 267–304.

11. Paul Gilroy, *Race and the Right to be Human* (Utrecht, Netherlands: Universiteit Utrecht Press, 2009), 11. For a comprehensive reconstruction of the relationship between decolonization, self-determination, and human rights consult Roland Burke, *Decolonization and the Evolution of International Human Rights* (Philadelphia: University of Pennsylvania Press, 2011).

12. Samera Esmeir, *Juridical Humanity: A Colonial History* (Palo Alto, CA: Stanford University Press, 2012), 2.

13. The Right of Peoples and Nations to Self-Determination, 637 (VII), 403rd Plenary Meeting Sess., United Nations (December 16, 1952).

14. Arendt, *The Origins of Totalitarianism*, 287–323; for an excellent analysis of Arendt's conception of human rights consult Peg Birmingham, *Hannah Arendt and Human Rights: The Predicament of Common Responsibility* (Bloomington: Indiana University Press, 2006).

15. Samuel Moyn's claim that the international political mobilization of the Holocaust started only during the 1970s is accordingly equivocal.

16. The issue we are raising here does not involve the "abuse" or "instrumentalization of the Holocaust." Instrumentalist and utilitarian critiques of the creation of Israel and its relationship with the history of human rights are both ethically problematic and heuristically useless. The issue here is rather one of genealogy: the genealogy of the relationship between human rights and the State of Israel, in which the Holocaust is relevant, but not as an instrument. We need to take into account the politico-historical processes that resulted in the creation of the first settler-humanitarian state. Our concern in this book is not with an alleged exploitation and manipulation of an experience of political violence by its victims, but rather with how the history of human rights and domination are intertwined, inseparable, and cosubstantial.

17. Alan Dowty, *Israel/Palestine* (Cambridge: Polity, 2012).

18. Middle East Research and Information Project, "Primer on Palestine, Israel and the Arab-Israeli Conflict," MERIP, http://www.merip.org/primer-palestine-israel-arab-israeli-conflict-new (accessed April 28, 2014).

19. Gerard Daniel Cohen, "The Holocaust and the 'Human Rights Revolution': A Reassessment," in Iriye, Goedde, and Hitchcock, *The Human Rights Revolution*, 53–72.

20. Israel's Law of Return states that "every Jew has the right to come to this country as an oleh [Jewish immigrant]," thus restricting the right of return to Israel/Palestine to Jews, and denying this right to the Palestinians expelled in 1948 as a result of the creation of the State of Israel. This law constitutes one of the pillars of Israel's settler colonial regime and the main obstacle to a settlement of the conflict according to international law.

21. Alexander Yakobson and Amnon Rubinstein, *Israel and the Family of Nations: The Jewish Nation-State and Human Rights* (London: Routledge, 2008), 2.

22. Convention on the Prevention and Punishment of the Crime of Genocide, A/P.V. 179, United Nations (December 9, 1948).

23. Robert Meister, *After Evil: A Politics of Human Rights* (New York: Columbia University Press, 2011), 198.

24. These authors problematized the often dehistoricized invocation of genocide and crimes against humanity that translate the European Holocaust into an isolated and primal manifestation of human evil. In her pioneer work *The Origins of Totalitarianism*, Arendt analyzed how the extermination of European Jews can be traced back to a deeper genealogy related to the development of modern nation-states and to their colonial and imperial expansion outside Europe. Along similar lines, Aimé Césaire, in his *Discourse on Colonialism*, criticized the "exceptionalization" of the Holocaust. According to Césaire, it would be a political and heuristic mistake to understand the European Holocaust as something unrelated to the various forms of political violence and domination

deployed by European nation-states in their colonies. The genocide after which the normative definition of "crimes against humanity" was instituted can be read, according to Césaire, as a return within the boundaries of European nation-states of the crimes that these states perpetrated "out of themselves," mainly in the settler colonies. Later, Mahmood Mamdani showed how some of the ethnic divisions and categories that had constituted the colonial systems have fueled genocides and political violence even after decolonization. Elsewhere Mamdani has also shown how some of the German techniques of extermination utilized during the final solution had already been experimented by Germany in its colonies. Mahmood Mamdani, "A Brief History of Genocide," *Transition* 10, no. 3 (2001), 26–47; Mahmood Mamdani, *When Victims Become Killers: Colonialism, Nativism, and the Genocide in Rwanda* (Princeton, NJ: Princeton University Press, 2001); Aimé Césaire, *Discourse on Colonialism* (New York: Monthly Review Press, 1972); Fanon, *Wretched of the Earth*; Arendt, *The Origins of Totalitarianism*. On German racial imperialism and the colonial dimension of the Holocaust see Carroll P. Kakel III, *The Holocaust as Colonial Genocide: Hitler's "Indian Wars" in the "Wild East"* (London: Palgrave Macmillan, 2013); Michael Rothberg, *Multidirectional Memory: Remembering the Holocaust in the Age of Decolonization* (Palo Alto, CA: Stanford University Press, 2009). On the relationship of filiation between colony and camp see also Ann Laura Stoler, "Colony," http://www.politicalconcepts.org/issue1/colony/, and "Colony and Camp: A Political Matrix," in *Durabilities of Imperial Duress* (Durham, NC: Duke University Press, forthcoming).

25. Victor Kattan has shown how the Zionist project in Palestine intertwined with international law and treaties in the first half of the twentieth century. The Zionist movement framed the creation of a Jewish national home in Palestine as an issue of consent among the nations informed by international law. In the decades preceding the 1947 partition of Palestine, the creation of a settler state in the Middle East was progressively constructed and legitimized through the treaties between the Great Powers. Victor Kattan, *From Coexistence to Conquest: International Law and the Origins of the Arab-Israeli Conflict, 1891–1949* (London: Pluto Press, 2009).

26. United Nations, "San Francisco Conference," http://www.un.org/en/aboutun/history/sanfrancisco_conference.shtml (accessed April 28, 2014).

27. Eliahu Elath, *Zionism at the UN: A Diary of the First Days* (Philadelphia, PA: Jewish Publication Society of America, 1976), 34.

28. John Snetsinger, *Truman, the Jewish Vote, and the Creation of Israel* (Palo Alto, CA: Hoover Press, 1974), 16–17. See also Baruch Kimmerling, *The Invention and Decline of Israeliness: State, Society, and the Military* (Berkeley: University of California Press, 2001); Cohen, "The Holocaust."

29. General Assembly, "Annexes, A/364," http://domino.un.org/unispal.nsf/c17b3a9d4bfb04c985257b28006e4ea6/fb6dd3f0e9535815852572dd006cc607?OpenDocument (accessed April 28, 2014).

30. United Nations Special Committee on Palestine, "Official Records of the Second Session of the General Assembly, Supplement no. 11," Report of the General Assembly, http://unispal.un.org/unispal.nsf/0/364a6ac0dc52ada785256e8b00716662?OpenDocument (accessed April 28, 2014).

31. Gershon Shafir, *Land, Labor and the Origins of the Israeli-Palestinian Conflict, 1882–1914* (Berkeley: University of California Press, 1989); Oren Yiftachel, *Ethnocracy: Land and Identity Politics in Israel/Palestine* (Philadelphia: University

of Pennsylvania Press, 2006); Baruch Kimmerling, *Zionism and Territory: The Socio-Territorial Dimensions of Zionist Politics* (Berkeley: University of California Press, 1983); Benny Morris, *The Birth of the Palestinian Refugee Problem, 1947–1949* (Cambridge: Cambridge University Press, 1987); Ilan Pappe, *A History of Modern Palestine: One Land, Two Peoples* (Cambridge: Cambridge University Press, 2006); Ahmad H. Sa'di and Lila Abu-Lughod, *Nakba: Palestine, 1948, and the Claims of Memory* (New York: Columbia University Press, 2007).

32. On the relationship between liberal rights theories, settler colonialism, and reparations see David L. Eng, *Reparations and the Human* (Durham, NC: Duke University Press, forthcoming). In his reconstruction of the "genealogy of the human" in Locke, Eng shows how Locke couched the colonial settler—instead of the dispossessed native—as "the paradigmatic injured subject of modernity" in need of reparations.

33. *The Specialist: Portrait of a Modern Criminal*, directed by Eyal Sivan and Rony Brauman (New York: Home Vision Entertainment, 2002).

34. William Schabas argues that "The pronouncements on universal jurisdiction in *Eichmann* are probably the most influential finding of the judgments. The legal reasoning was flimsy, defying clear evidence of the views of states, and yet it was almost immediately accepted as a precedent in international law," and that the "The *Eichmann* precedent on universal jurisdiction stands essentially unchallenged to this day" (692). In his article, Schabas tries to reconstruct what the trial did to human rights, but he never really tackles the issue of what human rights did in the trial, let alone the effects of the trial on the political history of the region. William Schabas, "The Contribution of the Eichmann Trial to International Law," *Leiden Journal of International Law* 26, no. 3 (2013), 667–699.

35. Hannah Arendt, *Eichmann in Jerusalem* (New York: Penguin, 2006), 270.

36. Shoshana Felman, *The Juridical Unconscious: Trials and Traumas in the Twentieth Century* (Cambridge, MA: Harvard University Press, 2002), 226.

37. On the Law of Return see note 20. Oren Yiftachel, "Planning and Social Control: Exploring the Dark Side," *Journal of Planning Literature* 12, no. 4 (1998), 395–406; Oren Yiftachel and Haim Yacobi, "Urban Ethnocracy: Ethnicization and the Production of Space in an Israeli Mixed City," *Environment and Planning D* 21, no. 6 (2003), 673–694.

38. Talal Asad, "What Do Human Rights Do? An Anthropological Enquiry," *Theory & Event* 4, no. 4 (2000).

39. Idith Zertal, *Israel's Holocaust and the Politics of Nationhood* (Cambridge: Cambridge University Press, 2005). See also Judith Butler, *Parting Ways: Jewishness and the Critique of Zionism* (New York: Columbia University Press, 2012).

40. Zertal, *Israel's Holocaust*, 173–175.

41. Gilbert Achcar, *The Arabs and the Holocaust* (London: Saqi Books, 2009), especially chapter 5, "The Nasser Years."

42. Statement to the Security Council by Foreign Minister Eban, June 6, 1967, United Nations Information System on the Question of Palestine (UNISPAL), http://unispal.un.org/UNISPAL.NSF/0/F0E5CF015592 D4D10525672700590136 (accessed April 29, 2014).

43. Abba Eban, interview with the German newspaper *Der Spiegel*, November 5, 1969.

44. Abba Eban at the United Nations in 1967, noted that: "had the Arabs won the war, there would be no Jewish refugees left, only two million more corpses, to add to the six million Shoah victims." Cited in Ada Yurman, "The Victimisation

Motif as a Guiding Principle of Israeli Discourse," *International Review of Victimology.* vol. 15, (2008) pp. 59-83. P. 67.

45. Neve Gordon, *Israel's Occupation* (Berkeley: University of California Press, 2008).

46. A study examining the use of the term *human rights* in the Israeli press reveals that 20 years of repressive occupation did not lead to the introduction of a human rights discourse in Israel in relation to the 1967 occupation and its effects. There was talk of civil rights, but human rights were absent from the political landscape. The eruption of the Palestinian revolt in the OPT and the iron fist policy deployed by Israel to quell the resistance triggered the adoption of the term *human rights* also within the colonial domestic setting. More specifically, four intricately tied factors related to the Intifada led to the introduction of the human rights discourse: the extent of the rights-abusive policies used to crush the resistance; the coalescing of a global human rights discourse and its prominence as a new form of international moral language; the widespread coverage of the events in the international media; and rapid institutionalization of human rights—namely, the creation of an organizational infrastructure of human rights activism both in the OPT and in Israel. Neve Gordon and Nitza Berkovitch, "Human Rights Discourse in Domestic Settings: How Does It Emerge?" *Political Studies* 55, no. 1 (2007), 243–266.

47. Stanley Cohen and Daphna Golan, "The Interrogation of Palestinians during the Intifada: Ill-Treatment, 'Moderate Physical Pressure' or Torture," B'Tselem—The Israeli Information Center for Human Rights in the Occupied Territories (Jerusalem, 1991); James Ron, Eric Goldstein, and Cynthia Brown, *Torture and Ill-Treatment: Israel's Interrogation of Palestinians from the Occupied Territories* (Human Rights Watch, 1994); Yehezkel Lein and Eyal Weizman, *Land Grab: Israel's Settlement Policy in the West Bank* (Jerusalem: B'Tselem, 2002); Emma Playfair, *International Law and the Administration of Occupied Territories: Two Decades of Israeli Occupation of the West Bank and Gaza Strip* (Oxford: Oxford University Press, 1992); Joost R. Hiltermann, "Israel's Strategy to Break the Uprising," *Journal of Palestine Studies* Vol. 19, No. 2 (1990), 87–98.

48. Sari Hanafi and Linda Tabar, *The Emergence of a Palestinian Globalized Elite: Donors, International Organizations, and Local NGOs* (Washington, DC: Institute of Jerusalem Studies, 2005).

49. Benoît Challand, *Palestinian Civil Society: Foreign Donors and the Power to Promote and Exclude* (London: Routledge, 2008).

50. Dotan Yoav, "Do the Haves Still Come Out Ahead—Resource Inequalities in Ideological Courts: The Case of the Israeli High Court of Justice," *Law & Society Review* 33, no. 2 (1999), 319–363.

51. Dafna Golan and Zvi Orr, "Translating Human Rights of the 'Enemy': The Case of Israeli NGOs Defending Palestinian Rights," *Law & Society Review* 46, no. 4 (2012), 781–814; David Kretzmer, *The Occupation of Justice: The Supreme Court of Israel and the Occupied Territories* (New York: SUNY Press, 2002); Eran Shor, "Conflict, Terrorism, and the Socialization of Human Rights Norms: The Spiral Model Revisited," *Social Problems* 55, no. 1 (2008), 117–138.

52. John Collins, *Global Palestine* (London: Hurst Publishers, 2011).

53. Lori Allen, *The Rise and Fall of Human Rights: Cynicism and Politics in Occupied Palestine* (Stanford, CA: Stanford University Press, 2013).

54. Rema Hammami, "Palestinian NGOs since Oslo: From NGO Politics to Social Movements?" *Middle East Report* no. 214 (2000), 16–48; Islah Jad, "The NGO-isation of Arab Women's Movements," *IDS Bulletin* 35, no. 4 (2004), 34–42.

55. Orna Ben-Naftali, Aeyal Gross, and Keren Michaeli, "Illegal Occupation: The Framing of the Occupied Palestinian Territory," *Berkley Journal of International Law* 23 (2005), 551; Baruch Kimmerling, "Religion, Nationalism, and Democracy in Israel," *Constellations* 6, no. 3 (1999), 339–363; Kretzmer, *The Occupation of Justice*.

56. George E. Bisharat, "Courting Justice? Legitimation in Lawyering under Israeli Occupation," *Law & Social Inquiry* 20, no. 2 (1995), 349–405.

57. Lisa Hajjar, *Courting Conflict: The Israeli Military Court System in the West Bank and Gaza* (Berkeley: University of California Press, 2005); see also Kretzmer, *The Occupation of Justice*.

58. Yoav, "Do the Haves."

59. Justus Reid Weiner, "Human Rights in the Israeli Administrated Areas during the Intifada: 1987–1990," *Wisconsin International Law Journal* 10 (1991), 185–222.

60. Here we trace a parallel between Israel's organic legal experts and Italy's organic intellectuals. By organic legal experts here we mean those law specialists whose work and arguments reinforce Israel's regime of violence through the production of a hegemonic discourse that legitimizes domination. Antonio Gramsci, *Selections from the Prison Notebooks*, ed. and trans. Geoffrey Nowell-Smith and Quintin Hoare (London: International Publishers, 1971).

61. Lisa Hajjar, "Human Rights in Israel/Palestine: The History and Politics of a Movement," *Journal of Palestine Studies* 30, no. 4 (2001), 21–38.

62. Michael Sfard, "The Price of Internal Legal Opposition to Human Rights Abuses," *Journal of Human Rights Practice* 1, no. 1 (2009), 48.

63. B'tselem, for example, documented the killing of 168 Palestinians during arrests in the West Bank between January 2004 and June 2006. At least 40 of those killed were civilians who were not connected in any way to the military operation, and another 54 were defined as "wanted" but were unarmed or otherwise *hors de combat* at the time they were shot and killed. None of these cases were investigated by the Military Police and consequently none of the soldiers were charged with unlawful shooting or any other offense. Letter to Prime Minister Ehud Olmert, from several human rights organizations, dated June 10, 2006, Ronen Shnayderman and Shaul Vardi, *Take No Prisoners: The Fatal Shooting of Palestinians by Israeli Security Forces during "Arrest Operations"* (Jerusalem: B'Tselem, 2005).

64. The numbers are taken from B'tselem's website. B'Tselem, "Statistics," http://www.btselem.org/statistics/fatalities/before-cast-lead/by-date-of-event (accessed April 29, 2014).

65. After the terrorist attack at the Munich Olympics, Golda Meir authorized the Mossad to assassinate all those who were involved in a bloody assault on Israeli targets. Neve Gordon, "Rationalising Extra-judicial Executions: The Israeli Press and the Legitimisation of Abuse," *International Journal of Human Rights* 8, no. 3 (2004), 305–324.

66. Renata Capella and Michael Sfard, *The Assassination Policy of the State of Israel* (Jerusalem: Public Committee Against Torture in Israel, 2002).

67. Jessica Montell, "Operation Defensive Shield," *Tikkun*, July–August 2002.

68. World Bank, *Twenty-Seven Months: Intifada, Closures and Palestinian Economic Crisis* (Jerusalem: World Bank, 2003).

69. For an example of a human rights report that exposes the structural elements of Israel's land regime consult Lein and Weizman, *Land Grab*.

70. G. Barzilai, *Communities and Law: Politics and Cultures of Legal Identities* (Ann Arbor: University of Michigan Press, 2003).

71. Irus Braverman, "Checkpoint Watch Bureaucracy and Resistance at the Israeli/ Palestinian Border," *Social & Legal Studies* 21, no. 3 (2012), 316.

72. Didier Fassin, "The Humanitarian Politics of Testimony: Subjectification through Trauma in the Israeli–Palestinian Conflict," *Cultural Anthropology* 23, no. 3 (2008), 531–558.

73. Ruthie Ginsburg, "Taking Pictures over Soldiers' Shoulders: Reporting on Human Rights Abuse from the Israeli Occupied Territories," *Journal of Human Rights* 10, no. 1 (2011), 17–33; Eyal Weizman, "Walking through Walls," *Radical Philosophy* 136 (2006), 8–22.

74. Lori Allen, "Getting by the Occupation: How Violence Became Normal during the Second Palestinian Intifada," *Cultural Anthropology* 23, no. 3 (2008), 453–487.

CHAPTER 2

1. Reuters, "Israel Kills Scores in Gaza Air Strikes," http://www.reuters.com/ article/2008/12/27/us-palestinians-israel-violence-idUSLR1342320081227 (accessed July 8, 2013).

2. B'Tselem, "Operation Cast Lead, 27 Dec. 08 to 18 Jan. 09," http://www.btselem. org/gaza_strip/castlead_operation (accessed January 14, 2013).

3. The mission had been established on April 3, 2009. In addition to Richard Goldstone, Christine Chinkin, Hina Jilani, and Desmond Travers were asked to serve on the commission.

4. Haviv Rettig Gur, "Goldstone to 'Post': Mandate of My Gaza Probe Has Changed," *Jerusalem Post*, July 17, 2009.

5. The State of Israel, *The Operation in Gaza: Factual and Legal Aspects* (Jerusalem: Ministry of Foreign Affairs, 2009).

6. Some of the interviews can be viewed and/or heard online at http://www. un.org/webcast/unhrc/archive.asp?go=090628 (accessed February 22, 2013).

7. R. Goldstone et al., *Human Rights in Palestine and Other Occupied Arab Territories: Report of the United Nations Fact Finding Mission on the Gaza Conflict* (Geneva: United Nations, 2009).

8. Subsequently, the Human Rights Council established two independent committees to examine whether the two sides actually initiated investigations. According to the final 2011 report, the Israeli government had conducted some 400 command investigations in relation to Operation Cast Lead, of which 52 were criminal investigations into allegations of wrongdoing. Nineteen investigations into serious violations of international humanitarian law and international human rights law reported by the fact-finding mission had been completed by the Israeli authorities with findings that no violations were committed. Two inquiries were discontinued for different reasons. Three investigations led to disciplinary action, including one in which criminal charges have been brought against an Israeli soldier (for theft of a credit card). The status of possible investigations into six additional incidents remains unclear. The committee emphasized that there was no indication that Israel has opened investigations into the actions of those who designed, planned, ordered, and oversaw Operation Cast Lead. Nonetheless, in May 2013, after the committee had completed its report and in response to a petition filed by different Israeli human rights organizations, the military notified the High Court of Justice that it would stop

using white phosphorous in populated areas. The committee also approached the Hamas government in Gaza, which was unwilling to conduct any investigations into the launching of rocket and mortar attacks against Israel, but did carry out a number of investigations into alleged human rights violations carried out by its security forces against Palestinians. Human Rights Council, *Report of the Committee of Independent Experts in International Humanitarian and Human Rights Laws to Monitor and Assess any Domestic, Legal or Other Proceedings Undertaken by Both the Government of Israel and the Palestinian Side, in the Light of General Assembly Resolution 64/254, Including the Independence, Effectiveness, Genuineness of These Investigations and Their Conformity with International Standards* (Geneva: United Nations, 2010).

9. JTA News Service, "Prodded by Danon, U.S. Lawyers Set to Sue Goldstone," http://www.jta.org/news/article/2011/04/07/3086766/american-jewish-lawyers-set-to-sue-goldstone (accessed January 10, 2013).

10. Benjamin Netanyahu, "Excerpts from PM Netanyahu's Speech at the Knesset Special Session," http://mfa.gov.il/MFA/PressRoom/2009/Pages/PM-Netanyahu-addresses-%20Knesset-Special-Session-23-Dec-2009.aspx (accessed July 25, 2013).

11. Letty Cottin, "The Un-Jewish Assault on Richard Goldstone," *Forward*, January 7, 2011. This strategy of "attacking the expert's conclusions, credentials, ethics and sanity" is by no means unique, since as Clifford Bob shows in his research, networks around the world often bring their own "stable of wise men—their own scientific wunderkinds, moral megastars, and celebrity hangers on"—in order to "yoke their foes to moral monstrosities, historical events or personages whose wickedness epitomizes the enemy's secret aim." Bob, *Global Right Wing*.

12. Nathan Guttman, "Israel, U.S. Working to Limit Damage of Goldstone Report," http://www.haaretz.com/print-edition/features/israel-u-s-working-to-limit-damage-of-goldstone-report-1.7116 (accessed May 1, 2014).

13. After two years of seemingly endless accusations that affected Goldstone's relationship with his own family, the South African judge finally bowed under the pressure. Donna Bryson, "South African Judge Says He Won't Attend Bar Mitzvah," Associated Press Online, April 17, 2010. Writing for the *Washington Post*, Goldstone recanted, renouncing his previous claim that Israel had intentionally targeted civilians. He (and not the other coauthors) thus accepted the Israeli government's claims that it had bombed civilian buildings because terrorists were hiding in them and that it had warned the Palestinian civilians before any bombing ensued. Irrespective of one's view regarding this debate, Goldstone's retraction regarding the accusation of intentionality was grabbed by the Israeli government and worded in such a way that people who had not read his newspaper article would think that the South African judge had disavowed the entire report, while demanding that the UN renounce all the findings. Carlo Strenger, "Richard Goldstone's Changed Mind on Israel Should Lead to Official Retraction," *Guardian*, April 4, 2011; R. Goldstone, "Reconsidering the Goldstone Report on Israel and War Crimes," *Washington Post*, April 1, 2011.

14. NGO Monitor, *Annual Report: A Year of Impact* (Jerusalem: NGO Monitor, 2011); see also Gerald Steinberg, "Gerald M. Steinberg," http://www.geraldsteinberg.com/ (accessed May 1, 2014).

15. NGO Monitor, "About Us," http://www.ngo-monitor.org/articles.php?type=about (accessed January 6, 2013).

16. NGO Monitor, "NGO Monitor at UN Human Rights Council, 25th Session," http://www.ngo-monitor.org/article/ngo_monitor_at_un_human_rights_council_th_session (accessed May 1, 2014).
17. Gerald Steinberg, "Monitoring the Political Role of NGOs," Jerusalem Center for Public Affairs, http://www.jcpa.org/jl/vp499.htm (accessed May 1, 2014).
18. Ibid.
19. UN Watch, "Mission & History," UN Watch, http://www.unwatch.org/site/c.bdKKISNqEmG/b.1313591/k.954F/Mission_History.htm (accessed May 1, 2014).
20. Global Jewish Advocacy, "On Zionism: Responses to Critics," AJC, http://www.ajc.org/atf/cf/%7Bf56f4495-cf69-45cb-a2d7-f8eca17198ee%7D/ON%20ZIONISM%20-%20MARCH%202013.PDF (accessed May 1, 2014).
21. Global Governance Watch, "About Global Governance Watch," http://www.globalgovernancewatch.org/about/ (accessed May 1, 2014); for a list and explanation about other organizations consult Institute for Policy Studies, "Right Watch," IPS, http://rightweb.irc-online.org/ (accessed May 1, 2014).
22. Meister, *After Evil*, 7.
23. Neve Gordon, "Human Rights as a Contingent Foundation: The Case of Physicians for Human Rights 1," *Journal of Human Rights* 5, no. 2 (2006), 163–184.
24. Douzinas, *The End of Human Rights*.
25. On the notion of translating human rights into local idioms consult Merry, "Transnational Human Rights"; M. Goodale and S. E. Merry, *The Practice of Human Rights: Tracking Law between the Global and the Local* (Cambridge: Cambridge University Press, 2007); Sally Engle Merry et al., "Law from Below: Women's Human Rights and Social Movements in New York City," *Law & Society Review* 44, no. 1 (2010), 101–128; Elizabeth Samson, *Warfare through Misuse of International Law* (Bar Ilan University, Israel: BESA Center, 2009).
26. Jetschke, *Human Rights and State Security*.
27. Gerald Steinberg, "NGOs Make War on Israel," *Middle East Quarterly* 11, no. 3 (2004), 13–25.
28. New Vilna Review, "Israel, Legitimacy and Human Rights: An Interview with Professor Gerald Steinberg of NGO Monitor," http://www.newvilnareview.com/features/israel-legitimacy-and-human-rights-an-interview-with-professor-gerald-steinberg-of-ngo-monitor.html (accessed May 1, 2014).
29. C. J. Dunlap Jr., "Law and Military Interventions: Preserving Humanitarian Values in 21st Century Conflicts" (Harvard University's Carr Center for Human Rights Policy, November 2001).
30. J. L. Austin, *How to Do Things with Words* (Cambridge, MA: Harvard University Press, 1975); Ole Wæver, "Securitization and Desecuritization," in *On Security*, ed. Ronnie D. Lipschutz (New York: Columbia University Press, 1998), 46–86.
31. B. Buzan, O. Wæver, and J. De Wilde, *Security: A New Framework for Analysis* (Boulder, CO: Lynne Rienner, 1998).
32. Lisa Hajjar, "Universal Jurisdiction as Praxis," in *When Governments Break the Law: The Rule of Law and the Prosecution of the Bush Administration*, ed. N. Hussain (New York: New York University Press, 2010), 87–120; D. Morrison and J. R. Weiner, "Curbing Enthusiasm for Universal Jurisdiction," *Publicist* 4 (2010), 1–11.
33. L. N. Sadat and J. Geng, "On Legal Subterfuge and the So-Called Lawfare Debate," *Case Western Reserve Journal of International* 43 (2010), 153–162.
34. A survey carried out by Amnesty International indicates that 166 (approximately 86 percent) of the 193 UN member states have defined one or more of

four crimes under international law (war crimes, crimes against humanity, genocide, and torture) as crimes in their national law, and 147 (approximately 76.2 percent) out of 193 states have provided for universal jurisdiction over one or more of these crimes. Amnesty International, *Universal Jurisdiction: A Preliminary Survey of Legislation around the World—2012 Update* (London: Amnesty International, 2012). An examination of when these countries amended their laws in order to include or broaden universal jurisdiction in their criminal code reveals that 91 of the 147 countries introduced amendments after the year 2000, and 118 countries introduced changes after 1990, underscoring the relative novelty of this phenomenon. And even though many of these countries have yet to exercise universal jurisdiction, the fact that the laws are in place renders it more likely that they will do so in the future. Moreover, a study carried out by Redress and FIDH about the exercise of extraterritorial jurisdiction among the EU's 27 member states reveals that the phenomenon is becoming more and more prevalent. Redress and FIDH, *Extraterritorial Jurisdiction in the EU: A Study of the Laws and Practice in the 27 Member States of the EU* (London and Paris: Redress and FIDH, 2010).

35. Michael Byers, "The Law and Politics of the Pinochet Case," *Duke Journal of Comparative and International Law* 10 (1999), 415–441; N. Roht-Arriaza, "The Pinochet Precedent and Universal Jurisdiction," *New England Law Review* 35 (2000), 311–320.

36. Redress and FIDH, *Extraterritorial Jurisdiction in the EU*, 1–276; Human Rights Watch, *Universal Jurisdiction in Europe: The State of the Art* (New York: HRW, 2006).

37. W. Kaleck, "From Pinochet to Rumsfeld: Universal Jurisdiction in Europe 1998–2008," *Michigan Journal of International Law* 30 (2009), 927–1273.

38. Department of Defense, *National Defense Strategy of the United States of America* (Washington, DC: Department of Defense, 2005).

39. Human Rights Watch, *Universal Jurisdiction in Europe*, 1–101.

40. David Sapsted, "Hundreds of War Crimes Lawsuits Filed against Israelis," *National*, October 11, 2009.

41. "The Lawfare Project" underscores the cooperation between US and Israeli conservatives. It defines lawfare as "the use of the law as a weapon of war, or more specifically the abuse of the law and legal systems for strategic political or military ends," which is then described as a strategy waged against the United States and Israel as a way to undermine democracy. The Lawfare Project, "Lawfare: The Use of the Law as a Weapon of War," http://www.thelawfareproject.org/what-is-lawfare.html (accessed January 13, 2013).

42. According to the Fédération Internationale des Ligues des Droits de l'Homme, 99 percent of referrals to the prosecutor at the ICC between the years 2002 and 2006 came from NGOs and individuals. Fédération Internationale des Ligues des Droits de l'Homme, *Israel, National Round Table on the International Criminal Court: "Raising Accountability of International Criminals"* (France: FIDH, 2007); see also Anne Herzberg, *NGO "Lawfare": Exploitation of Courts in the Arab-Israeli Conflict* (Jerusalem: NGO Monitor, 2010); NGO Monitor, "Goldstone Report: 575 Pages of NGO 'Cut and Paste'," http://www.ngo-monitor.org/article/goldstone_report_pages_of_ngo_cut_and_paste_ (accessed March 1, 2013); Im Tirtzu, "The Influence of the New Israel Fund Organizations on the Goldstone Report," http://imti.org.il/Uploads/NIFGoldstone25P.pdf (accessed December 22, 2012); Samson, *Warfare through Misuse*, 1–6.

43. BESA Center, "Our Mission," http://besacenter.org/about/mission/ (accessed August 7, 2013).
44. Samson, *Warfare through Misuse of International Law*, 1–6. Italics ours.
45. Anghie, *Imperialism, Sovereignty*, 1–30.
46. Jacques Derrida, "Force of Law: The 'Mystical Foundation of Authority'," *Cordova Law Review* 11 (2002), 950–970; Robert M. Cover, "Violence and the Word," *Yale Law Journal* (1986), 1601–1629.
47. Edward Said, *The Question of Palestine* (New York: Vintage Books, 1980), xix.
48. In reality, African leaders and paramilitaries have been the main target of lawfare, followed by officials from Latin America and the former Yugoslavia. Redress and FIDH, *Extraterritorial Jurisdiction in the EU*, 1–276.
49. Herzberg, *NGO "Lawfare"*, 41.
50. Ibid., 6.
51. Buzan, Wæver, and De Wilde, *Security*, 1–36.
52. The Goldstone Report is considered a watershed in terms of the strategies deployed against human rights organizations in Israel. Interview with Hadas Ziv from Physicians for Human Rights Israel, November 21, 2012. Interview with Hassan Jabareen, director of Adalah, February 3, 2013.
53. NGO Monitor, *Goldstone Report*.
54. The name comes from a famous quote about the creation of a Jewish state made by the Zionist visionary Theodore Herzl: "If you will it, it is no dream; and if you do not will it, a dream it is and a dream it will stay."
55. Im Tirtzu, "Our Mission," http://en.imti.org.il (accessed December 22, 2012).
56. NGO Monitor, "NIF-Funded NGOs: Goldstone's Building Blocks," http://www.ngo-monitor.org/article/nif_funded_ngos_goldstone_s_building_blocks (accessed December 22, 2012).
57. Im Tirtzu, "Influence of the New Israel Fund Organizations."
58. NGO Monitor, "NIF-Funded NGOs."
59. Ben Kaspit, "The Material from Which the Goldstone Is Made," *Ma'ariv*, January 29, 2010.
60. In Hebrew the word for horn is *keren*, which also means "fund."
61. Along similar lines, Reut Institute, a conservative Israeli think tank, published a monograph that aims to analyze and provide a "response to the erosion in Israel's diplomatic status over the past few years, which reached its peak with the Goldstone report." This attack, Reut asserts, "possesses strategic significance, and may develop into a comprehensive existential threat within a few years." Reut Institute, "Building a Political Firewall Against Israel's Delegitimization," http://reut-institute.org/data/uploads/PDFVer/20100310%20Delegitimacy%20Eng.pdf (accessed December 22, 2012); Gerald Steinberg and Anne Herzberg, eds., *The Goldstone Report "Reconsidered": A Critical Analysis* (Jerusalem: NGO Monitor and the Jerusalem Center for Public Affairs, 2011).
62. Steinberg and Herzberg, *The Goldstone Report Reconsidered*, p. 20.
63. Israeli Ministry of Foreign Affairs, "Goldstone Fact-Finding Report: A Challenge to Democracies Fighting Terror," http://www.mfa.gov.il/MFA/Terrorism-+Obstacle+to+Peace/Hamas+war+against+Israel/Goldstone+Fact-Finding_Report_Challenge_democracies_fighting+_error.htm (accessed November 23, 2012).
64. Israeli Ministry of Foreign Affairs, *Israel's Deputy Foreign Minister Danny Ayalon at the Israel Council on Foreign Relations, Jerusalem: Challenges for Israeli Foreign Policy*, http://bibireport.blogspot.co.il/2010/01/deputy-fm-ayalon-to-to-israel-council.html (accessed January 15, 2015).

65. Israeli Ministry of Foreign Affairs, "Deputy Foreign Minister Danny Ayalon: 'International Human Rights Day Has Been Transformed in Terror Rights Day'," in Hebrew, http://mfa.gov.il/MFAHEB/PressRoom/Spokesman/2010/Pages/DFM_Ayalon_Human_Rights_Day_091210.aspx (accessed June 26, 2013); see also Israeli Ministry of Foreign Affairs, "Press Conference Marking International Human Rights Day," http://mfa.gov.il/MFA/PressRoom/2010/Pages/Ayalon_Press_conference_International_Human_Rights_Day_9-Dec-2010.aspx (accessed June 26, 2013).

66. Barak Ravid and Jonathan Lis, "Lieberman Blasts PM, Likud Ministers for Refusing to Probe Left-Wing Groups," *Ha'aretz*, July 18, 2011.

67. Ibid.

68. Tomer Zarchin, "IDF: War Crime Charges over Gaza Offensive are 'Legal Terror'," *Ha'aretz*, February 19, 2009. It is interesting to note that this notion has been increasingly adopted in recent years in other geographical contexts in order to delegitimize human rights groups and label them as "disingenuous elements" who "misuse" existing human rights legislation, especially in India, in the framework of antirape laws. V. Harish Nair, "Inside the New 'Legal Terrorism': How Laws Are Being Abused to Settle Personal Scores," Media Online India, http://www.dailymail.co.uk/indiahome/indianews/article-2516150/Inside-new-legal-terrorism-How-laws-abused-settle-personal-scores.html (accessed May 1, 2014).

69. Israeli Ministry of Foreign Affairs, "FAQ: The Campaign to Defame Israel," http://www.mfa.gov.il/MFA/FAQ/FAQ_Attack_Israeli_Values (accessed January 12, 2013).

70. Ibid.

71. Jonathan Lis, "Leftist Groups: 'Witch Hunt' against Us Will Destroy Democracy in Israel," *Ha'aretz*, January 5, 2011.

72. Ibid.

73. ACRI, *Knesset Database* (Jerusalem: Association of Civil Rights in Israel, 2012); Adalah, *New Discriminatory Laws and Bills in Israel* (Haifa: Adalah: The Legal Center for the Arab Minority in Israel, 2012).

74. Ibid.

75. According to Hasan Jabareen from Adalah, the bill was shelved through pressure from the EU and the US State Department. Interview February 3, 2013.

76. Neve Gordon, "Human Rights as a Security Threat: Lawfare and the Campaign against Rights NGOs," *Law and Society Review* 48, no. 2 (2014), 311–344.

77. The two organizations are the Coalition for Women for Just Peace and Mada: The Palestinian Center for Development and Media Freedoms. According to Naomi Paiss, development director at NIF, the changes in guidelines were introduced because of a change of guard in the NIF's leadership. The campaigns, according to Paiss, only accelerated a process that was already underway. Interview with Naomi Paiss, February 12, 2013.

78. New Israel Fund, "We Are NIF," http://www.nif.org/about/wearenif (accessed January 25, 2013).

79. Interview with Naomi Paiss, February 12, 2013.

80. New Israel Fund, "Selected NIF Policies," http://www.nif.org/about/selected-nif-policies (accessed January 18, 2013).

81. Human Rights Watch, *Universal Jurisdiction in Europe*, 1–101.

82. Kretzmer, *The Occupation of Justice*.

83. B'Tselem was established in February 1989 "to document and educate the Israeli public and policymakers about human rights violations in the Occupied Territories, combat the phenomenon of denial prevalent among the Israeli public, and help create a human rights culture in Israel." The NGO has a staff of 43 people working in several departments, including a research department, a data department, a public outreach department, and an international relations department. It concentrates on documentation and advocacy, publishing numerous reports each year about human rights violations in order to provide as much information as possible to the Israeli public and decision-makers. Although it does not highlight its international advocacy on its website, it also distributes its reports, statements, and press releases to decision-makers and members of civil society in Europe, North America, and elsewhere. B'Tselem, "About B'Tselem," http://www.btselem.org/about_btselem (accessed May 1, 2014).

84. Amos Harel, "Hamas Military Chief Ahmed Jabari Killed by Israeli Strike," *Ha'aretz*, November 14, 2012.

85. Human Rights Council, *Report of the United Nations High Commissioner for Human Rights on the Implementation of Human Rights Council Resolutions S-9/1 and S-12/1* (Geneva: Human Rights Council, 2013).

86. Ibid.

87. Physicians for Human Rights et al. vs. The Prime Minister et al., HCJ 201/09 and HCJ 248/09, elyon1.court.gov.il/files_eng/09/010/002/n07/09002010. n07.pdf (accessed August 8, 2013).

88. Interview with Hadas Ziv from PHR-Israel, January 28, 2013.

89. B'Tselem, "Learning the Lessons of the Past to Protect Gaza Civilians," http://www.btselem.org/gaza_strip/20121115_gaza_operation (accessed August 3, 2013).

90. Yael Stein, *Human Rights Violations during Operation Pillar of Defense 14–21 November 2012* (Jerusalem: B'Tselem, 2013), 3–4.

91. Ibid.

92. B'Tselem, "Testimonies of Young People from Kibbutz Zikim on Rocket Damage at the Kibbutz, 2006," http://www.btselem.org/testimonies/20121117_rockets_in_zikim (accessed August 4, 2013).

93. Edmund Burke, *Reflections on the Revolution in France: A Critical Edition* (Palo Alto, CA: Stanford University Press, 2002).

94. Interestingly, cultural relativists also assume that human rights are poised against the state. This critique condemns human rights work as a new form of Western imperialism or neocolonialism because it conceives the source of human rights to be Western culture rather than some form of universal norm, and consequently does not accept the identification of human rights with freedom, liberation, or any other good. While the threat of human rights is different, focusing on culture, it is ultimately also a threat to the non-Western state.

CHAPTER 3

1. Kennedy, *Dark Sides of Virtue*, 294.
2. David Kennedy, *Of War and Law* (Princeton NJ: Princeton University Press, 2009).
3. Ibid., 139.
4. Achille Mbembe, "Necropolitics," *Public Culture* 15, no. 1 (2003), 11–40.
5. Paul Robinson, *Ethics Education in the Military* (London: Ashgate, 2013); see also Sidney Axinn, *A Moral Military* (Philadelphia, PA: Temple University Press,

2009); Anthony Joseph Coates, *The Ethics of War* (Manchester: Manchester University Press, 1997); and Jeff McMahan, *Killing in War* (Oxford: Oxford University Press, 2009).

6. Amnesty International, *Military Training 101*, 1–2.

7. Fort Benning, *Human Rights Training Classes*.

8. Kennedy, *Dark Sides of Virtue*, 195.

9. #IDFWithoutBorders, Map of IDF Aid Delegations Around the World, http://www.idfblog.com/2013/11/27/idfwithoutborders-map-idf-aid-delegations-around-world/ (accessed May 1, 2014).

10. David Kennedy, "Primitive Legal Scholarship," *Harvard International Law Journal* 27 (1986), 1–98.

11. St. Petersburg Declaration Renouncing the Use in Time of War of Explosive Projectiles under 400 Grammes Weight, 1868, 138 C.T.S. 297.

12. For a list of the treaties and the state parties to such treaties see http://www.icrc.org/ihl. Jody Williams, *My Name Is Jody Williams: A Vermont Girl's Winding Path to the Nobel Peace Prize* (Berkeley: University of California Press, 2013); Weizman, *Least of All Possible Evils*; Asa Kasher and Amos Yadlin, "Military Ethics of Fighting Terror: An Israeli Perspective," *Journal of Military Ethics* 4, no. 1 (2005), 3–32.

13. John A. Nagl et al., *The US Army / Marine Corps Counterinsurgency Field Manual* (Chicago: University of Chicago Press, 2008); see also Patricia Cohen, "Scholars and the Military Share a Foxhole, Uneasily," *New York Times*, December 22, 2007.

14. Professor Asa Kasher was active in drafting the new military ethical code, while the Association for Civil Rights in Israel instituted training programs for the border police. Kasher and Yadlin, "Military Ethics of Fighting Terror"; Asa Kasher and Amos Yadlin, "Assassination and Preventive Killing," *SAIS Review* 25, no. 1 (2005), 41–57; Neve Gordon, "Human Rights, Social Space and Power: Why Do Some NGOs Exert More Influence Than Others?" *International Journal of Human Rights* 12, no. 1 (2008), 23–39; Muhammad Ali Khalidi, "'The Most Moral Army in the World': The New 'Ethical Code' of the Israeli Military and the War on Gaza," *Journal of Palestine Studies* 39, no. 3 (2010), 6–23.

15. Kasher and Yadlin, "Assassination and Preventive Killing," 41–57.

16. Thomas W. Smith, "The New Law of War: Legitimizing Hi-Tech and Infrastructural Violence," *International Studies Quarterly* 46, no. 3 (2002), 355–374.

17. Steven Keeva, "Lawyers in the War Room," *American Bar Association Journal* 77 (1991), 52.

18. Ari Shavit, "Zvi Hauser Tells Ha'aretz What Israel Is Doing Wrong," *Ha'aretz*, August 16, 2013.

19. Weizman, *Least of All Possible Evils*, 99–136.

20. We use social space here in the sense attributed to it by Pierre Bourdieu, who argued that the more common properties agents, groups, or institutions have, the closer they are located to one another. The space an agent occupies is not only determined by the agent's properties, but the space itself also helps constitute the agent, suggesting that the space is inscribed in the bodies of the people and institutions who inhabit it. Thus, there is a dialectical relationship between an organization's properties and the place it occupies in social space. While Bourdieu focuses on individuals and groups rather than on institutions, his insights can, in our opinion, be extrapolated and used for analyzing institutions. The movement of personnel from the State Department to Amnesty

suggests that both institutions and their staff have a considerable number of common characteristics, ranging from tastes and use of language to a worldview; they share a set of dispositions—that is, practices, perceptions, and attitudes—that do not need to be consciously coordinated or governed by any "rule," but, nonetheless, do incline the agents to react in certain similar ways. Pierre Bourdieu, *The Logic of Practice*, trans. Richard Nice (Palo Alto, CA: Stanford University Press, 1990); Pierre Bourdieu, *In Other Words: Essays towards a Reflexive Sociology*, trans. Matthew Adamson (Palo Alto, CA: Stanford University Press, 1990).

21. Kennedy, *Of War and Law*, 139.
22. Thomas Hobbes, *Leviathan*, ed. Richard Tuck (Cambridge: Cambridge University Press, 1991), 91.
23. Ibid., 124.
24. Mbembe, "Necropolitics," 11.
25. Michel Foucault, *Society Must Be Defended: Lectures at the Collège De France, 1975–1976*, ed. François Ewald (New York: Macmillan, 2003), 240.
26. Hobbes, *Leviathan*, 124.
27. Michael C. Williams, "Hobbes and International Relations: A Reconsideration," *International Organization* 50 (1996), 213–236.
28. Hobbes, *Leviathan*, 124.
29. Achille Mbembe, *On the Postcolony* (Berkeley: University of California Press, 2001), particularly chapter 1.
30. Kennedy, *Of War and Law*, 9.
31. Khalili, *Time in the Shadows*, 241.
32. Michael Schmitt, "Human Shields in International Humanitarian Law," *Israel Yearbook on Human Rights* 38 (2008), 17–59.
33. Geneva Convention (IV) Relative to the Protection of Civilian Persons in Time of War, 1949, Article 28.
34. Protocol Additional to the Geneva Conventions of August 12, 1949, and Relating to the Protection of Victims of International Armed Conflicts, 1977, Art. 51(7), 1125 *U.N.T.S.* 3.
35. Statute of the International Criminal Court, 1998, Art. 8(2)(b)(xxiii), U.N. Doc. A/CONF. 183/9, 37 *I.L.M.* 1002 (1998). Art. 8(2) (b)xiii.
36. Stephen Graham, *Cities under Siege: The New Military Urbanism* (London: Verso, 2011), 16.
37. Yael Stein, *Human Shield: Use of Palestinian Civilians as Human Shields in Violation of High Court of Justice Order* (Jerusalem: B'tselem, 2002).
38. Miranda Sissons, *In a Dark Hour: The Use of Civilians during IDF Arrest Operations* (New York: Human Rights Watch, 2002).
39. Adalah: The Legal Center for Arab Minority Rights in Israel and others v. GOC Central Command and Others, HCJ 3799/02, Adalah, http://www.adalah.org/features/humshields/decision061005.pdf. (accessed May 1, 2014).
40. Jean Pictet, *The Geneva Conventions of 12 August 1949: Geneva Convention Relative to the Protection of Civilian Persons in Time of War* (Geneva: International Committee of the Red Cross, 1958).
41. *Adalah: The Legal Center for Arab Minority Rights in Israel and Others v. GOC Central Command and Others*, HCJ 3799/02.
42. Reuven Erlich, *Hezbollah's Use of Lebanese Civilians as Human Shields: The Extensive Military Infrastructure Positioned and Hidden in Populated Areas* (Tel-Aviv: Intelligence and Terrorism Information Center at the Center for Special Studies, 2006).

43. Ibid., 8, 10.
44. Intelligence and Terrorism Information Center, *Evidence of the Use of the Civilian Population as Human Shields* (Tel-Aviv: Intelligence and Terrorism Information Center, 2009).
45. Intelligence and Terrorism Information Center, *Using Civilians as Human Shields* (Tel-Aviv: Intelligence and Terrorism Information Center, 2009).
46. Eyal Weizman, "Lethal Theory," *Roundtable: Research Architecture* (2006).
47. According to preliminary data gather by the UN, at least 2,133 Palestinians were killed during the campaign. This figure includes 362 persons who could not be yet identified or their status established. Of the initially verified cases, 1,489 are believed to be civilians, including 500 children (187 girls and 313 boys), 257 women, and 282 members of armed groups. Many fatalities involved multiple family members, with at least 142 Palestinian families having three or more members killed in the same incident, for a total of 739 fatalities. United Nations, *Gaza: Initial Rapid Assessment* (East Jerusalem: United Nations Office for the Coordination of Humanitarian Affairs, Occupied Palestinian Territory, 2014).
48. Georgio Agamben, *Homo Sacer: Sovereign Power and Bare Life*, trans. Daniel Heller-Roazen (Palo Alto, CA: Stanford University Press, 1998); Georgio Agamben, *L'uso dei corpi* (Vicenza, Italy: Neri Pozza, 2014).
49. Elie Weisel, "Jews rejected child sacrifice 3,500 years ago. Now it's Hamas turn." Ad published in *The Guardian*, September 10, 2014 online at http://www.algemeiner.com/wp-content/uploads/2014/08/Elie-Wiesel-Hamas-Child-Sacrifice.pdf (accessed October 10, 2014).
50. The Iron Dome system was developed by Israel in order to intercept rockets launched from Gaza and southern Lebanon. It consists of batteries of missiles placed in the proximity to Israeli cities and strategic assets and is able to intercept the majority of the projectiles.
51. Intelligence and Terrorism Information Center, *Evidence of the Use*, 1–9.
52. Israeli Security Agency, "Selected Examples of Interrogations Following Operation Cast Lead," http://www.shabak.gov.il/English/EnTerrorData/Archive/Operation/Pages/cast-lead-Interrogations.aspx (accessed October 1, 2013).
53. Ibid.
54. On the ethics of witnessing consult Michal Givoni, "The Ethics of Witnessing and the Politics of the Governed," *Theory, Culture & Society* 31, no. 1 (2014), 123–142.
55. Fassin, "Humanitarian Politics of Testimony," 536.
56. Israeli Security Agency, "Selected Examples of Interrogations."
57. Majd Badr and Abeer Baker, *Exposed: The Treatment of Palestinian Detainees during Operation "Cast Lead"* (Jerusalem: Public Committee Against Torture, 2010), 12.
58. Israeli Security Agency, "Selected Examples of Interrogations."
59. Badr and Baker, *Exposed*, 1–45.
60. Human Rights Council, *Report of the United Nations High Commissioner.*
61. Stein, *Human Rights Violations*, 1–30.
62. Ibid., 4.
63. Ibid., 4–5.
64. Political scientist Thomas Smith explains that the "new military technology invariably has been matched by technical virtuosity in the law. New legal interpretations, diminished ad bellum restraints, and . . . the new law of war

burnishes hi-tech campaigns and boosts public relations, even as it undercuts customary limits on the use of force and erodes distinctions between soldiers and civilians." Moreover, the "vogue today is the 'Strategic Ring Theory' of striking critical nodes of infrastructure in order to induce 'strategic paralysis' in one's enemy. International law sanctions the destruction of dual-use facilities so long as the intention is to choke off the military effort." So even though "precise targeting" may have reduced the number of civilian deaths in the midst of battle, the law sanctions infrastructural campaigns that often lead to extensive civilian deaths in the following months and years, as demonstrated by the thousands of civilian deaths in the aftermath of the aerial attacks during the first Gulf War. Smith, "New Law of War."

65. Stein, *Human Rights Violations*, 4.
66. In the sense, B'Tselem follows just war theorist Michael Walzer, "Targeted Killing and Drone Warfare," *Dissentmagazine.Org* (2013). http://www. dissentmagazine.org/online_articles/targeted-killing-and-drone-warfare (accessed October 26, 2014).
67. Khalili, *Time in the Shadows*, 241.
68. Nonetheless, B'Tselem indicates that the "military *may* have acted unlawfully at least in some cases." Stein, *Human Rights Violations*, 5.
69. Chamayou, *Manhunts*, 37.
70. Protocol Additional to the Geneva Conventions of August 12, 1949, and Relating to the Protection of Victims of International Armed Conflicts, 1977, Art. 51(3), 1125 *U.N.T.S.* 3.
71. Yoram Dinstein, *The Conduct of Hostilities under the Law of International Armed Conflict* (Cambridge: Cambridge University Press, 2004), 131. Italics added.
72. Cited in Schmitt, "Human Shields," 51.
73. Cited in ibid.
74. A. P. V. Rogers and P. Malherbe, *Fight It Right: Model Manual on the Law of Armed Conflict for Armed Forces* (Geneva: ICRC, 1999).
75. Antony Anghie, "Finding the Peripheries: Sovereignty and Colonialism in Nineteenth-Century International Law," *Harvard International Law Journal* Vol. 40 (1999), 1-71.
76. Erik Ringmar, "'How to Fight Savage Tribes': The Global War on Terror in Historical Perspective," *Terrorism and Political Violence* 25, no. 2 (2013), 264-283.; Christiane Wilke, "Civilians, Combatants, and Histories of International Law," *Critical Legal Thinking*, http://criticallegalthinking.com/2014/07/28/civilians-combatants-histories-international-law/ (accessed 01/07, 2015).
77. Mbembe, "Necropolitics." Mbembe goes on to argue that "Under Jus publicum, a legitimate war is, to a large extent, a war conducted by one state against another or, more precisely, a war between 'civilized' states. The centrality of the state in the calculus of war derives from the fact that the state is the model of political unity, a principle of rational organization, the embodiment of the idea of the universal, and a moral sign."
78. Schmitt, "Human Shields," 17–21.
79. Ibid.
80. Recently, the prohibition of using human shields has been extended to noninternational armed conflict; namely, armed conflict that is not carried out between two sovereign states as in the case of the conflict between Israel and the Palestinians.
81. Smith, "New Law of War."

CHAPTER 4

1. Regavim, *On the Perversion of Justice* (Jerusalem: Regavim, 2010).
2. On the role of the Israeli High Court of Justice in extending Israel's colonial policies see D. Kretzmer, "Targeted Killing of Suspected Terrorists: Extra-judicial Executions or Legitimate Means of Defence?" *European Journal of International Law* 16, no. 2 (2005), 171–212; Kimmerling, "Religion, Nationalism, and Democracy"; Ben-Naftali, Gross, and Michaeli, *Illegal Occupation*, 551.
3. Derek Gregory, *The Colonial Present: Afghanistan, Palestine, Iraq* (Oxford: Blackwell, 2004).
4. See chapter 1 of this book.
5. Interview with Yitzhak Rabin, *Yedioth Ahronoth*, September 3, 1993, 4.
6. Dan Izenberg, "State Attorney Rejects Har-Shefi Retrial Petition," *Jerusalem Post*, October 17, 2010.
7. After their evacuation from the Jewish settlements in Sinai, many settlers were relocated by the state in the Jewish settlements in the West Bank and Gaza. See Maha Samman Mansour, "Israeli Colonial Contraction: The Cases of the Israeli Peninsula and the Gaza Strip," working paper, Ibrahim Abu-Lughod Institute of International Studies, Birzeit University, 2011.
8. In reality, outposts are new settlements. Today, there are more than 100 outposts throughout the West Bank. Around 50 were established after March 2001. Not unlike other settlements, these outposts were established with the goal of creating a continuity of Israeli presence by taking over as much Palestinian land as possible and creating a barrier between the various Palestinian population centers. Peace Now, "Settlements and Outposts," Peace Now, http://peacenow.org.il/eng/content/settlements-and-outposts (accessed May 1, 2014); see also Talia Sasson, "Report on Unauthorized Outposts: Submitted to the Prime Minister," Prime Minister's Office (Jerusalem, 2005).
9. Dror Etkes and Hagit Ofran, *Construction of Settlements upon Private Land* (Tel-Aviv: Peace Now, 2006).
10. For an overview of the Israeli policy of house demolitions see The Israeli Committee Against House Demolitions, "Homepage," ICHAD, http://www.icahd.org (accessed May 1, 2014).
11. For a report on the lack of law enforcement in relation to settler activity see Ron Dudai, *Free Rein: Vigilante Settlers and Israel's Non-enforcement of the Law* (Jerusalem: B'Tselem, 2001); Yehezkel Lein, *The Performance of Law Enforcement Authorities in Responding to Settler Attacks on Olive Harvesters* (Jerusalem: B'Tselem, 2002).
12. For an interesting analysis of the use of human rights language by settlers during the evacuation as well as tropes from the Holocaust see Shor, "Utilizing Rights and Wrongs."
13. For an analysis of the disengagement from Gaza see Joyce Dalsheim, *Unsettling Gaza: Secular Liberalism, Radical Religion, and the Israeli Settlement Project* (Oxford: Oxford University Press, 2011); Sara M. Roy, *Failing Peace: Gaza and the Palestinian-Israeli Conflict* (London: Pluto Press, 2007).
14. On the protraction of the Israeli policies of closure in Gaza after the disengagement see Darryl Li, "The Gaza Strip as Laboratory: Notes in the Wake of Disengagement," *Journal of Palestine Studies* 35, no. 2 (2006), 38–55.
15. Ha'etzni Elyakim, "The Shock of Surrender," *Nativ: A Journal of Politics and the Arts* 10 (April 2006), http://www.acpr.org.il/ENGLISH-NATIV/10-issue/haetzni-10.htm. (accessed October 12, 2014).

16. I. Bam, Yitzhak Klein, and Shmuel Meidad, *Israeli Government Violations of Disengagement Opponents' Civil Rights* (Jerusalem: Israel Policy Center, 2005), http://www.eretzyisroel.org/~jkatz/Pinui_Final_for_Web.pdf. It is interesting to note that this publication was funded by the Norwegian Israel Center Against Anti-Semitism and the Union of Orthodox Congregations of America.

17. Ibid., i.

18. Ibid., 2. With the use of this term, Yesha clearly tries to reconnect the events of the disengagement from Gaza to the broader human rights debate on the violation of the freedom of movement of the Palestinians in the Occupied Territories. The violation of the freedom of movement is one of the key focuses of advocacy by local and international organizations. For an overall picture of this issue see the official website of the United Nations Office for the Coordination of Humanitarian Affairs in the Occupied Territories: http://www.ochaopt.org/.

19. Bam, Klein, and Meidad, *Israeli Government Violations*, 10.

20. Ibid., 36.

21. Ibid., 1.

22. Nicola Perugini, interview with Ari Briggs, August 29, 2013.

23. Neve Gordon, "The Israeli Peace Camp in Dark Times," *Peace Review* 15, no. 1 (2003), 39–45.

24. The Amona Pogrom, SOS Israel, http://www.sos-israel.com/3418.html (accessed May 2, 2014).

25. Nicola Perugini and Kareem Rabie, interview with Dror Etkes, July 18, 2010.

26. In a 2008 report, for example, Yesha for Human Rights calculated that there are more policemen per capita in the West Bank than anywhere else in Israel, that the police initiate 56 percent more investigations in the region, and that proportionally to the Jewish population in the pre-1976 borders they submit a much higher number of indictments, but, as the new rights NGO showed, the rate of convictions in the West Bank was actually much lower. All of which reveals, according to Yesha for Human Rights, that when it comes to law enforcement the settler population is discriminated against. See Yesha for Human Rights, *Law Enforcement in Judea and Samaria* (no place mentioned, 2008) (Hebrew). That same year, B'Tselem published a report reiterating the fact that in the West Bank there are two separate systems of law, which apply to persons based on their nationality—one for Palestinians and the other for Israeli settlers. Palestinians are subject to a military regime that denies many of their rights. Settlers, on the other hand, are considered by the authorities as part of the sovereign State of Israel and, as such, enjoy the same rights as the state's citizens. This division, the rights group claims, applies to every area of life, so when Palestinians harm settlers, the authorities take considerable efforts, sometimes by illegal means, and in violation of the human rights of Palestinians, to prosecute the perpetrators. Contrarily, the same authorities refrain from providing proper protection to Palestinians from physical harm and from damage to their property at the hands of Israeli civilians. B'Tselem, *Human Rights in the Occupied Territories: Annual Report* (Jerusalem: B'Tselem, 2008).

27. Nicola Perugini and Kareem Rabie, interview with Meir Deutsch, July 25, 2012.

28. Nicola Perugini and Kareem Rabie, interview with Bimkom legal expert, August 3, 2010.

29. The fact that Yael Tamir resigned from the position of chairwoman of the Association for Civil Rights in Israel (ACRI) and overnight became a minister in Ehud Barak's 1999 government reveals that the movement is not merely

between settler human rights NGOs and the government, but also from liberal human rights NGOs to the government. Tamir's relocation was not an isolated incident. The minister of police chose a leading ACRI member to head a committee investigating the rise in police violence, and ACRI's chief lawyer left his position to become the government's deputy legal advisor. Gordon, "Human Rights, Social Space and Power."

30. Nicola Perugini and Kareem Rabie, interview with Dror Etkes, July 18, 2010.
31. Nicola Perugini and Kareem Rabie, interview with Dror Etkes, July 18, 2010.
32. Nicola Perugini and Kareem Rabie, "The Human Right to the Colony," in *Shifting Borders: European Perspectives on Creolization*, ed. S. Jacoviello and T. Sbriccolo (Cambridge: Cambridge Scholars Publishing, 2012), 35–56.
33. Aeyal M. Gross, "Human Proportions: Are Human Rights the Emperor's New Clothes of the International Law of Occupation?" *European Journal of International Law* 18, no. 1 (2007), 1–35.
34. Another significant example is from Israel's protracted siege on Gaza, where the distance between state apparatuses administering the infliction of military violence and the human rights world has been progressively dwindling. In this case, Marc Garlasco, a Human Rights Watch expert who carried out investigations for the Goldstone-led international commission of enquiry about violations committed by Israel in Gaza during the 2008–2009 offensive, had previously served as a military expert for the Pentagon. At the Pentagon, Garlasco was in charge of determining the number of tolerable civilian casualties—29 civilians per bombing—for the US operations of "targeted killings" in Iraq. In Gaza he helped determine the kinds of weapons and military techniques deployed to destroy houses and kill civilians. Weizman, *Least of all Possible Evils*, 99–138.
35. Nicola Perugini and Kareem Rabie, interview with Bimkom legal expert, August 3, 2010.
36. On the multiple strategies of Israeli dispossession, at the border between legal, architectural, landscape, environmental, and other kinds of arguments consult Eyal Weizman, *Hollow Land: Israel's Architecture of Occupation* (London: Verso Books, 2012).
37. Patrick Wolfe, *Settler Colonialism* (London: Continuum, 1999); Lorenzo Veracini, *Settler Colonialism: A Theoretical Overview* (London: Palgrave Macmillan, 2010); Fiona Bateman and Lionel Pilkington, *Studies in Settler Colonialism: Politics, Identity and Culture* (London: Palgrave Macmillan, 2011).
38. Didier Fassin, *Les économies morales revisitées* (Paris: Editions de l'EHESS, 2009), 1257.
39. Didier Fassin, "A Contribution to the Critique of Moral Reason," *Anthropological Theory* 11, no. 4 (2011), 481–491.
40. Nicola Perugini, "The Moral Economy of Settler Colonialism: Israel and the Evacuation Trauma," *History of the Present* 4, no. 1 (2014), 49–74.
41. James C. Scott, *Weapons of the Weak: Everyday Forms of Peasant Resistance* (New Haven, CT: Yale University Press, 2008). For an analysis of the universe of settler's meaning in this context see Nicola Perugini, "'The Frontier Is Where the Jews Live': A Case of Israeli Democratic Colonialism," *Journal of Law and Social Research* 1, no. 1 (2009), 73–90.
42. Nicola Perugini, interview with Ari Briggs, August 29, 2013.
43. For a petition asking the state to demolish a Palestinian school village see HCJ 5083/10, Regavim and Others vs. Defense Minister and Others; and HCJ

8806/10, Regavim vs. Prime Minister and Others; for a petition demanding the destruction of a mosque see HCJ 5790/10, Regavim and Others vs. Defense Minister and Others; for the demolition of a quarry see HCJ 2407/10, Regavim and Others vs. Defense Minister and Others and villas in Husan and Birzeit see HCJ 10424/09, Regavim and Others vs. Defense Minister and Others; for a petition asking the state to demolish Bedouin houses in the Negev see HCJ 648/13, Regavim and Others vs. Prime Minister and Others. For similar petitions submitted by the Legal Forum for the Land of Israel see HCJ 4704/06, Legal Forum for the Land of Israel and Others vs. the Israeli Government and Others, HCJ 10517/08, Legal Forum for the Land of Israel vs. Defense Minister and Others.

44. Nicola Perugini, interview with Ari Briggs, August 29, 2013.

45. Dror Etkes explained how both the settlement administration and Regavim utilize the same scouts for monitoring Palestinian construction and preventing the lands controlled by the administration from being "invaded" by Palestinians. Nicola Perugini and Kareem Rabie, interview with Dror Etkes, July 18, 2010.

46. Ari Briggs, "Is Government and Supreme Court Inaction Poisoning our Children?" *Jerusalem Post*, July 15, 2012.

47. When in 2010 construction companies started to build the new Palestinian city of Rawabi, an "environmentally friendly" real estate project close to the Palestinian town of Birzeit (sponsored by the Palestinian Authority and funded by a Gulf Company and a Palestinian investor), Regavim's cofounder, Yehuda Eliyahu, immediately denounced it as a political provocation, a security threat to the State of Israel and an environmental liability: "The city's only purpose is to create territorial continuity between Ramallah and Samaria. It was planned in a rush, without proper infrastructure and without a solution for the sewage that will go flowing into the valleys. It's part of a wider move of setting up a de-facto Palestinian state." Cited in Chaim Levinson, "Settlers: New Palestinian City Will Harm Security, the Environment," *Ha'aretz*, February 24, 2010.

48. Regavim, *"There is a Solution" Program* (Jerusalem: Regavim, 2010), 3–4.

49. Ari Briggs, "He Came, He Saw, He Posted: Now He's Branded Racist," *Jerusalem Post*, April 5, 2013.

50. By the early 1950s most of the over 100,000 Palestinian Bedouin who had lived in the Negev before the establishment of Israel had fled or had been expelled to Jordan, Gaza, and Egypt. Many of the 12,000 who remained were uprooted from the lands they had inhabited for generations and resettled in the mostly barren area of the northeast Negev known as the *siyagh* (enclosure). Now cleared of Palestinians, the Negev's most fertile areas were given to new kibbutzim and moshavim. The Bedouin were subject to military rule until 1966, their movement restricted and basic rights denied. When this ended, the Bedouin still occupied too much of the Negev for the state's liking, and it decided to concentrate the population into seven semiurban townships. Most of the families who moved to the townships renounced their land rights. They also had to abandon their pastoral way of life. The townships rapidly became overcrowded and today are home to about 135,000 people; all have high unemployment rates, high birth rates, dilapidated infrastructure, and third-rate schools. Prawer's plan assumes that the Bedouin have no land rights. In the 1970s, when Israel first began to relocate them, some 3,200 petitions were filed with the Justice Ministry claiming a right to property that had belonged to Bedouin

families for generations. Two-thirds of these claims were for property belonging to individuals and the rest for land used in common for pasture. The majority of the cases have been rejected; claims over about 550,000 dunams, or 4 percent of the Negev, are still to be settled.

51. Meir Deutsch, *There Is a Solution* (Jerusalem: Regavim, 2010), 3–4. In Hebrew.
52. Regavim, "The Truth about the Bedouin," http://www.israelnationalnews.com/Articles/Article.aspx/14722#.U2EPIFePwm8 (accessed May 1, 2014).
53. Havatzelet Yahel, Ruth Kark, and Seth J. Frantzman, "Are the Negev Bedouin an Indigenous People?" *Middle East Quarterly* 19, no. 3 (2012), 3–14. For a very different perspective consult Oren Yiftachel, "Naqab/Negev Bedouins and the (Internal) Colonial Paradigm," in *Indigenous (in)Justice: Law and Human Rights among the Bedouins in the Naqab/Negev*, ed. Ahmad Amara, Ismael Abu-Saad, and Oren Yiftachel (Cambridge, MA: Harvard University Press, 2013), 289–318.
54. Benny Tocker, "Bedouin Invaders and Insolent [Hebrew]," Mako, http://www.tbk.co.il/article/2500344 (accessed April 28, 2014).
55. Regev Goldman, "Bedouin Invaders in the Coastal Region? The War Is Here," NRG, 2012 (in Hebrew), http://www.nrg.co.il/online/54/ART2/322/464.html (accessed April 28, 2014); Teni Goldstein, "Is There a Solution to the Bedouin Land Problems in the Negev?" Ynet, 2010 (in Hebrew), http://www.ynet.co.il/articles/0,7340,L-3944146,00.html (accessed April 28, 2014).
56. Migel Deutch, "Why It Is Wrong to Spray the Fields of Bedouin Invaders," *Ha'aretz*, April 26, 2007.
57. Homi K. Bhabha, *The Location of Culture* (New York: Routledge, 1994), 87–88.
58. David Lev, "Interview: Yesha Jews have Rights, Too, Says Orit Strook," Arutz Sheva, http://www.israelnationalnews.com/Controls/SendFriend.ashx?print=1&type=0&item=142562 (accessed April 28, 2014).
59. Press release, "Knesset Members to Barak: It is Prohibited to Enforce the Law Discriminately," Jerusalem, Knesset, October 18, 2008 (in Hebrew).
60. Arie Eldad, The 91st Meeting of the 18th Knesset, Jerusalem, Knesset Protocols, December 29, 2009 (in Hebrew).
61. Uri Makleb, Constitution, Law and Judicial Committee Protocol 523, Jerusalem, Knesset Protocols, November 8, 2010 (in Hebrew).
62. Ari Briggs, interview with Nicola Perugini, August 29, 2012.
63. Edmund Levy, Tchia Shapira, and Alan Baker, *Report on the Legal Status of Building in Judea and Samaria* (Jerusalem: Government of Israel 2010) (in Hebrew).
64. Hillel Fendel, "Statistics Show Police Discrimination against Yesha Jews," Arutz Sheva, http://www.israelnationalnews.com/News/News.aspx/128809#.UZPMucpOA3U (accessed April 27, 2014); Tzvi Ben Gedalyahu, "Expose: Blatant Anti-Jewish Policy in Yesha," Arutz Sheva, http://www.israelnationalnews.com/News/News.aspx/147583#.UZPP88pOA3U (accessed April 27, 2014).
65. Rafael Castro, "Settlers and Human Rights," Ynet, http://www.ynetnews.com/articles/0,7340,L-4323209,00.html (accessed April 27, 2014).
66. Efrat Weiss, "West Bank Turned into Thieves' Heaven, Says Yesha Council," Ynet, http://www.ynetnews.com/articles/0,7340,L-3473453,00.html (accessed April 27, 2014); Orit Strook, "What about Jewish Farmers?" Ynet, http://www.ynetnews.com/articles/0,7340,L-3965059,00.html (accessed April 27, 2014); Fern Sidman, "Interview: Pushing Back against Arab Land Grabs," Arutz Sheva, http://www.israelnationalnews.com/News/News.aspx/140335 (accessed April 28, 2014); Caroline Glick, "Do Jews Have Civil Rights?," *Jerusalem Post*,

http://www.jpost.com/Opinion/Columnists/Article.aspx?id=190179 (accessed April 28, 2014); Ophir Falk, Ynet, http://www.ynetnews.com/articles/ 0,7340,L-3963438,00.html (accessed April 28, 2014); Yair Altman, "Settlers Call on Ministers Not to Extend Freeze," Ynet, http://www.ynetnews.com/ articles/0,7340,L-3964337,00.html (accessed April 28, 2014); Arutz Sheva, "Legal Forum: UN should Know International Law," Arutz Sheva, http://www. israelnationalnews.com/News/Flash.aspx/196135#.UZJpQq487qs (accessed April 28, 2014).

67. During the "freeze," settlement construction continued, and any settlers who were forced to stop building were compensated by the state. The end result of the "settlement freeze" was the expansion of the settlements.

68. Karni Eldad, "Settlement Freeze Is Like Racial Segregation in U.S.," *Ha'aretz*, December 29, 2009.

69. Not by chance, in 2013 Orit Strook, the aforementioned founder of the conservative Yesha for Human Rights, won a seat in the Knesset with Naftali Bennet's "liberal" settler party HaBaiyt HaYehuda and joined the Israeli government. Strook's rapid and relatively effortless move from an oppositional position that struggles against government violations to a position within the government is due to the proximity of the settlers and the state institutions within Israeli social space. The party, which is part of the coalition, seems to be very proud of her profile as a human rights defender and therefore parades her "legal, public, and parliamentary battles against restraining orders, weapons confiscations, damage to children during expulsions, property damage during expulsions, violation of prisoners' rights, and violation of the right to protest." HaBaiyt HaYehuda, "Official Website," http://baityehudi.org.il/englp/strok.htm (accessed May 1, 2014).

CONCLUSION

1. CTV News, "Netanyahu: Jew Free Palestinian State Would Be Ethnic Cleansing," CTV News, http://www.ctvnews.ca/video?clipId=274474&playlistId= 1.1639771&binId=1.810401&playlistPageNum=1#274474 (accessed April 28, 2014).

2. For general background on the ethnic cleansing carried out in 1948 consult Morris, *Birth of the Palestinian Refugee Problem*. For background on the ethnic cleansing carried out in 1967 consult Avi Raz, *The Bride and the Dowry: Israel, Jordan, and the Palestinians in the Aftermath of the June 1967 War* (New Haven, CT: Yale University Press, 2012).

3. Yonah Jeremy Bob, "Israeli Lawyer Goes After Abbas, Hamas in ICC," *Jerusalem Post*, http://www.jpost.com/International/Israeli-lawyer-goes-after-Abbas-Hamas-in-ICC (accessed April 28, 2014).

4. Arendt, *The Origins of Totalitarianism*, 293.

5. Ibid.

6. For a cogent analysis of Arendt's ontology of human rights see Birmingham, *Hannah Arendt and Human Rights*, 45–46.

7. Benjamin, "The Task of the Translator."

8. Roth, "Defending Economic, Social and Cultural Rights," 64.

9. Ibid., 69; HRW's founding executive director also holds that the methodology should determine the organization's operations, consult Neier, *Misunderstanding our Mission*, 69.

10. Human Rights Watch, *"Between a Drone and Al-Qaeda": The Civilian Cost of US Targeted Killings in Yemen* (New York: HRW, 2013), 1.

11. Ibid.

12. Amnesty International, *"Will I Be Next?" US Drone Strikes in Pakistan* (London: Amnesty International, 2013).

13. Nitza Berkovitch and Neve Gordon, "The Political Economy of Transnational Regimes: The Case of Human Rights," *International Studies Quarterly* 52, no. 4 (2008), 881–904.

14. Barzilai, *Communities and Law*.

15. Duncan Kennedy, *Legal Education and the Reproduction of Hierarchy: A Polemic against the System* (New York: NYU Press, 2004).

16. Brown and Halley, *Left Legalism / Left Critique*.

17. Makau Mutua, *Human Rights NGOs in East Africa: Political and Normative Tensions* (Philadelphia: University of Pennsylvania Press, 2009).

18. Roth, "Defending Economic, Social and Cultural Rights," 64.

19. Gordon, "Human Rights, Social Space and Power," 24.

20. Bourdieu, *In Other Words*, 137–138.

21. Ibid.

22. Pierre Bourdieu, "Identity and Representation," in *Language and Symbolic Power*, trans. **Gino Raymond and Matthew Adamson** (Cambridge: Polity Press, 1991), 220–228.

23. Pierre Bourdieu and Loïc Wacquant, *An Invitation to Reflexive Sociology* (Cambridge: Polity, 1992).

24. Riles, "Anthropology, Human Rights."

25. Bourdieu, *The Logic of Practice*, 108.

26. Mandela, *Long Walk to Freedom*, 612.

27. This, we think, is similar to the conclusion reached by Hopgood, *Endtimes of Human Rights*, 162–182.

BIBLIOGRAPHY

Abu-Lughod, Lila. *Do Muslim Women Need Saving?* Cambridge, MA: Harvard University Press, 2013.

Achcar, Gilbert. *The Arabs and the Holocaust*. London: Saqi Books, 2009.

Adalah. *New Discriminatory Laws and Bills in Israel*. Haifa: Adalah: The Legal Center for the Arab Minority in Israel, 2012.

Agamben, Georgio. *Homo Sacer: Sovereign Power and Bare Life*. Trans. Daniel Heller-Roazen. Palo Alto, CA: Stanford University Press, 1998.

———. *L'uso dei corpi*. Vicenza, Italy: Neri Pozza, 2014.

Allen, Lori. "Getting by the Occupation: How Violence Became Normal during the Second Palestinian Intifada." *Cultural Anthropology* 23, no. 3 (2008), 453–487.

———. *The Rise and Fall of Human Rights: Cynicism and Politics in Occupied Palestine*. Palo Alto, CA: Stanford University Press, 2013.

Alston, P. and R. Goodman. *International Human Rights in Context: Law, Politics, Morals*. New York: Oxford University Press, 2007.

Amnesty International. *Military Training 101: Human Rights and Humanitarian Law*. London: Amnesty International, 2002.

———. *Universal Jurisdiction: A Preliminary Survey of Legislation around the World—2012 Update*. London: Amnesty International, 2012.

———. *"Will I Be Next?" US Drone Strikes in Pakistan*. London: Amnesty International, 2013.

Anghie, Antony. "Finding the Peripheries: Sovereignty and Colonialism in Nineteenth-Century International Law." *Harvard International Law Journal* 40 (1999), 1–71.

———. *Imperialism, Sovereignty and the Making of International Law*. Cambridge: Cambridge University Press, 2007.

Arendt, Hannah. *Eichmann in Jerusalem*. New York: Penguin, 2006.

———. *The Origins of Totalitarianism*. New York: Mariner Books, 1973.

Asad, Talal. "Reflections on Violence, Law, and Humanitarianism." *Critical Inquiry* Online Features, March 9, 2013.

———. "What Do Human Rights Do? An Anthropological Enquiry." *Theory & Event* 4, no. 4 (2000).

Association of Civil Rights in Israel (ACRI). *Knesset Database*. Jerusalem: Association of Civil Rights in Israel, 2012.

Austin, John. *How to Do Things with Words*. Cambridge, MA: Harvard University Press, 1975.

Axinn, Sidney. *A Moral Military*. Philadelphia, PA: Temple University Press, 2009.

Badr, Majd and Abeer Baker. *Exposed: The Treatment of Palestinian Detainees during Operation "Cast Lead"* Jerusalem: Public Committee Against Torture, 2010.

Balfour, Ian and Eduardo Cadava. "The Claims of Human Rights: An Introduction." *South Atlantic Quarterly* 103, no. 2 (2004), 277–296.

Bam, I., Yitzhak Klein, and Shmuel Meidad. *Israeli Government Violations of Disengagement Opponents' Civil Rights.* Jerusalem: Israel Policy Center, 2005.

Barzilai, Gad. *Communities and Law: Politics and Cultures of Legal Identities.* Ann Arbor: University of Michigan Press, 2003.

Bateman, Fiona and Lionel Pilkington. *Studies in Settler Colonialism: Politics, Identity and Culture.* London: Palgrave Macmillan, 2011.

Benford, Robert D. and David A. Snow. "Framing Processes and Social Movements: An Overview and Assessment." *Annual Review of Sociology* 26, no. 1 (2000), 611–639.

Benjamin, Walter. "The Task of the Translator." In *Illuminations,* trans. Harry Zohn, ed. Hannah Arendt, 69–82. New York: Schocken, 1968.

Ben-Naftali, Orna, Aeyal Gross, and Keren Michaeli. "Illegal Occupation: The Framing of the Occupied Palestinian Territory." *Berkeley Journal of International Law* 23 (2005), 551–614.

Bensouda, Fatou. "The Truth about the ICC and Gaza." *Guardian,* August 29, 2014.

Berkovitch, Nitza and Neve Gordon. "The Political Economy of Transnational Regimes: The Case of Human Rights." *International Studies Quarterly* 52, no. 4 (2008), 881–904.

Bhabha, Homi K. *The Location of Culture.* New York: Routledge, 1994.

Bialke, Joseph P. "Al-Qaeda and Taliban: Unlawful Combatant Detainees, Unlawful Belligerency, and the International Laws of Armed Conflict." *Air Force Law Review* 55 (2004), 1–85.

Birmingham, Peg. *Hannah Arendt and Human Rights: The Predicament of Common Responsibility.* Bloomington: Indiana University Press, 2006.

Bisharat, George E. "Courting Justice? Legitimation in Lawyering under Israeli Occupation." *Law & Social Inquiry* 20, no. 2 (1995), 349–405.

Bob, Clifford. *The Global Right Wing and the Clash of World Politics.* Cambridge: Cambridge University Press, 2012.

Bourdieu, Pierre. *In Other Words: Essays towards a Reflexive Sociology.* Trans. Matthew Adamson. Palo Alto, CA: Stanford University Press, 1990.

———. *Language and Symbolic Power* Trans. Gino Raymond and Matthew Adamson. Cambridge: Polity Press, 1991.

———. *The Logic of Practice.* Trans. Richard Nice. Palo Alto, CA: Stanford University Press, 1990.

Bourdieu, Pierre and Loïc Wacquant. *An Invitation to Reflexive Sociology.* Cambridge: Polity Press, 1992.

Braverman, Irus. "Checkpoint Watch Bureaucracy and Resistance at the Israeli/Palestinian Border." *Social & Legal Studies* 21, no. 3 (2012), 297–320.

Bricmont, Jean. *Humanitarian Imperialism: Using Human Rights to Sell War.* Delhi, India: Aakar Books, 2007.

Briggs, Ari. "Is Government and Supreme Court Inaction Poisoning Our Children?" *Jerusalem Post,* July 15, 2012.

———. "He Came, He Saw, He Posted: Now He's Branded Racist." *Jerusalem Post,* April 5, 2013.

Brown, Steven P. *Trumping Religion: The New Christian Right, the Free Speech Clause, and the Courts.* Birmingham: University of Alabama Press, 2002.

Brown, Wendy. "'The Most We Can Hope for . . .': Human Rights and the Politics of Fatalism." *South Atlantic Quarterly* 103, no. 2 (2004), 451–463.

Brown, Wendy and Janet Halley, eds. *Left Legalism / Left Critique*. Durham, NC: Duke University Press, 2002.

B'Tselem. *Human Rights in the Occupied Territories: Annual Report*. Jerusalem: B'Tselem, 2008.

———. "Learning the Lessons of the Past to Protect Gaza Civilians." Accessed August 3, 2013, http://www.btselem.org/gaza_strip/20121115_gaza_operation.

———. "Operation Cast Lead, 27 Dec. 08 to 18 Jan. 09." Accessed January 14, 2013, http://www.btselem.org/gaza_strip/castlead_operation.

———. "Testimonies of Young People from Kibbutz Zikim on Rocket Damage at the Kibbutz, 2006." Accessed August 4, 2013, http://www.btselem.org/testimonies/20121117_rockets_in_zikim.

Burke, Edmund. *Reflections on the Revolution in France: A Critical Edition*. Palo Alto, CA: Stanford University Press, 2002.

Burke, Roland. *Decolonization and the Evolution of International Human Rights*. Philadelphia: University of Pennsylvania Press, 2011.

Butler, Judith. *Parting Ways: Jewishness and the Critique of Zionism*. New York: Columbia University Press, 2012.

———. *Precarious Life: The Powers of Mourning and Violence*. London: Verso, 2006.

Buzan, Barry, Ole Wæver, and Jaap De Wilde. *Security: A New Framework for Analysis*. Boulder, CO: Lynne Rienner, 1998.

Byers, Michael. "The Law and Politics of the Pinochet Case." *Duke Journal of Comparative & International Law* 10 (1999), 415–441.

Camus, Albert. *The Just*. New York: Penguin, 1970.

Capella, Renata and Michael Sfard. *The Assassination Policy of the State of Israel*. Jerusalem: Public Committee Against Torture in Israel, 2002.

Carling, Jørgen. "Migration Control and Migrant Fatalities at the Spanish-African Borders." *International Migration Review* 41, no. 2 (2007), 316–343.

Césaire, Aimé. *Discourse on Colonialism*. New York: Monthly Review Press, 1972.

Challand, Benoît. *Palestinian Civil Society: Foreign Donors and the Power to Promote and Exclude*. London: Routledge, 2008.

Chamayou, Grégoire. *Manhunts: A Philosophical History*. Princeton, NJ: Princeton University Press, 2012.

Chandler, David. *From Kosovo to Kabul and Beyond: Human Rights and International Intervention*. Ann Arbor, MI: Pluto, 2006.

Chomsky, Noam. *The New Military Humanism: Lessons from Kosovo*. Monroe, ME: Common Courage Press, 1999.

Clark, Ann Marie. *Diplomacy of Conscience: Amnesty International and Changing Human Rights Norms*. Princeton, NJ: Princeton University Press, 2010.

Coates, Anthony Joseph. *The Ethics of War*. Manchester: Manchester University Press, 1997.

Cohen, Gerard Daniel. "The Holocaust and the 'Human Rights Revolution': A Reassessment." In *The Human Rights Revolution: An International History*, ed. Akira Iriye, Petra Goedde, and William I. Hitchcock, 53–72. Oxford: Oxford University Press, 2012.

Cohen, Stanley and Daphna Golan. "The Interrogation of Palestinians during the Intifada: Ill-Treatment, 'Moderate Physical Pressure' or Torture." B'Tselem—The Israeli Information Center for Human Rights in the Occupied Territories (Jerusalem, 1991).

Collins, John. *Global Palestine*. London: Hurst Publishers, 2011.

Conklin, Alice L. "Colonialism and Human Rights, a Contradiction in Terms? The Case of France and West Africa, 1895–1914." *American Historical Review* 103, no. 2 (1998), 419–442.

Cottin, Letty. "The Un-Jewish Assault on Richard Goldstone." *Forward* January 7, 2011.

Cover, Robert M. "Violence and the Word." *Yale Law Journal* 95, no. 8 (1986), 1601–1629.

Dalsheim, Joyce. *Unsettling Gaza: Secular Liberalism, Radical Religion, and the Israeli Settlement Project*. Oxford: Oxford University Press, 2011.

Department of Defense. *National Defense Strategy of the United States of America*. Washington, DC: Department of Defense, 2005.

Derrida, Jacques. "Force of Law: The 'Mystical Foundation of Authority.'" *Cordova Law Review* 11 (2002), 950–970.

———. *Writing and Difference*. Trans. Alan Bass. Chicago: University of Chicago Press, 1980.

Deutsch, Meir. *There Is a Solution*. Jerusalem: Regavim, 2010. In Hebrew.

Dinstein, Yoram. *The Conduct of Hostilities under the Law of International Armed Conflict*. Cambridge: Cambridge University Press, 2004.

Donnelly, Jack. *International Human Rights*. Boulder, CO: Westview Press, 2012.

———. *Universal Human Rights in Theory and Practice*. Ithaca, NY: Cornell University Press, 2003.

Dörmann, Knut. "The Legal Situation of 'Unlawful/Unprivileged Combatants'." *International Review—Red Cross* 85 (2003), 45–74.

Douzinas, Costas. *The End of Human Rights: Critical Legal Thought at the Turn of the Century*. Oxford: Hart, 2000.

———. "Humanity, Military Humanism and the New Moral Order." *Economy and Society* 32, no. 2 (2003), 159–183.

———. *Human Rights and Empire: The Political Philosophy of Cosmopolitanism*. London: Routledge, 2007.

Dowty, Alan. *Israel/Palestine*. Cambridge: Polity, 2012.

Dudai, Ron. *Free Rein: Vigilante Settlers and Israel's Non-enforcement of the Law*. Jerusalem: B'Tselem, 2001.

Dunlap, C. J., Jr. "Law and Military Interventions: Preserving Humanitarian Values in 21st Century Conflicts." Harvard University's Carr Center for Human Rights Policy, November 2001.

Elath, Eliahu. *Zionism at the UN: A Diary of the First Days*. Philadelphia, PA: Jewish Publication Society of America, 1976.

Erlich, Reuven. *Hezbollah's Use of Lebanese Civilians as Human Shields: The Extensive Military Infrastructure Positioned and Hidden in Populated Areas. From within the Lebanese Towns and Villages Deliberate Rocket Attacks Were Directed against Civilian Targets in Israel*. Tel-Aviv: Intelligence and Terrorism Information Center at the Center for Special Studies, 2006.

Esmeir, Samera. *Juridical Humanity: A Colonial History*. Palo Alto, CA: Stanford University Press, 2012.

Etkes, Dror and Hagit Ofran. *Construction of Settlements upon Private Land*. Tel-Aviv: Peace Now, 2006.

Fanon, Frantz. *The Wretched of the Earth*. Trans. Constance Farrington. New York: Grove Press, 1965.

Fassin, Didier. "A Contribution to the Critique of Moral Reason." *Anthropological Theory* 11, no. 4 (2011), 481–491.

————. *Les économies morales revisitées*. Paris: Editions de l'EHESS, 2009.

————. "The Humanitarian Politics of Testimony: Subjectification through Trauma in the Israeli-Palestinian Conflict." *Cultural Anthropology* 23, no. 3 (2008), 531–558.

Fédération Internationale des Ligues des Droits de l'Homme. *Israel, National Round Table on the International Criminal Court: "Raising Accountability of International Criminals."* France: FIDH, 2007.

Felman, Shoshana. *The Juridical Unconscious: Trials and Traumas in the Twentieth Century*. Cambridge, MA: Harvard University Press, 2002.

Forsythe, D. P. *Human Rights in International Relations*. Cambridge: Cambridge University Press, 2012.

Foucault, Michel. "Nietzsche, Genealogy, History." *Semiotexte* 3, no. 1 (1978), 78–94.

————. *Society Must Be Defended: Lectures at the Collège de France, 1975–1976*. Ed. and trans. François Ewald. New York: Macmillan, 2003.

Foucault, Michel, Graham Burchell, and Colin Gordon. *The Foucault Effect: Studies in Governmentality*. Chicago: University of Chicago Press, 1991.

Gilroy, Paul. *Race and the Right to Be Human*. Utrecht, Netherlands: Universiteit Utrecht Press, 2009.

Ginsburg, Ruthie. "Taking Pictures over Soldiers' Shoulders: Reporting on Human Rights Abuse from the Israeli Occupied Territories." *Journal of Human Rights* 10, no. 1 (2011), 17–33.

Givoni, Michal. "The Ethics of Witnessing and the Politics of the Governed." *Theory, Culture & Society* 31, no. 1 (2014), 123–142.

Golan, Dafna and Zvi Orr. "Translating Human Rights of the 'Enemy': The Case of Israeli NGOs Defending Palestinian Rights." *Law & Society Review* 46, no. 4 (2012), 781–814.

Goldstone, Richard. "Reconsidering the Goldstone Report on Israel and War Crimes." *Washington Post*, April 1, 2011.

Goldstone, R., C. Chinkin, H. Jilani, and D. Travers. *Human Rights in Palestine and Other Occupied Arab Territories: Report of the United Nations Fact Finding Mission on the Gaza Conflict*. Geneva: United Nations, 2009.

Goodale, Mark. "Introduction to 'Anthropology and Human Rights in a New Key.'" *American Anthropologist* 108, no. 1 (2008), 1–8.

————. "Toward a Critical Anthropology of Human Rights." *Current Anthropology* 47, no. 3 (2006), 485–511.

Goodale, Mark and Sally E. Merry. *The Practice of Human Rights: Tracking Law between the Global and the Local*. Cambridge: Cambridge University Press, 2007.

Gordon, Joy. "The Concept of Human Rights: The History and Meaning of Its Politicization." *Brooklyn Journal of International Law* 23 (1997), 689–737.

Gordon, Neve. "Human Rights as a Contingent Foundation: The Case of Physicians for Human Rights 1." *Journal of Human Rights* 5, no. 2 (2006), 163–184.

————. "Human Rights, Social Space and Power: Why Do Some NGOs Exert More Influence Than Others?" *International Journal of Human Rights* 12, no. 1 (2008), 23–39.

————. "Rationalising Extra-judicial Executions: The Israeli Press and the Legitimisation of Abuse." *International Journal of Human Rights* 8, no. 3 (2004), 305–324.

————. *Israel's Occupation*. Berkeley: University of California Press, 2008.

Gordon, Neve and Nitza Berkovitch. "Human Rights Discourse in Domestic Settings: How Does It Emerge?" *Political Studies* 55, no. 1 (2007), 243–266.

Gordon, Neve, Jacinda Swanson, and Joseph Buttigieg. "Is the Struggle for Human Rights a Struggle for Emancipation?" *Rethinking Marxism* 12, no. 3 (2000), 1–22.

Graham, Stephen. *Cities under Siege: The New Military Urbanism*. London: Verso, 2011.

Gramsci, Antonio. *Selections from the Prison Notebooks*. Ed. and trans. Geoffrey Nowell-Smith and Quintin Hoare. London: International Publishers, 1971.

Gregory, Derek. *The Colonial Present: Afghanistan, Palestine, Iraq*. Oxford: Blackwell, 2004.

Grewcock, Michael. "Shooting the Passenger: Australia's War on Illicit Migrants." In *Human Trafficking*, ed. Maggy Lee, 178–200. London: Routledge, 2007.

Gross, Aeyal. "Human Proportions: Are Human Rights the Emperor's New Clothes of the International Law of Occupation?" *European Journal of International Law* 18, no. 1 (2007), 1–35.

Gur, Haviv Rettig. "Goldstone to 'Post': Mandate of My Gaza Probe Has Changed." *Jerusalem Post*, July 17, 2009.

Habermas, Jürgen. *Between Facts and Norms*. Trans. William Rehg. Cambridge, MA: MIT Press, 1996.

———. "Remarks on Legitimation through Human Rights." *Modern Schoolman* 75 (1998), 87–100.

Hajjar, Lisa. *Courting Conflict: The Israeli Military Court System in the West Bank and Gaza*. Berkeley: University of California Press, 2005.

———. "Human Rights in Israel/Palestine: The History and Politics of a Movement." *Journal of Palestine Studies* 30, no. 4 (2001), 21–38.

———. "International Humanitarian Law and 'Wars on Terror': A Comparative Analysis of Israeli and American Doctrines and Policies." *Journal of Palestine Studies* 36, no. 1 (2006), 21–42.

———. "Universal Jurisdiction as Praxis." In *When Governments Break the Law: The Rule of Law and the Prosecution of the Bush Administration*, ed. N. Hussain, 87–120. New York: New York University Press, 2010.

Hammami, Rema. "Palestinian NGOs since Oslo: From NGO Politics to Social Movements?" *Middle East Report* (2000), 16–48.

Hanafi, Sari and Linda Tabar. *The Emergence of a Palestinian Globalized Elite: Donors, International Organizations, and Local NGOs*. Washington, DC: Institute of Jerusalem Studies, 2005.

Hardt, Michael and Antonio Negri. *Empire*. Cambridge, MA: Harvard University Press, 2001.

Heintze, Hans-Joachim. "On the Relationship between Human Rights Law Protection and International Humanitarian Law." *International Review of the Red Cross* 86, no. 856 (2004), 789–814.

Henkin, Louis. *The Age of Rights*. New York: Columbia University Press, 1990.

Herzberg, Anne. *NGO "Lawfare": Exploitation of Courts in the Arab-Israeli Conflict*. Jerusalem: NGO Monitor, 2010.

Hiltermann, Joost R. "Israel's Strategy to Break the Uprising." *Journal of Palestine Studies* (1990), 87–98.

Hirschkind, Charles and Saba Mahmood. "Feminism, the Taliban, and Politics of Counter-insurgency." *Anthropological Quarterly* 75, no. 2 (2002), 339–354.

Hobbes, Thomas. *Leviathan*. Ed. Richard Tuck. Cambridge: Cambridge University Press, 1991.

Hopgood, Stephen. *The Endtimes of Human Rights*. Ithaca, NY: Cornell University Press, 2013.

Human Rights Council. *Report of the Committee of Independent Experts in International Humanitarian and Human Rights Laws to Monitor and Assess Any Domestic, Legal or Other Proceedings Undertaken by Both the Government of Israel and the Palestinian Side, in the Light of General Assembly Resolution 64/254, Including the Independence, Effectiveness, Genuineness of these Investigations and Their Conformity with International Standards.* Geneva: United Nations, 2010.

———. *Report of the United Nations High Commissioner for Human Rights on the Implementation of Human Rights Council Resolutions S-9/1 and S-12/1.* Geneva: Human Rights Council, 2013.

Human Rights Watch. *"Between a Drone and Al-Qaeda": The Civilian Cost of US Targeted Killings in Yemen.* New York: HRW, 2013.

———. *Universal Jurisdiction in Europe: The State of the Art.* New York: HRW, 2006.

Ignatieff, Michael. "The Attack on Human Rights." *Foreign Affairs* 80, no. 6 (2001), 102–116.

———. *Human Rights as Politics and Idolatry.* Princeton, NJ: Princeton University Press, 2001.

Intelligence and Terrorism Information Center. *Evidence of the Use of the Civilian Population as Human Shields.* Tel-Aviv: Intelligence and Terrorism Information Center, 2009.

———. *Using Civilians as Human Shields.* Tel-Aviv: Intelligence and Terrorism Information Center, 2009.

Iriye, Akira, Petra Goedde, and William I. Hitchcock. *The Human Rights Revolution.* New York: Oxford University Press, 2012.

Jacoby, Tamar. "The Reagan Turnaround on Human Rights." *Foreign Affairs* 64 (Summer 1986), 1066–1086.

Jad, Islah. "The NGO-isation of Arab Women's Movements." *IDS Bulletin* 35, no. 4 (2004), 34–42.

James, Cyril Lionel Robert. *The Black Jacobins: Toussaint L'Ouverture and the San Domingo Revolution.* London: Penguin, 2001.

Jetschke, Anja. *Human Rights and State Security: Indonesia and the Philippines.* Philadelphia: University of Pennsylvania Press, 2010.

Kakel, Carroll P., III. *The Holocaust as Colonial Genocide: Hitler's "Indian Wars" in the "Wild East".* London: Palgrave Macmillan, 2013.

Kaleck, W. "From Pinochet to Rumsfeld: Universal Jurisdiction in Europe 1998–2008." *Michigan Journal of International Law* 30 (2009), 927–1273.

Kandiyoti, Deniz. "Old Dilemmas or New Challenges? The Politics of Gender and Reconstruction in Afghanistan." *Development and Change* 38, no. 2 (2007), 169–199.

Kasher, Asa and Amos Yadlin. "Assassination and Preventive Killing." *SAIS Review* 25, no. 1 (2005), 41–57.

———. "Military Ethics of Fighting Terror: An Israeli Perspective." *Journal of Military Ethics* 4, no. 1 (2005), 3–32.

Kaspit, Ben. "The Material from Which the Goldstone Is Made." *Ma'ariv*, January 29, 2010.

Kattan, Victor. *From Coexistence to Conquest: International Law and the Origins of the Arab-Israeli Conflict, 1891–1949.* London: Pluto Press, 2009.

Keck, Margaret E. and Kathryn Sikkink. *Activists beyond Borders: Advocacy Networks in International Politics.* Cambridge: Cambridge University Press, 1998.

Keeva, Steven. "Lawyers in the War Room." *American Bar Association Journal* 77 (1991), 52.

Kennedy, David. *The Dark Sides of Virtue: Reassessing International Humanitarianism.* Princeton, NJ: Princeton University Press, 2011.

———. *Of War and Law.* Princeton, NJ: Princeton University Press, 2009.

———. "Primitive Legal Scholarship." *Harvard International Law Journal* 27 (1986), 1–98.

Kennedy, Duncan. "The Critique of Rights in Critical Legal Studies." In *Left Legalism / Left Critique,* ed. Wendy Brown and Janet Halley, 178–226. Durham, NC: Duke University Press, 2002.

———. *Legal Education and the Reproduction of Hierarchy: A Polemic against the System.* New York: New York University Press, 2004.

Keys, Barbara. *Reclaiming American Virtue.* Cambridge, MA: Harvard University Press, 2014.

Khalidi, Muhammad Ali. "'The Most Moral Army in the World': The New 'Ethical Code' of the Israeli Military and the War on Gaza." *Journal of Palestine Studies* 39, no. 3 (2010), 6–23.

Khalili, Laleh. *Time in the Shadows: Confinement in Counterinsurgencies.* Palo Alto, CA: Stanford University Press, 2012.

Kimmerling, Baruch. *The Invention and Decline of Israeliness: State, Society, and the Military.* Berkeley: University of California Press, 2001.

———. "Religion, Nationalism, and Democracy in Israel." *Constellations* 6, no. 3 (1999), 339–363.

———. *Zionism and Territory: The Socio-Territorial Dimensions of Zionist Politics.* Berkeley: University of California Press, 1983.

Kolakowski, Leszek. "Marxism and Human Rights." *Daedalus* 112, no. 4 (1983), 81–92.

Kretzmer, David. *The Occupation of Justice: The Supreme Court of Israel and the Occupied Territories.* New York: SUNY Press, 2002.

———. "Targeted Killing of Suspected Terrorists: Extra-judicial Executions or Legitimate Means of Defence?" *European Journal of International Law* 16, no. 2 (2005), 171–212.

Lein, Yehezkel. *The Performance of Law Enforcement Authorities in Responding to Settler Attacks on Olive Harvesters.* Jerusalem: B'Tselem, 2002.

Lein, Yehezkel and Eyal Weizman. *Land Grab: Israel's Settlement Policy in the West Bank.* Jerusalem: B'Tselem, 2002.

Lemkin, Raphael. "Genocide as a Crime under International Law." *American Society of International Law* 41, no. 1 (1947), 145–151.

Levy, Edmund, Tchia Shapira, and Alan Baker. *Report on the Legal Status of Building in Judea and Samaria.* Jerusalem: Government of Israel, 2012. In Hebrew.

Lio, Shoon, Scott Melzer, and Ellen Reese. "Constructing Threat and Appropriating 'Civil Rights': Rhetorical Strategies of Gun Rights and English Only Leaders." *Symbolic Interaction* 31, no. 1 (2008), 5–31.

Mamdani, Mahmood. "A Brief History of Genocide." *Transition* 10, no. 3 (2001), 26–47.

———. *When Victims Become Killers: Colonialism, Nativism, and the Genocide in Rwanda.* Princeton, NJ: Princeton University Press, 2001.

Mandela, Nelson. *Long Walk to Freedom: The Autobiography of Nelson Mandela.* New York: Hachette Digital, 2008.

Mann, Michael. *The Dark Side of Democracy: Explaining Ethnic Cleansing.* Cambridge: Cambridge University Press, 2005.

Marx, Karl. "On the Jewish Question." In *The Marx-Engels Reader,* ed. Robert C. Tucker, 26–46. New York: W. W. Norton, 1978.

Mbembe, Achille. *Critique de la raison nègre*. Paris: La Découverte, 2013.

———. "Necropolitics." *Public Culture* 15, no. 1 (2003), 11–40.

———. *On the Postcolony*. Berkeley: University of California Press, 2001.

McMahan, Jeff. *Killing in War*. Oxford: Oxford University Press, 2009.

Meister, Robert. *After Evil: A Politics of Human Rights*. New York: Columbia University Press, 2011.

Merry, Sally Engle. "Transnational Human Rights and Local Activism: Mapping the Middle." *American Anthropologist* 108, no. 1 (2008), 38–51.

Merry, Sally Engle, P. Levitt, M. Ş Rosen, and D. H. Yoon. "Law from Below: Women's Human Rights and Social Movements in New York City." *Law & Society Review* 44, no. 1 (2010), 101–128.

Mitchell, Timothy. "The Limits of the State: Beyond Statist Approaches and Their Critics." *American Political Science Review* 85, no. 1 (1991), 77–96.

Montell, Jessica. "Operation Defensive Shield." *Tikkun*, July–August 2002.

Morris, Benny. *The Birth of the Palestinian Refugee Problem, 1947–1949*. Cambridge: Cambridge University Press, 1987.

Morrison, Diane and Justus Reid Weiner. "Curbing Enthusiasm for Universal Jurisdiction." *Publicist* 4 (2010), 1–11.

Moyn, Samuel. "Imperialism, Self-Determination, and the Rise of Human Rights." In *The Human Rights Revolution: An International History*, ed. Akira Iriye, Petra Goedde, and William I. and Hitchcock, 159–178. Oxford: Oxford University Press, 2012.

———. *The Last Utopia: Human Rights in History*. Cambridge, MA: Harvard University Press, 2010.

Mudde, Cas. *Populist Radical Right Parties in Europe*. Cambridge: Cambridge University Press, 2007.

Mutua, Makau. *Human Rights NGOs in East Africa: Political and Normative Tensions*. Philadelphia: University of Pennsylvania Press, 2009.

———. "Savages, Victims, and Saviors: The Metaphor of Human Rights." *Harvard International Law Journal* 42 (2001), 201–246.

Nagl, John A., James F. Amos, Sarah Sewall, and David H. Petraeus. *The US Army / Marine Corps Counterinsurgency Field Manual*. Chicago: University of Chicago Press, 2008.

Neier, Aryeh. "Misunderstanding our Mission." Open Global Rights, Accessed September 18, 2014, https://www.opendemocracy.net/openglobalrights/ aryeh-neier/misunderstanding-our-mission.

New Vilna Review. "Israel, Legitimacy and Human Rights: An Interview with Professor Gerald Steinberg of NGO Monitor." Accessed May, 2014, http:// www.newvilnareview.com/features/israel-legitimacy-and-human-rights-an-interview-with-professor-gerald-steinberg-of-ngo-monitor.html.

NGO Monitor. *Annual Report: A Year of Impact*. Jerusalem: NGO Monitor, 2011.

Norton, Anne. *On the Muslim Question*. Princeton, NJ: Princeton University Press, 2013.

Nossel, Suzanne. "Smart Power." *Foreign Affairs* 83, no. 2 (2004), 131–142.

Orakhelashvili, Alexander. "The Interaction between Human Rights and Humanitarian Law: Fragmentation, Conflict, Parallelism, or Convergence?" *European Journal of International Law* 19, no. 1 (2008), 161–182.

Orford, Anne. *Reading Humanitarian Intervention: Human Rights and the Use of Force in International Law*. Cambridge: Cambridge University Press, 2003.

Panikkar, Raimundo. "Is the Notion of Human Rights a Western Concept?" *Diogenes* 30, no. 120 (1982), 75–102.

Pappe, Ilan. *A History of Modern Palestine: One Land, Two Peoples*. Cambridge: Cambridge University Press, 2006.

Perugini, Nicola. "The Frontier Is Where the Jews Live": A Case of Israeli 'Democratic Colonialism.'" *Journal of Law and Social Research* 1, no. 1 (2009), 73–90.

———. "The Moral Economy of Settler Colonialism: Israel and the 'Evacuation Trauma'." *History of the Present* 4, no. 1 (2014), 49–74.

Perugini, Nicola and Kareem Rabie. "The Human Right to the Colony." In *Shifting Borders: European Perspectives on Creolization*, ed. S. Jacoviello and T. Sbriccolo, 35–56. Cambridge: Cambridge Scholars, 2012.

Pictet, Jean. *The Geneva Conventions of 12 August 1949: Geneva Convention Relative to the Protection of Civilian Persons in Time of War*. Geneva: International Committee of the Red Cross, 1958.

Playfair, Emma. *International Law and the Administration of Occupied Territories: Two Decades of Israeli Occupation of the West Bank and Gaza Strip* New York: Oxford University Press, 1992.

Pollis, Adamantia and Peter Schwab. "Human Rights: A Western Construct with Limited Applicability." In *Human Rights: Cultural and Ideological Perspectives*, ed. Adamantia Pollis, Peter Schwab, and Nigel Eltringham, 1–18. New York: Praeger, 1979.

Rancière, Jacques. "Who Is the Subject of the Rights of Man?" *South Atlantic Quarterly* 103, no. 2 (2004), 297–310.

Raz, Avi. *The Bride and the Dowry: Israel, Jordan, and the Palestinians in the Aftermath of the June 1967 War*. New Haven, CT: Yale University Press, 2012.

Redress and FIDH. *Extraterritorial Jurisdiction in the EU: A Study of the Laws and Practice in the 27 Member States of the EU*. London: Redress and FIDH, 2010.

Regavim. *"There is a Solution" Program*. Jerusalem: Regavim, 2010.

Riles, Annelise. "Anthropology, Human Rights, and Legal Knowledge: Culture in the Iron Cage." *American Anthropologist* 108, no. 1 (2006), 52–65.

Risse, Thomas, Stephen C. Ropp, and Kathryn Sikkink. *The Persistent Power of Human Rights: From Commitment to Compliance*. Cambridge: Cambridge University Press, 2013.

———. *The Power of Human Rights: International Norms and Domestic Change*. Cambridge: Cambridge University Press, 1999.

Robinson, Paul. *Ethics Education in the Military*. London: Ashgate, 2013.

Rogers, A. P. V. and P. Malherbe. *Fight It Right: Model Manual on the Law of Armed Conflict for Armed Forces*. Geneva: ICRC, 1999.

Roht-Arriaza, N. "The Pinochet Precedent and Universal Jurisdiction" *New England Law Review* 35 (2000), 311–320.

Ron, James, Eric Goldstein, and Cynthia Brown. *Torture and Ill-Treatment: Israel's Interrogation of Palestinians from the Occupied Territories*. New York: Human Rights Watch, 1994.

Roth, Kenneth. "Defending Economic, Social and Cultural Rights: Practical Issues Faced by an International Human Rights Organization." *Human Rights Quarterly* 26, no. 1 (2004), 63–73.

Rothberg, Michael. *Multidirectional Memory: Remembering the Holocaust in the Age of Decolonization*. Palo Alto, CA: Stanford University Press, 2009.

Roy, Arundhati. *War Talk*. Boston: South End Press, 2003.

Roy, Sara M. *Failing Peace: Gaza and the Palestinian-Israeli Conflict*. London: Pluto Press, 2007.

Sadat, L. N. and J. Geng. "On Legal Subterfuge and the So-Called Lawfare Debate." *Case Western Reserve Journal of International* 43 (2010), 153–162.

Sa'di, Ahmad H. and Lila Abu-Lughod. *Nakba: Palestine, 1948, and the Claims of Memory.* New York: Columbia University Press, 2007.

Said, Edward. "Nationalism, Human Rights, and Interpretation." *Raritan* 12, no. 3 (1993), 26–51.

———. *The Question of Palestine.* New York: Vintage Books, 1980.

Samson, Elizabeth. *Warfare through Misuse of International Law.* Bar Ilan University, Israel: BESA Center, 2009.

Sasson, Talia. "Report on Unauthorized Outposts: Submitted to the Prime Minister." Jerusalem, Prime Minister's Office (2005).

Schabas, William. "The Contribution of the Eichmann Trial to International Law." *Leiden Journal of International Law* 26, no. 3 (2013), 667–699.

Schmitt, Michael. "Human Shields in International Humanitarian Law." *Israel Yearbook on Human Rights* 38 (2008), 17–59.

Scott, James C. *Weapons of the Weak: Everyday Forms of Peasant Resistance.* New Haven, CT: Yale University Press, 2008.

Scott, Joan Wallach. *The Politics of the Veil.* Princeton, NJ: Princeton University Press, 2009.

Sfard, Michael. "The Price of Internal Legal Opposition to Human Rights Abuses." *Journal of Human Rights Practice* 1, no. 1 (2009), 37–50.

Shafir, Gershon. *Land, Labor and the Origins of the Israeli-Palestinian Conflict, 1882–1914.* Berkeley: University of California Press, 1989.

Shnayderman, Ronen and Shaul Vardi. *Take No Prisoners: The Fatal Shooting of Palestinians by Israeli Security Forces during "Arrest Operations."* Jerusalem: B'Tselem, 2005.

Shor, Eran. "Conflict, Terrorism, and the Socialization of Human Rights Norms: The Spiral Model Revisited." *Social Problems* 55, no. 1 (2008), 117–138.

———. "Utilizing Rights and Wrongs: Right-Wing, the 'Right' Language, and Human Rights in the Gaza Disengagement." *Sociological Perspectives* 51, no. 4 (2008), 803–826.

Simmons, Beth A. *Mobilizing for Human Rights: International Law in Domestic Politics.* Cambridge: Cambridge University Press, 2009.

Sissons, Miranda. *In a Dark Hour: The Use of Civilians during IDF Arrest Operations.* New York: Human Rights Watch, 2002.

Sivan, Eyal and Rony Brauman. *The Specialist: Portrait of a Modern Criminal.* New York: Home Vision Entertainment, 2002.

Smith, Thomas W. "The New Law of War: Legitimizing Hi-Tech and Infrastructural Violence." *International Studies Quarterly* 46, no. 3 (2002), 355–374.

Snetsinger, John. *Truman, the Jewish Vote, and the Creation of Israel.* Palo Alto, CA: Hoover Press, 1974.

Snow, David A. and Robert D. Benford. "Ideology, Frame Resonance, and Participant Mobilization." *International Social Movement Research* 1, no. 1 (1988), 197–217.

Spijkerboer, Thomas. "The Human Costs of Border Control." *European Journal of Migration and Law* 9, no. 1 (2007), 127–139.

State of Israel. *The Operation in Gaza: Factual and Legal Aspects.* Jerusalem: Ministry of Foreign Affairs, 2009.

Stein, Yael. *Human Rights Violations during Operation Pillar of Defense 14–21 November 2012.* Jerusalem: B'Tselem, 2013.

———. *Human Shield: Use of Palestinian Civilians as Human Shields in Violation of High Court of Justice Order.* Jerusalem: B'Tselem, 2002.

Steinberg, Gerald. "NGOs Make War on Israel." *Middle East Quarterly* 11, no. 3 (2004), 13–25.

Steinberg, Gerald and Anne Herzberg, eds. *The Goldstone Report "Reconsidered": A Critical Analysis*. Jerusalem: NGO Monitor and the Jerusalem Center for Public Affairs, 2011.

Strenger, Carlo. "Richard Goldstone's Changed Mind on Israel Should Lead to Official Retraction." *Guardian*, April 4, 2011.

United Nations. Convention on the Prevention and Punishment of the Crime of Genocide. A/P.V. 179 United Nations (December 9, 1948, a).

———. *Gaza: Initial Rapid Assessment*. East Jerusalem: United Nations Office for the Coordination of Humanitarian Affairs, Occupied Palestinian Territory, 2014.

United Nations Assistance Mission in Afghanistan. *Annual Report 2012: Protection of Civilians in Armed Conflict*. Geneva: United Nations, 2013.

Van den Eynde, Laura. "An Empirical Look at the Amicus Curiae Practice of Human Rights NGOs before the European Court of Human Rights." *Netherlands Quarterly of Human Rights* 31, no. 3 (2013), 271–313.

Van Houtum, Henk and Freerk Boedeltje. "Europe's Shame: Death at the Borders of the EU." *Antipode* 41, no. 2 (2009), 226–230.

Veracini, Lorenzo. *Settler Colonialism: A Theoretical Overview*. London: Palgrave Macmillan, 2010.

Wæver, Ole. "Securitization and Desecuritization." In *On Security*, ed. Ronnie D. Lipschutz, 46–86. New York: Columbia University Press, 1998.

Walzer, Michael. "Targeted Killing and Drone Warfare." *Dissentmagazine.Org* (2013).

Weiner, Justus Reid. "Human Rights in the Israeli Administrated Areas during the Intifada: 1987–1990." *Wisconsin International Law Journal* 10 (1991), 185–222.

Weizman, Eyal. *Hollow Land: Israel's Architecture of Occupation*. London: Verso, 2012.

———. *The Least of All Possible Evils: Humanitarian Violence from Arendt to Gaza*. London: Verso, 2012.

———. "Lethal Theory." *Roundtable: Research Architecture* (2006).

———. "Walking through Walls." *Radical Philosophy* 136 (2006), 8–22.

Williams, Michael C. "Hobbes and International Relations: A Reconsideration." *International Organization* 50 (1996), 213–236.

Williams, Jody. *My Name Is Jody Williams: A Vermont Girl's Winding Path to the Nobel Peace Prize*. Berkeley: University of California Press, 2013.

Williams, Randall. *The Divided World: Human Rights and Its Violence*. Minneapolis: University of Minnesota Press, 2010.

Wolfe, Patrick. *Settler Colonialism*. London: Continuum, 1999.

World Bank. *Twenty-Seven Months: Intifada, Closures and Palestinian Economic Crisis*. Jerusalem: World Bank, 2003.

Yahel, Havatzelet, Ruth Kark, and Seth J. Frantzman. "Are the Negev Bedouin an Indigenous People?" *Middle East Quarterly* 19, no. 3 (2012), 14.

Yakobson, Alexander and Amnon Rubinstein. *Israel and the Family of Nations: The Jewish Nation-State and Human Rights*. London: Routledge, 2008.

Yiftachel, Oren. *Ethnocracy: Land and Identity Politics in Israel/Palestine*. Philadelphia: University of Pennsylvania Press, 2006.

———. "Naqab/Negev Bedouins and the (Internal) Colonial Paradigm." In *Indigenous (in)Justice: Law and Human Rights among the Bedouins in the Naqab/Negev*, ed. Ahmad Amara, Ismael Abu-Saad, and Oren Yiftachel, 289–318. Cambridge, MA: Harvard University Press, 2013.

———. "Planning and Social Control: Exploring the Dark Side." *Journal of Planning Literature* 12, no. 4 (1998), 395–406.

Yiftachel, Oren and Haim Yacobi. "Urban Ethnocracy: Ethnicization and the Production of Space in an Israeli Mixed City'." *Environment and Planning D* 21, no. 6 (2003), 673–694.

Yoav, Dotan. "Do the Haves Still Come Out Ahead—Resource Inequalities in Ideological Courts: The Case of the Israeli High Court of Justice." *Law & Society Review* 33, no. 2 (1999), 319–363.

Zertal, Idith. *Israel's Holocaust and the Politics of Nationhood.* Cambridge: Cambridge University Press, 2005.

Zolo, Danilo. *Terrorismo umanitario: Dalla guerra del Golfo alla strage di Gaza.* Rome: Diabasis, 2009.

INDEX

Illustrations are indicated by italicized page numbers.

proportionality principle and, 97
Yemen, US drone attacks in, 131
Civilizing mission of colonialism, 15
Clausewitz, Carl von, 62
Coalition for Women for Just Peace,
157n77
Coalition to Stop Gun Violence, 10
Cohen, Daniel, 31
Colonialism. *See also* British colony of
Palestine; Dispossession; Right
to colonize
founding violence necessary for
peace, 79
hierarchy of humans in, 18
human rights used to advance and
legitimate, 15, 16, 23, 37, 47,
149n32, 158n94. *See also*
Domination
IHL legacies of, 98–100
validation by Palestinian interaction with Israeli courts and
military, 41
Conklin, Alice, 24
Conservative NGOs, 6. *See also*
Regavim; Yesha for Human
Rights
appropriation of human rights
discourse by, 22. *See also*
Appropriation of human
rights discourse
characterizing liberal NGOs as
national security threat, 25,
47, 51, 54–59, 61
convergence with liberals in use of
human rights discourse. *See*
Convergence in use of human
rights discourse
fighting to make government
adhere to ethnocratic
commitments, 123
Context-driven human rights, 17–18,
22
Convention on the Prevention and
Punishment of the Crime of
Genocide (1948), 28
Convergence in use of human rights
discourse
liberals and conservatives, 5–7, 12,
22, 53, 98
right to dominate and, 127

right to kill and, 80, 94–98
settlers and liberal NGOs and Civil
Administration, 111,
114–116
Crimes against humanity, 26, 37, 50,
56, 128, 148n24
Cultural relativists, 158n94

The Dark Sides of Virtue (Kennedy), 72,
77
Decolonization, 29, 98, 127, 148n24
*De Indis Noviter Inventis and De Jure
Bellis Hispanorum in Barbaros*
(Francisco de Vitoria), 74
Democracy's development in Europe,
145n83
Demolition
of Jewish homes. *See* Evacuation of
Jewish outposts
of Palestinian homes. *See*
Dispossession
Denmark, freedom of expression in, 5
"Denunciation routine," 47
Depoliticized original of human rights
declarations and conventions, 17
Dershowitz, Alan, 50, 60
Detention without due process, 18, 40,
41, 107, 133
Deutsch, Meir, 112–113
Dignity, 7, 13, 29, 33
Dinstein, Yoram, 97
Discourse on Colonialism (Césaire),
147–148n24
Dispossession
in colonization process (generally),
23
human rights to protect against, 34
moral economy of settler
colonialism, 112
Israeli Jews at risk for, 101. *See also*
Evacuation of Jewish
outposts; Regavim; Settler
human rights NGOs
of Palestinians and demolitions of
their homes, 25, 40, 105, 117,
133, 165–166n43
Bedouins viewed as invaders,
120–123
economy of human rights and,
70

Dispossession (*continued*)
    environmental justification for,
        119
    forms of dispossession, 115
    geographic nonrecognition of
        Bedouin villages in Negev,
        120
    Holocaust as justification for, 37,
        47. *See also* Holocaust
    Israeli courts as arbiters of, 41,
        115
    liberal human rights NGOs
        focusing on, 45
    Regavim petitions seeking. *See*
        Regavim
Doctors Without Borders, 45–46, 73
Domination. *See also* Colonialism
    asymmetry in, 69, 83, 88, 99,
        137
    defined, 3
    economy of, 70
    human rights and, 10, 12–13, 118
        appropriation of. *See*
            Appropriation of human
            rights discourse
        continued life and redefinition of
            human rights, 129
        defining who can be subjected to
            legitimate killing, 100. *See*
            also Right to kill
        Eichmann trial's role, 35–36
        hydraulic model of human
            rights, 13–15, 129
        legitimization of domination,
            16, 19, 21, 24, 43, 47, 80,
            128, 137
        perpetuation by reshaping
            culture of, 14
        reinstituted in
            counterdomination, 129,
            138
        treating violations as separate
            cases, 133
    normalizing, 37, 43–47
        court cases and, 45
        evidence production methods
            and, 46
        mental health approach to effect
            of human rights violations
            and, 46

    military checkpoint
        bureaucratization and, 45
    violence associated with, 3, 98–100,
        133. *See also* Violence
    Western culture's goal of, 15–16
Donnelly, Jack, 14, 27
Douzinas, Costas, 6
Drone use, 99, 131–132, 136

East Timor tribunal, 56
Eban, Abba, 37, 47, 149n44
Economy of human rights, 15, 70
Egypt, decolonization of, 29
Eichmann trial, 24, 34–36, 149n34
Elath, Eliahu, 32–33
Elites, 137
Eliyahu, Yehuda, 166n47
Empowerment of the weak, 13–15, 129
    participation by those who have
        been wronged, 134
Eng, David L., 149n32
Environmental issues, 119
Epistemic framework, human rights as,
    12–13
Equality issues, 14, 27, 64, 101–102,
    106, 118
Esmeir, Samera, 29
Ethical use of violence. *See* Violence
Ethnic cleansing, 105, 106, 127–128,
    145n83
Ethnicity and value of life, 23
Etkes, Dror, 111, 114–115, 166n45
European Court of Human Rights, 7,
    20, 56
Evacuation of Jewish outposts,
    105–108, *107*, 110–111
    relocation of settlers from Sinai in
        West Bank and Gaza, 163n7
Evidence of the Use of the Civilian
    Population as Human Shields
    (ITIC), 83–84
Evidence production methods, 46–47,
    90, 91, 107, 112
Existential threats, 59–61, 156n61
Experts
    lawyers' unique human rights
        expertise, 134
    organic legal experts, 56, 151n60
    vilification for criticizing Israeli
        tactics, 50, 153n11, 153n13

Inter-American Court of Human
Rights, 56
International Commission of Jurists,
6, 39
International Committee of the Red
Cross, 11, 97–98
International Court of Justice (ICJ),
56, 58, 61
International Criminal Court (ICC), 20,
56, 58, 61, 128, 155n42. *See also*
Rome Statute
International humanitarian law (IHL)
arbitrary and discriminatory
conduct not in accordance
with, 131
human shields and, 81–83
in justification of state violence
against civilians, 91, 97
lawfare using, 56
legitimate vs. illegitimate
application of, 62, 98
merged with international human
rights law, 11
Operation Pillar of Cloud (2012)
and, 67, 95
relationship with war, 71–72
settlements opposition using, 110
unlawful combatants and, 18
International human rights law
arbitrary and discriminatory
conduct not in accordance
with, 131
in Israel/Palestine situation, 24
lawfare using, 56
legitimate vs. illegitimate
application of, 62
merged with international
humanitarian law, 11
to secure rights of the weak, 14
state sovereignty restricted by, 14,
27
war, relationship with, 71–72
International juridical humanity,
29–30
International law. *See also*
International humanitarian law;
International human rights law
Eichmann abduction and, 34
extraterritoriality of, 55. *See also*
Universal jurisdiction

favoring high-tech states, 23
human rights NGOs' use of,
57–58
right to colonize and, 102
right to kill and, 25, 73, 80
state power and, 23, 27
weapons use and, 23, 67
International Refugee Organization,
31
International Security Assistance
Force, 1
International Society for Human
Rights, 8
International solidarity, 138
Inversions, 8–10
between colonizer and colonized,
123, 127
in Israel/Palestine, 21–22
by settler human rights NGOs, 112,
117, 120
Iraq-Iran war, 98
Iraq war
human shielding in, 98
legitimizing and justifying, 5
sovereign violence in, 79
Iron Dome system (Israel), 88,
161n50
Islamophobia, 8, 141n32
Israel. *See also* History of human rights
in Israel; Israel/Palestine;
headings starting "Israeli"
Associations Law, 63
creation of
as destruction of Palestinian
settlements, 33
as reparation for human rights
violations, 24, 30–34, 47,
148n25. *See also* Holocaust
ethnocentric nationalism in, 35, 69
Income Tax Ordinance, 63
lawfare suits against, 56
pre-*Eichmann* trial "selective
amnesia" toward Holocaust,
36
testimonies provided by Israelis
in Operation Pillar of Cloud,
68
Israel Defense Forces (IDF)
aid delegations from, serving all
around the world, 73

Israel Defense Forces (IDF) (*continued*)
  evacuation of Jewish outposts by,
    110. *See also* Evacuation of
    Jewish outposts
  house vs. home defined by, 84–85
  on human rights and
    humanitarianism, 73
  human shields, use of, 82
  Intelligence and Terrorism
    Information Center. *See*
    Intelligence and Terrorism
    Information Center
  posters, 73, 74. *See also* Posters
  social media use by, 84, 89, 95–96
Israeli attitude toward human rights
  organizations, 63–64
*Israeli Government Violations of
  Disengagement Opponents' Civil
  Rights* (Yesha for Human Rights
  et al.), 106–108
Israeli High Court of Justice, 41, 45,
  65, 67, 82–83, 101–104, 110,
  114, 117–119, 122, 152n8,
  163n2
Israeli Ministry of Defense, 83
Israeli Ministry of Environment, 119
Israeli Ministry of Foreign Affairs, 50,
  61, 62, 90, 91
Israeli Ministry of Justice, 166n50
Israeli Security Agency. *See* Shabak
Israel/Palestine. *See* British colony of
  Palestine; Colonialism;
  Dispossession; Domination;
  Palestinians; Right to colonize;
  Right to kill
Israel Yearbook on Human Rights
  (Schmitt), 98
Italian courts exercising universal
  jurisdiction, 56
ITIC. *See* Intelligence and Terrorism
  Information Center
Izz Al-Din Al-Qassam Brigades, 66

Jabari, Ahmad, 66
Jaber, Salim Bin Ali, 131
Jaber, Walid bin Ali, 131
Jerusalem Post op-ed on environmental
  issues, 119
Jewish Agency, 32
Jews. *See also* Holocaust; Law of Return

in Nazi Germany, 18. *See also*
  Holocaust
Palestinians displacing as victims of
  human rights violations, 42
as perpetual victims of human
  rights violations, 22, 37, 106
post-Holocaust Jews as refugees, 31
privileged in Israel over non-Jews,
  35
Juridical humanity, 29
Jus in bello, 11
Justice, advanced by human rights
  discourse, 25, 28, 129, 138

Kasher, Asa, 75, 159n14
Kattan, Victor, 148n25
Kennedy, David, 71, 75, 77, 80
Kennedy, Duncan, 10
Khalili, Laleh, 11, 80–81
Killing. *See* Civilian casualties; Right to
  kill
Kirshenbaum, Fania, 63
Knesset
  antidemocratic bills (2009–2013),
    63
  Constitution, Law and Judicial
    Committee, 124
  inquiry into funding of liberal
    rights groups, 62–63
  Regavim's lobbying of, 117
Koran, 5
Kosovo, NATO intervention in, 140n10

Law and litigation. *See also* Israeli High
    Court of Justice
  colonialism and, 24
  conduct of war and, 11
  creating false symmetry between
    colonizer and colonized, 115
  Human Rights Watch not pursuing
    litigation, 130
  ideological crime of
    antidisengagement
    protestors, 108
  legalistic approach to human rights
    advantages of, 133
    impoverishment of, 134
  nonlegal perspective as means to
    liberate human rights
    discourse, 136–137

Palestinian NGOs filing lawsuits in Israeli courts and international tribunals, 40, 41. *See also* Lawfare

nature of suits obscuring structural underpinnings of domination, 45

Regavim petitions to force displacement of Palestinians, 115, 118–119, 165–166n43

universal jurisdiction, 55–56

Law enforcement

discriminatory allegations used by both settler and liberal NGOs, 111–112, 124, 164n26

evacuation of Jewish outposts by, 105–108, *107*, 110–111

petitions against "lack of law enforcement," 101, 115, 120

Regavim's mission to address void in, 113, 117, 119

Lawfare, 51, 54–59, 155n41

African and Latin American officials and, 156n48

defined, 55, 58

as form of terrorism, 61–64

Israeli conservative response to, 61–62, 109–110

universal jurisdiction and, 55–56, 58

Law of Return, 31, 35, 147n20

Lawyers

unique human rights expertise of, 134

working with military on decisions affecting combat, 75–76, 96

Lebanon War (2006), 83

Lefever, Ernest, 142n37

Legal Forum for the Land of Israel, 103, 117, 126

Lemkin, Raphael, 27

Le Pen, Marine, 5

Levy, Edmund, 125

Levy Commission, 125

Liberal NGOs, 10. *See also* B'Tselem

becoming part of the system and working within the system, 45–46

characterized as national security threat, 25, 47, 51, 54–59, 61

fighting excesses arising from state's Jewish character, 123

focus after Second Intifada, 45

human rights discourse of, 22. *See also* Convergence in use of human rights discourse

authoritarian appropriation, 19. *See also* Appropriation of human rights discourse

on human shields, 82

international law invoked by, 23

lawsuits by, using universal jurisdiction, 58. *See also* Universal jurisdiction

psychological discourse of, 46

systematizing evidence production, 46–47

Liberia, 98

Lieberman, Avigdor, 61

Likud, 63

Litigation. *See* Law and litigation

Local context, human rights within, 17–18, 22

Locke, John, 149n32

Ma'ariv article attacking Goldstone Report, 60

Mada: The Palestinian Center for Development and Media Freedoms, 157n77

Mamdani, Mahmood, 32, 148n24

Mandela, Nelson, 3, 137

Mann, Michael, 145–146n83

Mavi Marmara (Turkish ship), 76

Mbembe, Achille, 78, 79, 143n49, 162n77

Media coverage of human rights abuses, 39, 40, 125–126, 150n46

Meir, Golda, 151n65

Mental health support in OPT, 46

Merry, Sally, 17

Middle East Watch, 39

Military. *See also* Israel Defense Forces (IDF); headings starting with "Operation"

checkpoints in OPTs, 44, 45

humanitarian endeavors of, 4

human rights training of, 11, 71–72, 75, 80

human shields used in. *See* Human shields

liberal NGOs focused on Israeli human rights violations in. *See* B'Tselem; Liberal NGOs

mental health support in, 46

military operations in. *See headings starting with "Operation"*

transformation into restricted military zones (2002), 44

withdrawal from (1967) equated to Holocaust's persistence, 37

On the Jewish Question (Marx), 15

On the Law of War and Peace (Grotius), 74

On the Perversion of Justice (Regavim), 101

On the Postcolony (Mbembe), 79

Operation Cast Lead (2008–2009), 48–51, 67, 68, 83, 90, 91, 99
   investigations following, 152–153n8, 165n34. *See also* Goldstone Report

Operation Condor (1975), 56

Operation Defensive Shield (2002), 44, 82

Operation of Protective Edge (2014), 20, 81, 84–90, 99

Operation Pillar of Cloud (2012), 66–69, 94–95, 99

OPTs. *See* Occupied Palestinian Territories

Orford, Anne, 145n78

Organic legal experts, 56, 151n60

"Original" of human rights
   illusion of, 15–19, 53
   translation of, 17, 19

"Original state," Regavim's construction of, 122

Origins of Totalitarianism (Arendt), 16, 128, 147n24

Oslo Accords (1993), 40, 103

Oslo settlers, 104

"Other," 145n78

Paiss, Naomi, 157n77

Pakistan, US drone attacks in, 131

Palestinian Authority
   coordinating with Palestinian NGOs, 40
   creation of, 103
   failure to sign Rome Statute, 20

Palestinians. *See also* Hamas; Occupied Palestinian Territories
   Bedouins as indigenous population, 120–123
   boycott, divestment, and sanctions (BDS) movement of, 138
   casualties of. *See* Civilian casualties
   displacing Jews as victims of human rights violations, 42
   dispossession and demolitions of homes of. *See* Dispossession
   globalization of situation of, 40
   as human shields. *See* Human shields
   liberal NGOs advocating for. *See also* B'Tselem; Liberal NGOs
   outposts in southern Negev of, 112–116, *113*, 118, 120–123, 166–167n50
   portrayal by settler human rights NGOs, 22
   as stateless persons, 41
   testimonies of, 68, 90–94
   as threat to human rights of Israeli Jews, 37, 117–118
   as victims of colonial abuse, 16, 38–40

Paris Declaration Respecting Maritime Law (1856), 74

Participation by those who have been wronged, 134

Peace Now, 110, 115

Peres, Shimon, 50

Philippines, Typhoon Haiyan assistance from Israel for, 73

Physicians for Human Rights USA, 39

Pictet, Jean, 82

Pinochet, Augusto, 56

Politicization of human rights, 12, 17–19, 51–69
   defined, 52
   existential threats and, 59–61, 156n61
   Human Rights Watch's choice to reject, 130
   "illusion of the original" and, 53

Right to dominate. *See* Domination

Right to education, 18

Right to kill, 25, 71–100

　assassination as protection for citizens of state, 75, 151*n*65

　colonial legacies and, 98–100

　human rights and

　　convergence with, 80, 94–98

　　dominant allowed to kill, 133

　　military training, 71–72

　human shields, 81–84, 97–98. *See also* Human shields

　international humanitarian law used to justify killing of Palestinian civilians, 25

　moral killing, 73–77, 80. *See also* Violence, ethical use of

　not to breach international humanitarian and human rights law, 80

　Operation Protective Edge (2014), 84–90

　social contract and, 78–79

　sovereign right, 77–81, 91

　war conventions, 74. *See also* Geneva Conventions

Right to life, 75

Right to movement, restrictions on, 44, 45, 107, 164*n*18, 166*n*47

Right to property, 18, 166*n*50

Rome Statute, 56, 81

Roth, Kenneth, 130–131

Roy, Arundhati, 4

Rubinstein, Amnon, 31

Rule of law, 57, 132

Rumsfeld, Donald, 56

Russia's antigay law, 6

Rutherford Institute, 6

Rwanda

　international law, applicability of, 99

　tribunal (1994), 56

Said, Edward, 25, 26, 58

St. Petersburg Declaration (1868), 74

Samson, Elizabeth, 57

Scandinavia, anti-immigrant policies of, 140*n*19

Schabas, William, 149*n*34

Schmitt, Michael, 98–99

Second-generation human rights, 19

Second Intifada (2000), 24–25, 43

　human shields and, 82

　trauma discourse used in, 45–46

Self-censorship, 51

Self-determination, 29–30

　in British colony of Palestine, 31, 32

　human rights of Palestinians and, 39

　UN resolutions and, 38

"Semiotic warfare," 58

Senegal, training of military in laws of war and human rights in, 71

Settlement freeze, 104, 126, 168*n*67

Settlement Watch, 110

Settler human rights NGOs, 22, 101–102. *See also* Regavim; Right to colonize; Yesha for Human Rights

　creation and strategies of, 102, 105

　framing settlement as human right, 117, 124

　Jewish outposts and, 104–106

　lawsuits to stop outpost evacuations, 106–107

　universal pretensions of, 24

Sewall, Sarah, 75

Sfard, Michael, 43

Shabak (Israeli Security Agency), 91–94, 100, 108, 113

Shalit, Gilad, 94

Sharon, Ariel, 57, 106

Shas (religious party), 124

Shurat HaDin, 128

Sierra Leone

　human shielding in, 98

　tribunal, 56

Slavery as protection of inferior humanity, 143*n*49

Smart power, 4

Smith, Thomas, 99, 161–162*n*64

Social contract theory, 78–79

Social media use by Israeli military, 84, 89, 95–96

Social space, 12, 76, 117, 159*n*20, 168*n*69

Somalia

　human shielding in, 98

　US drone attacks in, 131

SOS Israel, 110

South Africa's anti-apartheid struggle
  as struggle to change laws and
    social practices, 14
  violence in, 3
Sovereign power, 84
Sovereign right to kill, 77–81, 91
Spain seeking extradition of Pinochet,
  56
State-building of Palestinians. *See*
  Palestinian Authority
State Department, US
  evaluation of human rights records
    by, 141–142*n*37
  personnel moving to Amnesty
    International from, 76–77,
    159–160*n*20
Stateless persons, 29. *See also* The weak
  Palestinians as, 41
State power
  economy of human rights and, 15
  human rights and
    decentralized state power, 20
    as limit and restraint on, 14, 27,
      128
    operating in service of, 15, 28,
      69–70
    state as violating entity, 29
  international law and, 23, 27
  in post-World War II human rights
    regime, 20–21, 27–28
  right to kill and, 77–81, 162*n*77
  sovereign power, 84, 128–129
Steinberg, Gerald, 51, 52, 54, 55, 60
Steinitz, Youval, 50
Strategic Ring Theory, 162*n*64
Strook, Orit, 104–105, 123–124,
  168*n*69
Subsidiarity, 65
Sudan, 99
Swiss People's Party, 8, *9*
Symbolic power of human rights, 135
Syria
  failure to adhere to liberal
    humanitarian and human
    rights principles, 81
  international law, applicability of,
    99

Tamir, Yael, 164–165*n*29
Tea Party (US), 7

Terrorism, 61–64. *See also* War on
  terror
This World: The Values Network, 87
Threat of human rights, 48–70, 103
  characterized as national security
    threat, 25, 47, 51, 54–59, 61,
    69
  existential threats, 59–61
  Operation Cast Lead (2008–2009)
    and Goldstone Report (2009)
    and, 48–51. *See also*
    Goldstone Report
  politicization, 17–19, 51–69. *See also*
    Politicization of human
    rights
Torture, 18, 41, 55, 56, 81, 94, 133
Translation of human rights, 17, 19
Trauma discourse, 45–46
Truman, Harry S, 33
The Truth about the Negev Bedouin
  (Regavim), 122
Typhoon Haiyan assistance from Israel
  for Philippines, 73

Union of Orthodox Congregations of
  America, 164*n*16
United Kingdom's Manual of the Law
  of Armed Conflict, 97
United Nations
  adopting reports of political NGOs,
    58
  advocating violence to protect
    human rights, 3–4
  on Afghani fatalities in Afghanistan
    war, 139*n*1
  British colony of Palestine, creation
    of Israel out of, 31
  condemning Israel's rights-abusive
    policies, 38
  convergence of liberals with
    conservatives in use of
    human rights in, 53
  Economic and Social Council, 52
  General Assembly resolution "The
    Right of Peoples and Nations
    to Self-Determination," 30
  Goldstone Report on Operation
    Cast Lead damages in Gaza
    (2008–2009). *See* Goldstone
    Report

Human Rights Council, 49, 52, 61,
152n8
monitoring accountability and
transparency of, 53
on Operation Pillar of Cloud (2012),
66
Special Committee on Palestine
(UNSCOP), 33
United States
Air Force on human shields, 97
drone attacks by US military,
131–132
lawfare suits against, 56
lawyers as consultants on decisions
affecting combat, 75
military training in human rights,
11, 72
opposition to ICC, 56
prohibition on new settlements in
OPT and. *See* Settlement freeze
war on terror and, 56–57
Universal Declaration of Human Rights
(1948), 6, 10, 26, 27–28, 29, 31
Universal human rights
creation of new states and, 29
of evacuated Jewish settlers, 106
within local contexts, 17–18, 22
in opposition to liberal human
rights NGOs, 69
"symbolic" universal, 22–23
Universal jurisdiction, 55–56, 58,
154–155n34
Eichmann trial and, 149n34
NIF opposition to, 64–65
Unlawful combatants, 18
UN Watch, 52
Urban areas as arenas of contemporary
warfare, 82, 84, 85, 92
US Army's Armor and Infantry schools,
11

Vilification of experts who criticize
Israeli tactics, 50, 153n11,
153n13
Violation of one human right by
protection of another human
right, 14
Violence. *See also* First Intifada (1987);
Military; Right to kill; Second
Intifada (2000)

ethical use of, 73, 77, 80–81, 85,
91–92, 96, 98
high-tech, 99–100
human rights used to
scrutinize, 28
legal vs. illegal, 23
legitimatization of
due to Hamas' use of hostages
and human shields,
87–88
by humanitarian and human
rights law, 77
by IDF, 86
by Israeli High Court, 65
to protect human rights, 3, 14
state's monopoly over legitimate use
of, 78
Vitoria, Francisco de, 74

Walzer, Michael, 162n66
War conventions, 74
War crimes, 20, 23, 50, 56–57, 61,
68–69, 95, 128
Warfare in urban areas, 82, 84, 85,
92
War of 1967, 36, 37
War on terror, 55, 56–57, 58
The weak
asymmetry with dominant. *See*
Domination
human rights' purpose to empower,
13–15, 129
Weapons use
air attacks, no legal requirements
for, 99
drones, 99, 131–132, 136
indiscriminate weapons vs. precise
weapons, 23, 131
Iron Dome system (Israel), 88,
161n50
pinpoint surgical strikes to
minimize civilian casualties,
96–100, 162n64
Weber, Max, 78
Weiner, Justus Reid, 41–42, 43
Weizman, Chaim, 33
Weizman, Eyal, 76, 84
West Bank. *See also* Occupied
Palestinian Territories
drone surveillance in, 126

CPSIA information can be obtained
at www.ICGtesting.com
Printed in the USA
BVHW032023101019
560697BV00003B/5/P